Ethiopian Jewish
Immigrants in Israel

Ethiopian Jewish Immigrants in Israel

The Homeland Postponed

Tanya Schwarz

LONDON AND NEW YORK

First published 2001 by Curzon Press

Published 2016 by Routledge
2 Park Square, Milton Park, Abingdon, Oxon OX14 4RN
711 Third Avenue, New York, NY 10017, USA

Routledge is an imprint of the Taylor & Francis Group, an informa business

Copyright © 2001 Tanya Schwarz

Typeset in Photina by LaserScript Ltd, Mitcham, Surrey

All rights reserved. No part of this book may be reprinted or reproduced or utilised in any form or by any electronic, mechanical, or other means, now known or hereafter invented, including photocopying and recording, or in any information storage or retrieval system, without permission in writing from the publishers.

Notice:
Product or corporate names may be trademarks or registered trademarks, and are used only for identification and explanation without intent to infringe.

Credits and acknowledgments borrowed from other sources and reproduced, with permission, in this textbook appear on appropriate page within text.

British Library Cataloguing in Phublication Data
A catalogue record of this book is available from the British Library

Library of Congress Cataloguing in Publication Data
A catalogue record for this book has been requested

ISBN: 9781138969025 (pbk)

I dedicate this book to my family – Walter, Dorothy, Tanya, Habie, Simon, Ben, Frederique, Zoe, Zac, Chloe, Max, and Noé – with appreciation for your ongoing support, however far I go from you.

Contents

Acknowledgements	ix
1 Introduction	1
2 From Ethiopia to Israel	26
Part One Living Well and Becoming Deaf in the Homeland	39
3 An Ethiopian Village in Urban Israel	41
4 Israel the Homeland	72
5 Young Ethiopian Israelis	98
6 Rejected	114
7 On Becoming Deaf	127
8 Losing Control	145
Part Two Overcoming Difficulties	175
9 Being Together as Ethiopians	177
10 Proud Ethiopians	189
11 The Purest of Jews	200
12 Subverting Negative Ascriptions	220
13 The Homeland Postponed	234
Conclusion	250
Notes	253
Bibliography	275
Index	285

Acknowledgements

I thank the Economic and Social Research Council for a Postgraduate Research Award and generous fieldwork allowance that enabled me to pursue the research required for this book. I thank the Royal Anthropological Institute (Radcliffe-Brown/Sutasoma Award) and the London School of Economics (Malinowski Memorial Fund) for additional support. In addition, I thank Emma Rothschild at the Centre for History and Economics, King's College, Cambridge for funding a preliminary year of post-graduate study.

In Israel, my Ethiopian adoptive family and neighbours and the Ethiopian Jewish community as a whole received me with boundless courtesy and hospitality. They rarely tired of my questions and allowed me to share their joys and sorrows for close to two years. My adoptive father became a veritable parent, cherishing me and guiding me, and I formed close friendships with many of his relatives and neighbours. I learned much from Ethiopian Jews on a personal level; their grace, hospitality, and remarkable ability to adapt to a totally new lifestyle, remain a source of inspiration. It is impossible to adequately thank them.

Several non-Ethiopians helped to make fieldwork enjoyable. Shmulick Porat, a tireless community worker, shared much of his insights and knowledge of Ethiopian Jews. Jonathan Miran and researchers Dr Chaim Rosen, Dr Steven Kaplan and Dr Lisa Anteby, foremost experts on Ethiopian Jewry, offered me friendship, guidance and encouragement. My relatives in Israel, and my friend Sarojini Vittachi in Jordan, provided welcome breaks.

In Ethiopia, I was received regally by my Ethiopian Israeli adoptive family's former neighbours in the village of Gomange Mariam, Gondar. I travelled in Ethiopian villages for over two months, and I thank all my hosts there, as well as Dr Alula Pankhurst and Dr Rick Hodes for welcoming me into their homes in Adis Abeba.

Without the inspiration and encouragement of my supervisor, Professor Maurice Bloch, the PhD thesis which led to this book would not have been started, and never completed. He has greatly enhanced the quality of my work and I owe him an enormous debt. Dr David Lan generously contributed his enthusiasm and anthropological perceptions. Dr Michael Stewart's approach to anthropology has influenced my own, and his critical insight and encouragement over the years have been invaluable. I also thank the staff and postgraduate students of the LSE Anthropology Department, London, for a stimulating environment in which to conduct research. My PhD thesis examiners, Drs Charles Stewart and Tom Selwyn encouraged me to publish and made several useful suggestions. Drs Steven Kaplan and Lisa Anteby both generously commented on the PhD thesis, and pointed out a number of errors. I am extremely grateful to Dr Tudor Parfitt for commissioning this book and for his editorial assistance.

I wrote my manuscript in idyllic conditions thanks to the generous hospitality of my aunt Tanya Morgan, my grandmother Cissie Morgan, and my friend Josh Mailman, in whose homes I lived, and to friends and family who periodically hosted me and my computer in their beautiful homes in the French, English, South African and Mozambican countryside.

My family and friends, and my parents and elder sister in particular, have been invaluable to me throughout this project. Special thanks to my army of proof-readers for the PhD thesis: my parents, my sisters, Miranda, Tom, Tom II, Tom III, Matthew, Lucy, Kenny, Daniel and Maya. And thanks to Kenny for filling the last year of my thesis-writing with love, lyrics, laughter, and lots of emails. For the book, I thank my parents and Edwin for their editorial help and loving encouragement.

Finally, I thank my beloved Niall for carting the proofs to and from London and Johannesburg, and for sharing with me the excitement of the final months prior to publication.

1

Introduction

The time had arrived to return to Jerusalem, and reclaim the inheritance of their ancestors. All shared in this hope of speedy redemption, and a crowd of poor, simple-minded individuals resolved to start for Jerusalem ... In less time than is required in Europe to get ready for a short excursion, a sizeable group of Falashas had started to go to Jerusalem ...[1]

This group of Ethiopian Jews, which set off on foot for Jerusalem in the early 1860s, never reached their destination: the hoped-for miracle that aided Moses' flight from Egypt, the parting of the Red Sea, failed to materialise. Many members of the group perished on the journey, others settled beyond the reach of the European Protestant Missionaries they were fleeing. Over one hundred years later, a miracle of a different kind assisted their descendants: in huge jumbo-jets sent by the state of Israel, they reached the promised land.

The Ethiopian Jews, otherwise known as Beta Israel, have long captured the Western imagination – ever since Jewish envoys, travelling in Ethiopia in the 1860s, brought back reports of 'Black Jews', apparently direct descendants of ancient Israelites, who retained a strict form of Biblical Judaism in the midst of 'primitive' Africans.[2] In recent years, the Beta Israel made the headlines when the Israeli government conducted two airlifts into Israel, bringing six thousand seven hundred from Sudanese refugee camps in 1984, and another fourteen thousand from Addis Abeba, in only thirty-six hours, in May 1991.

The Ethiopian Jews soon found that Israel was not the Jerusalem of their dreams. Although their living standards soared and their children were educated – they felt that, as in Ethiopia, they were cast in the bottom strata of society. Their customs, the colour of their skin – even their Jewishness – were devalued in Israel. Like many other immigrant groups, the Ethiopian Jews of Israel feel they are losing control of their lives – and losing influence on their children who speak Hebrew while they speak only Amharic. In their bewilderment, they say that they are 'becoming deaf'.

This book details the remarkable strategies that Ethiopian Jews have developed to cope with the difficulties of immigration and the psychological trauma of feeling disparaged in their homeland. They have recreated tight communal bonds, developed strong ethnic pride and reaffirmed their religious and cultural customs. They turn round the doubts cast on their Jewishness, insisting that *they* are the true Jews – glorying in a more authentic and purer religious tradition than other Israelis. In addition, they maintain faith in an ideal homeland of the future in which all Jews will be united in a colour-blind world of material plenty and Jewish purity.

Fieldwork

In December 1993, visiting Israel to find out whether it was feasible to conduct research amongst Ethiopian Jewish immigrants, I met academics,[3] a number of Israelis working with Ethiopians,[4] and Ethiopian Jewish community leaders.[5] This last group introduced me to Ethiopian families, one of whom hosted me for ten days in Beersheva. The joy and exuberance of the Ethiopians I met and their warm welcome gave me both the courage and enthusiasm to proceed. Back in London, I studied Amharic with an Ethiopian student, and with help from the proofs of Dr Appleyard's forthcoming book *Colloquial Amharic*,[6] I learned the basics of the language.

I returned to Israel to start fieldwork in November 1994. I chose Afula Tse'era ('Young Afula'), a newly-built neighbourhood of the small Northern town of Afula, home to one of the highest concentrations of Ethiopians in the country. In Afula, with a population of approximately 21,300 (1993 figures), five percent of households were Ethiopian, which given large Ethiopian family sizes, amounted to approximately a ten percent Ethiopian population[7] – compared to approximately one percent nationally. In my immediate vicinity, nearly one household in five was Ethiopian (ninety-six out of five hundred).

As soon as I arrived in Afula, I sought an Ethiopian Israeli family to live with. On my first day, an Ethiopian community worker took me to the local Ethiopian elders' club. With no warning, he put me in front of the group of men and told me to introduce myself – in Amharic. The men clapped their hands in delight at this white girl, who had come all the way from England, who knew no Hebrew but wanted to learn Amharic and the customs of the Ethiopian Jews. On my second day, I returned to the club, and the Israeli keep-fit instructor urged me to join the class. Foolishly, I agreed and ended doing jumping jacks with a group of Ethiopian elders! Luckily, the latter had the tact never to recall the incident – which totally contravened Ethiopian etiquette.

I sat on benches in the main street during the sociable hours in the late afternoon, and I attended the children's after-school clubs, the women's handicrafts class, and a few Hebrew classes. Soon, I received invitations to drink coffee in Ethiopian homes. In a country as strange to them as Israel, I was simply another strangeness.

Fantanesh became my first and best friend. She was, and still is, a popular, bubbly woman in her forties, short and plump with a very large tummy, her face nearly always smiling.

Fantanesh loved to tell visitors from other parts of the country, who marvelled at the presence of an Amharic-speaking White foreigner who ate *injera* (Ethiopian pancake), the story of how I settled in the neighbourhood: 'Tanya arrived here and went to the classes. She spoke just a little Amharic, learned in England from an Ethiopian there called Yalew Kebede. I saw her sitting on the bench below and invited her in to drink tea. She brought *bamba* (a savoury snack) for the children. She came often afterwards. People said that I should not let her in my house like this because maybe she was a *savaki* [Fantanesh explained this term as someone who wants to change people into a different religion, like the Pentecostals]. But I said "No, she has come to study, to learn about our culture and our religion."'

Fantanesh is at the centre of a small group of female neighbours. She is the one who tends to organise the local women to visit together a house of mourning, a woman who has given birth or a sick neighbour – calling out to them from the street. As I lived opposite her, I often heard the call, and joined in. I called Fantanesh '*imaye*' ('my mother'). She cared for me emotionally – listened to my tales of woe when I had problems with other Ethiopians, was unwell or homesick, counselled and comforted me, and fed me. Even though she spoke no English, from my first day in the field, she was always able to understand my imperfect Amharic, and conversely was able to make me understand anything she wanted, and often helped me to follow conversations.

Grinding coffee. Che'era, Gondar, 1995.

Like Fantanesh, most Ethiopian Israelis understood rapidly the purpose of my study. In view of their abrupt change in environment, questions relating to cultural change, religious identity, and the experience of immigration, were daily concerns. Apart from anything else, they are fiercely proud of their cultural heritage and religious practices, and it was therefore unsurprising that I should want to learn from them.

Two weeks after my arrival in Afula, Abba Negusse, a tall old man, with an open, bright face, a missing tooth, and sharp eyes, invited me for coffee. As I walked in, in spite of his wife's stern expression, I knew that I had reached my Ethiopian Israeli home. I sought the help of Fantanesh. She likes to repeat the story:

'Tanya said to me one day: 'I am looking for a place to live, here in your house would be so good but you have so many children and *imita* [grandmother], so you have no room. There at Abba Negusse's they only have one daughter at home. Are they good people?' 'Yes' I said. She asked me to ask them if she could live there because she was too afraid to ask herself. ... Abba Negusse was happy to have her. After a while, her parents came, and they too stayed in Abba Negusse's house and they came here for coffee. Her parents gave Abba Negusse a bedcover from England. Tanya gave me earrings and a head-scarf. She also went to Ethiopia and gave Mama Itaktu [a former neighbour] fifty Birr [approx. £10] and some coffee. She took a photo of her while she was grinding coffee!'

I lived for twenty months with Abba Negusse and his wife Mama Alefash. I paid them a modest rent, which significantly increased their monthly income, and I contributed to household expenses. I shared a room with their twenty-five year-old daughter Aveva and soon became a daughter of the house myself. This meant, much to my irritation at times, that I was expected to help daily with household chores and to entertain guests. I remember one day resting in my room, a rare moment of quiet and privacy after an intense forty-eight hour gathering of relatives. A guest came, I pretended not to notice, and stayed in my room – but I was called out to serve him tea. At other times, I was snatching a few moments to write up notes before the next event, when Mama Alefash would start cleaning and expect me to help. I often failed her in my duties, and my relationship with her suffered as a consequence. But to have been a proper Ethiopian daughter would have been a full time occupation.

In other ways, I failed to show Mama Alefash proper respect: *injera* (Ethiopian sour pancake), the staple food, was the problem. I sometimes accepted my neighbours' offer of food, and returning home satiated, declined her offers. Other women were sensitive to this slight, and did not press *injera* on me when I said that 'Mama Alefash has *injera* for me at home'. When my stomach resisted *injera* three times a day, I managed to avoid it altogether by telling my neighbours that I was eating at home, and Mama Alefash that I was eating at the neighbours. In fact, I sneaked a sandwich in town, or prepared hot food at home when the house was empty. On reflection, my hosts were probably aware of my ruse, but kept quiet, so as not to force me to blatantly defy Ethiopian etiquette – they understood the difficulties of a new environment, and the comforts provided by the food of one home's country…

Abba Negusse became a veritable father, guiding me in my studies, attentive to my wellbeing, and, with great pride, taking me with him wherever he went whenever I wanted to join him. He rejoiced at my successes – in Amharic and in my learning of Ethiopian customs and etiquette – and berated me gently when I erred. One night, after a lively party, I sat on the street bench chatting and laughing with a couple of young Ethiopian male guests. Abba Negusse walked straight past, with no greeting, a clear mark of discontent: a daughter of his should not talk to men late at night. Mama Alefash and I never achieved such closeness, but we grew to respect each other and to live together in peace. Their daughter Aveva and I shared our joys and tribulations, until she left home after her wedding. A number of Abba Negusse's other children, nieces, nephews and grandchildren became my companions, friends, and invaluable informants. In particular Telahun, one of Abba Negusse's many grandchildren, who partly lived in our home – he had lived with his grandfather as a child, since his grandfather had no boys at home, his own children having left for Israel. Telahun was at this time an eighteen year-old boarding school student, and his weekends home were highlights of my time in Afula.

I spent my days with my neighbours: drinking coffee, chatting, visiting the sick, shopping, playing, attending funerals and celebrations. I was welcomed into their lives and homes, and within a year, they began to take my presence for granted. By contrast, when I travelled to other neighbourhoods, I often grew exhausted and irritated by the attention I received and the incessant questions I had to answer. My reaction was unfair in view of my own endless stream of questions. During my first year of fieldwork, I hardly left my neighbourhood: daily life was so absorbing that I feared I would miss too much if I left even for the week-end. Later however, once intrigues became more familiar, and my familiarity with the relatives of my adoptive family and close neighbours who lived in other parts of the country increased, I travelled further afield. I wanted to gain a wider perspective on the Ethiopian Jewish population. But I always learned the most from my immediate neighbours, because they dropped their reserve in front of me and because our growing bonds of friendship added to their eagerness for me to learn. Indeed, when I quarrelled with someone close to me, s/he knew exactly what would upset me most: to intentionally withhold information.

In the middle of fieldwork I visited Ethiopia for two months. I lived for three weeks in the village of Gomange Mariam, a few hours by bus and foot from the town of Gondar, amongst the former Christian friends, neighbours and co-Godparents of my Beta Israel hosts. I also travelled extensively throughout the region and the Simien mountains. On my return, I delighted the Beta Israel with pictures and stories from their former villages. The trip enabled me to see quite how drastic the change in environment has been for Ethiopian Jews.

I conducted fieldwork in Amharic. After a year, I could follow simple group conversations and engage in more complex one-to-one discussions. Most of the information in the following chapters was obtained by participating in Beta Israel life: observing what Ethiopian Israelis did and said to me and to each other. Once fuller trust was established with my informants, and my research questions better defined, I taped about fifteen hours of semi-structured interviews.[8] The transcripts proved invaluable, not only to confirm many of the intuitions I had gained through participant observation, but also to provide many of the quotes which fill these pages. I never learned Hebrew: Amharic was hard enough without taking on another language. Whilst my lack of Hebrew hindered my communication with Ethiopian Israeli children, it made me closer to Ethiopian adults. We shared a common disorientation in the country, and this created an unspoken bond. It also allowed for role reversals: when I went to the bank and the clerk did not speak English, one of my Ethiopian companions would translate the Hebrew into Amharic for me, and back again from Amharic to Hebrew. At the bank, and when the story was repeated many times over coffee, everyone laughed.

Israel as a country of immigration

Israel is an immigrant's country *par excellence*. The majority of its Jewish population, either first or second generation immigrants, emanates from over sixty countries. All share a sense of common identity as Jews.

Jewish population and immigration figures[9] clearly show the rapid Jewish population growth, especially since the creation of the state of Israel in 1948:

- In 1880, Jewish population of 25,000;
- In 1922, Jewish population of 85,000 (chiefly idealistic pioneers from Russia);
- Between 1924 and 1936, approximately 282,000 immigrants, mostly from Poland and Western European countries, nearly tripled the Jewish population;
- Prior to independence, Jewish population stood at 630,000 of which just 10% were from Middle-Eastern origin;
- In the first three and a half years of statehood (1948–51), 700,000 immigrants (half from Europe and half from Asia and Africa) doubled the population;

- Numbers grew steadily with mass immigration in the mid-1950s (over 160,000 mostly from Morocco, Tunisia and Poland) and mid-1960s (215,000 especially from Morocco and Rumania);
- In 1989, population of four million Jews, half from North African or Asian origin;
- From 1989 to 1995, 710,000 people immigrated to Israel, mainly from the former USSR.

Israeli Jews cohabit with a large and growing minority of Arab citizens. On the eve of the establishment of the State of Israel in 1948, there were about 1,200,000 Arabs in Palestine – nearly twice the Jewish population. Only 156,000 remained after the first Arab-Israeli war. A high natural growth has gradually increased the population and Arab Israelis now account for close to twenty percent of the population of Israel (this figure does not include non-Israeli citizens, namely Palestinians from the West Bank and Gaza).[10]

These diverse populations create complex and dynamic ethnic relations. Israel is divided between Jewish and Arab citizens and the two groups are residentially segregated with few ties of friendships or marriage. Within these two broad groups, there are numerous sub-ethnic groups. Arabs comprise Muslims, Christians, Bedouins and Druze, each with their own group allegiances. Within Jewish society, Israelis are broadly divided into two categories: the 'Ashkenazim' who came mostly from Europe and America, and the 'Mizrachim', often called 'Sephardim' or 'Orientals', who came from the Middle East and North Africa.[11] These two categories are further differentiated into Jews from each of their countries of origin, which in turn maintain their own internal distinctions, often according to their previous geographical locality.[12]

Originally, the formation of the State of Israel was based on the assumption of the essential unity of the Jewish people. Reminiscent of the American idea of the 'melting pot', the ideology which pervaded the early waves of immigration, was *'kibbutz hagaluyot'* (the in-gathering of the exiles) and the *'mizug hagaluyot'* (the mixing of the exiles).[13] However, this model was gradually rejected by the general public and social scientists alike because the 'fusion' failed to materialise and Ashkenazi-dominated elites retained their political and economic position and their claims to cultural superiority. For, in practice, the 'in-gathering of the exiles' meant Oriental immigrants, who generally arrived in Israel with no economic resources and a lower educational background than the resident

Ashkenazi elites, were expected to abandon their own customs and traditions, to adapt unidirectionally to the dominant norms and values within the framework of 'modernisation' as defined by state policy. In modern-day Israel, there is no official discrimination in government institutions, the army or the educational system; there is upward social mobility on the part of Orientals; and inter-ethnic marriages, a standard measure of integration in Israel, are increasing between the Sephardim and Ashkenazim (from 9% of all marriage in 1957, to 24% in 1985). However, the social, economic and political gap between Europeans and Middle Easterners remains large to this day. Israeli towns have 'ethnic' neighbourhoods, with high concentrations of particular *edot* (ethnic groups) and this residential segregation results in de facto educational segregation.[14]

Partly as a result of such socio-economic disparities, ethnicity has become a live issue in Israel.[15] It breaks into politics (e.g. creation of ethnic political parties) and is expressed in the rise in ethnic festivals, such as the *mimuna* of the Moroccans and pilgrimages to the tombs of Saints, and public discourse on ethnic lines.[16] In the Israel of the 1980s and 90s, to which the Beta Israel emigrated, the standard rhetoric is that Israel must not repeat the 'mistakes of the 1950s', where large waves of Afro-Asian Jewish immigrants were treated as 'primitives', cultural *tabula rasa* capable of being turned into modern-day Israelis. As Kaplan and Rosen put it: 'Cultural pluralism is [now] high on the agenda of political correctness'.[17] Ethiopian immigrants have clearly benefited from this new attitude, but as their experience testifies, it is often enacted more in discourse than in practice.[18]

Social studies of Israeli immigrants[19]

The first sociological work in Israel, in the early 1950s, started from the assumption that Israeli citizens formed a uniform society, into which immigrants were 'assimilated' and 'absorbed'. Immigrants supposedly rejected their native traditions to strive to adopt society's 'uniform cultural orientation'.[20] As an early exponent put it:

> In this country ... there are no ethnic groups possessing definite cultures, but only one society characterised by a rather uniform cultural orientation ... and on the margins an ever increasing number of individuals and groups which have not yet been absorbed in it ...[21]

Shmuel Eisenstadt's *The Absorption of Immigrants*, published in 1954, was a more sophisticated version of this thesis and it became the founding stone for most sociological studies of Israeli immigrant groups. 'Absorption' into Israeli society was a special sort of acculturation: the ability of Oriental Jews to modernise in harmony with 'Israeli' norms.

Since 'absorption' turned out to be a less straightforward and rapid process than originally imagined, social scientists have turned to an analysis of the persisting differences between the 'European' and the 'Asian-African' segments of the population – systematic differences in income, occupation, and education between these two broad categories, i.e. what has come to be called 'the social gap'.[22]

Anthropologists of Israeli society have focussed on specific groups of immigrants, with particular attention to the remoulding of their cultural and social institutions in the new country. One of the earliest examples of this approach is Raphael Patai's *Israel between East and West*, published in 1953. The book concerns itself with the 'cultural crisis' resulting from the impact of culturally Western Israel on the first Eastern immigrants in the new state of Israel. Characteristic of Israeli social science, the book contains an element of advocacy, calling for 'cultural synthesis instead of cultural absorption; an in-gathering of cultural contributions from each ethnic element in the country, instead of the assimilation of all to the Western culture of Ashkenazi Jewry.'[23]

A number of anthropological works on Oriental immigration, particularly on the settlers in agricultural communities, followed.[24] A more flexible conception of tradition and modernity was developed, and in contrast to the views of the early sociologists, it was demonstrated that cultural continuity with a pre-migration past (i.e. 'tradition') did not hinder successful absorption into Israeli society, but rather contributed to it.[25] Further, as Eisenstadt himself recognised, 'traditional forms' did more than 'persist', they shaped the contours of Israeli society itself.[26]

Deshen and Shokeid took the studies of specific ethnic groups further. They looked at ways in which Moroccan and Tunisian Jews refashion their native understandings, interests, and symbols as they accommodated to their new Israeli circumstances.[27] Several anthropological works followed.[28] Kevin Avruch[29] for example sensitively depicts American Jewish immigrants' ambivalence about their American and Israeli identity. American Israelis tend to adopt a radical espousal of their Israeli identity when they first arrive in

Israel, and proudly assert a strong Zionist ideology. But soon, their American identity comes back to prominence and they miss American qualities in Israel. But when they return to America on visits, they remember why they migrated to Israel. In Israel, they remain frustrated by the constant label of 'American', when they strive so hard to be Israeli, as this young American Israeli illustrates:

> The first guy who reached me when I was wounded [in the army] started talking to me *in English*. I mean, the shell exploded, and I was lying there in gore and shock, and this Israeli comes running up and bends over me, screaming 'Medic!' and whispers [in a heavy Israeli accent], 'Not vorry, Dovid, not worry.' And I started cursing him, the worst profanities, in Hebrew and Arabic – I was hysterically enraged, crying like a baby – yelling in Hebrew: 'Why *English*! I just paid the price to be an Israeli, you bastard!'[30]

Herbert Lewis attempts to explain how and why Yemenites who reside in an ethnically mixed town maintain their separate identity and find there their sense of self-worth and dignity.[31] Lisa Gilad's rich ethnography of Yemeni Jewish women – both immigrant women and their Israeli-born adult daughters – is the study I have found closest to my own.[32] She describes Yemeni dissatisfaction with low-status jobs, and their efforts to succeed in Israel by Israeli standards and to be accepted as equal citizens.[33] My study is complementary to Gilad's because it is situated within the first decade after immigration and charts the origins of the processes Gilad analysed at a later stage of development, forty years after immigration.

Ethiopian Jews in the literature

When I first went to Israel, in December 1993, I was often greeted with a joke popular among both Ethiopians and Israelis: 'There are more anthropologists studying Ethiopian Jews than there are Ethiopian Jews!' However, despite several excellent scholarly histories of the Beta Israel, no thorough ethnography of the group had yet been completed. As Steven Kaplan, a leading scholar on Ethiopian Jewry has remarked: 'Of all the gaps that exist in Beta Israel studies, none appears as painful as the absence of a single first-rate ethnography of the group.'[34]

The Beta Israel have been given a variety of labels.[35] They used to be referred to, by both Ethiopians and foreigners, as the 'Falasha', a term thought to derive from the Ge'ez[36] words *falasa* (to separate/ emigrate/exile) or *falasyan* (foreigner/wanderer).[37] However, this appellation has been gradually abandoned because of its derogatory associations with landless and marginalised people.[38] The terms 'Ethiopian Jews' and '*Beta Israel*' ('House of Israel') have now been adopted by most scholars and educated Israelis. The advantage of the term 'Ethiopian Jew' is that this appellation places them squarely alongside other Jews, since it is equivalent to the labels of other Jews such as 'Yemeni Jews' and 'British Jews'. I rarely heard a non-educated Ethiopian Jew use the term 'Beta Israel': they refer to themselves as '*Israel*' (or sometimes in the plural '*Israelotch*')[39] or as '*havesha*' (the Ethiopian term for 'Abyssinian'). To avoid confusion with the country name Israel, I have not followed my informants in either of these two appellations: 'Israel' could be too easily confused with the country name and *havesha* is too imprecise, given that it also includes non-Jewish Highlanders. I have opted for the terms Beta Israel, Ethiopian Jews, and Ethiopian Israelis.[40] Sometimes, for simplicity, I also use the short hand term 'Ethiopian'.

Ethnographies of Beta Israel in Ethiopia

While the literature on the Beta Israel after their migration to Israel grows, it is a great misfortune that no thorough ethnography was ever written about their lives in Ethiopia.[41] Accounts from travellers, Protestant Missionaries such as Flad (1889) and Stern 1868), and Jewish Emissaries such as Halevy (1869) and Faitlovitch (1905) provide illuminating details about social and religious life. In the 1950s, Wolf Leslau (1951, 1957) wrote in greater detail about Beta Israel religious beliefs and practices.[42] In the 1970s, more extensive fieldwork was conducted,[43] although, as Abbink notes, 'one cannot suppress a certain feeling of disappointment with the analytical level' of the resulting ethnographies.[44] Michelle Schoenberger provides a succinct account of daily life in a Falasha village, although much of her data comes from one educated informant with whom she spoke in Hebrew, and she therefore presents a somewhat formal perspective, missing out the intricacies and contradictions of daily life.[45] In the 1980s, Kay Shelemay studied Beta Israel religion and music.[46] Hagar Salamon's thesis has reconstructed Beta Israel life in Ethiopia, particularly their relations with their Christian neighbours, from interviews and secondary accounts.[47]

The Beta Israel were culturally close to their Amhara Christian and Muslim neighbours, but there is a similar lack of quality ethnography on Amhara society. Levine's *Wax and Gold*,[48] a general account of Amhara society and culture, remains the seminal work, even though the author never undertook prolonged fieldwork in a rural area. Hoben provides a detailed description and analysis of land tenure systems[49] and Messing details more general aspects of daily life.[50] Gamst's study of the Qemant, a Hebrao-pagan group, which has converted to Christianity this century, offers interesting parallels to twentieth century Beta Israel life in Ethiopia.[51] More recently, two ethnographies, conducted by fluent Amharic speakers, consider various aspects of Amhara society: Helen Pankhurst focuses on women's daily life in a village in Shoa,[52] while Alula Pankhurst describes a displaced Amhara-speaking population.[53]

The Beta Israel in Israel: The Falasha *Phenomenon*[54]

A large number of articles and books have been written on the Ethiopian Jews after their migration to Israel;[55] Several journals have dedicated whole issues to the subject,[56] a society of researchers on Ethiopian Jewry has held four international conferences,[57] and a comprehensive bibliography is regularly updated.[58]

A growing number of books about Ethiopian Jews in Israel are aimed at the general reader.[59] Published compilations of articles and papers are another accessible source, from the early Michael Ashkenazi & Alex Weingrod volume (1987), to the most recent edited by Tudor Parfitt (1999). Soroff (1996) and Schindler & Ribner (1997) have written about the process of integration. Several anthropological theses have been completed to date. Jan Abbink wrote on life in the absorption centre in the early 1980s, when there were only a few thousand Beta Israel in the country. Marylin Herman (1993) analysed concepts of 'identity and honour' by studying the lyrics of a music group. Gadi Ben Ezer (1995) studied the narratives of migration of Ethiopian Jews who came to Israel via the Sudan. Malka Shabtay (1996) analysed questions of identity with soldiers in the Israeli army. Don Seeman (1997) focused on the relations between Ethiopian Jews, the Falash Mura and the Israeli state. Jennifer Phillips Davids studied fertility changes (forthcoming). Lisa Anteby (1996)'s thesis is the first comprehensive ethnography of Ethiopian Jewish immigrants, focusing on the transition of a semi-literate population into a literate society. She eloquently describes

Beta Israel daily life, practices and beliefs, from their arrival with Operation Solomon in 1991 to settlement in permanent housing in 1994.

Many articles and papers concentrate on specific aspects of Beta Israel absorption: religion (Ben-Dor 1986, Trevisan-Semi 1985 Alvarez-Peryre & Ben Dor 1999), housing (Rosen 1995, Benita and Goam 1995), education (Holt 1995), women (Doleve-Gandelman 1990, Leitman 1995, Leitman ad Weinbaum 1999), the army (Shabtay 1995, Shabtay 1999), medical practices (Nudelman 1995, Reiff 1999), and work (Rosen 1995). Following Kaplan & Rosen's (1993) seminal article 'Between preservation of culture and invention of tradition', a number of articles have focused on cultural aspects of Ethiopian Jewish life in Israel: for example, new forms of communication (Anteby 1994, 1999), rituals of birth and death in Israel (Anteby 1995), women's changing traditions (Doleve-Gandelman 1990), and representations of leadership (Weil 1995). Rosen (e.g. 1987, 1989, 1995) has written extensively and perceptively on many aspects of Beta Israel culture, with a special focus on helping Israeli absorption workers deal with cultural misunderstandings. Several researchers are turning their attention to less mainstream activities of Ethiopian Jewish immigrants: dancing at the disco (Horwitz 1999) and encounters with evangelicals (Seeman 1999).

Altogether this literature gives a varied picture of Ethiopian Jewish life in Israel. However, other than a few exceptions,[60] it is disappointing. Most researchers have undertaken short-term studies, using interviews rather than more in-depth participant observation. These interviews are conducted in Hebrew, for which interpreters are required for the older age group, and is the second language for the younger age group. As a consequence, many of the accounts offer formal descriptions of belief and practice, rather than lived experience: they often give findings which are little more than truisms when not backed with sound ethnography. Leitman and Weinbaum (1999), for example, concludes that younger Ethiopian Jewish women are adapting faster than the older generation. Her conclusion is correct, albeit predictable, in its general formulation. However, she does not address the many contradictions which young women face in their process of adaptation;[61] characteristic of this literature as whole, the resulting picture is incomplete.

The literature on religion, the most widely researched and written about aspect of Beta Israel life, illustrates well the shortcomings of these studies. Steven Kaplan, a foremost scholar of Ethiopian Jewry, concludes that current approaches, which seek to demonstrate the similarities and alleged historical links between the Beta Israel beliefs and rituals and those of other Jewish groups, have reached a 'methodological dead-end'. Data is largely collected from texts and religious leaders, and almost totally ignore the daily practice of religion and its social context.[62] Moreover, the majority of the literature is partisan – trying to find ways of affirming the Judaism of the group.[63] Note for example Rabbi Waldman who has published widely on the Beta Israel:

'The religious customs of the [Beta Israel] community distinguish them from the other tribes in Ethiopia ... Their special customs, in many ways different from those practised elsewhere in the Jewish world are the result of the community's total isolation from the rest of world Jewry and centres of learning and the fact that they have had to survive in a hostile and primitive environment ... The years of isolation and hardship led to a blurring of the commandments, even though they are explicit in the Tora. Thus mitzvot such as tzitzit, tefillin, ... and others have disappeared ... similarly, a number of customs, foreign to the spirit of Judaism, such as tattooing and Nazirite seclusion, have penetrated under the influence of time and the Gentile environment.'[64]

The themes of *Ethiopian Jewish Immigrants in Israel*

This is an ethnographic study of the Ethiopian Jews, otherwise known as Beta Israel or Falashas, a few years after their migration from rural Ethiopia to urban Israel. It analyses the experience of immigration from the Beta Israel's own perspective. In particular, it focuses on the factors which contribute to the Beta Israel's sense of well-being in Israel, the problems and difficulties the Beta Israel experience, and the strategies they are developing to overcome these difficulties.

The Beta Israel are characterised by a combination of factors, which makes their experience of migration particularly interesting and unusual.

1 Within a few years, the Beta Israel underwent a radical transformation in their social, economic, political and natural environment: from a rural African background to an urban Israeli setting.

2 The whole Beta Israel population migrated in a very short space of time, leaving no significant reference group behind,[65] and with little possibility of return. The Beta Israel therefore have to imagine and re-create their future entirely in the host-country.
3 Other immigrant groups are usually motivated to emigrate by harsh political and economic conditions in their home country. Their home country remains their homeland and they dream of returning there when its economic and/or political situation improves.[66] The Beta Israel motivations for migration, on the other hand, were primarily ideological. Like other immigrants to Israel, they had a prior sense of 'belonging' to the host country, which they thought of as their 'homeland' to which they were returning after over two thousand years of exile.[67]
4 While many recent immigrants from Africa and Asia are accepted, at times reluctantly, into Western countries as workers or political refugees, the Beta Israel were actively sought, and Israel spent enormous sums of money and effort for their immigration, granted them full citizenship on arrival and invested further expenditure on their successful absorption into Israeli society.[68]

These characteristics elicit a number of questions:

1 How do the Beta Israel make the transition from an African village to a modern urban setting? How do they adapt their customs and traditions?
2 How does the fact that the Beta Israel are returning to a perceived homeland affect their immigration experience?
3 How do the Beta Israel respond to the ambivalence of a sense of belonging to Israel on the one hand, and feeling rejected by its population on the other? How, in particular, does the older generation react when their leadership role is doubly challenged – by Israeli religious and welfare institutions and also by the new models followed by their own children?
4 How do they reconcile their often contradictory reactions to their new home – appreciation and disappointment?

Before considering these questions, it is important to guard against reifying the experience of immigration, and attributing to it all socio-cultural change and conflicts. While Ethiopian immigrants are shedding many of their former customs, this process had already begun in Ethiopia as a consequence of modernisation, urbanisation and education. Emigration has merely accentuated this process. It is equally important to avoid opposing an unchanging and unproblematic past to a difficult present. Lisa Gilad's[69] otherwise excellent ethnography of Yemeni Jewish immigrants in Israel falls into this trap. For example, she implies that Yemeni women's search for identity prior to migration was unproblematic – 'Middle Eastern women have never had any doubts about their own identities...'[70] – before proceeding to explain immigrant women's difficulties in identity formation. Middle Eastern women, as for example Abu Lughod[71] demonstrates, like other women, have their own share of identity problems, irrespective of migration.

1 How do the Beta Israel make the transition from an African village to modern urban setting? How do they adapt their customs and traditions?

The Beta Israel have experienced a dramatic change in their social, economic, political and natural environment. From rural Africa to urban Israel, from a Black society to a White one. Everything is different in their new country: the climate, the work, the landscape, urban life. This change forces them to abandon or substantially modify long held cultural practices. As for the younger generation, they are propelled into a world with radically new social norms, expectations and opportunities.

How would Ethiopian Jews deal with this abrupt transition? When I began fieldwork, I was full of preconceptions about the 'trauma' of migration[72] and cultural chaos that Ethiopian Jewish immigrants would experience as a result of their abrupt transition. I was soon struck however by how cheerful Ethiopians were, and how 'normal' their life had become, just a few years after their upheaval from rural Ethiopia to urban Israel. I did not see an aggrieved population, downtrodden and self-effacing, struggling with the trappings of modern life. As they often said themselves, 'this is a good country' and 'we are well in this country'. They had very rapidly adapted to modern society.

But this does not mean that Ethiopians rapidly forego their cultural heritage to better fit into Israeli society. Indeed, contemporary Israel exemplifies how people, from many different countries of origin, can adopt modern lifestyles and a new national identity while still retaining their cultural heritage and diversity. As Harvey Goldberg, a leading Israeli anthropologist, noted in the late 1980s: 'Immigrants and their children have been socialised into

Israeli skills, roles, and styles, while preserving and reshaping significant elements of their particular traditions'.[73] Integration, in reality, is a complex process of immigrants identifying with their new society whilst building and maintaining difference.

The recent anthropology of immigration shows how immigrants actively maintain and recreate selected cultural forms from the home society.[74] Indigenous cultural concepts and social and ritual practices are abandoned with ease or remoulded to suit new conditions. For example, detailing the growth of the dowry system among Sikhs in Britain, Bhachu demonstrates how a traditional practice can grow after migration, particularly since the cultural and religious effervescence that has taken place amongst Sikhs in the 1980s and 1990s.[75] Persian Jewish immigrants in Israel went further and began to organise a new ritual in Israel, a ceremony which was associated with a Muslim order in Iran.[76]

An unusual example of innovation in religious ritual is provided by Moroccan Jewish immigrants in Israel. At first, they preserved the form of their practice of hagiolatry by venerating tombs of local Israeli Saints, thus using various compensatory substitutes for the tombs that had been left behind in Morocco. However, as Bilu explains, 'in order to preserve the content, rather than merely the form, of Jewish Moroccan hagiolatry, a more direct and daring accommodation had to be called for, namely, the symbolic transfer of saints from Morocco to Israel and their reinstallation in the new country'.[77] The most celebrated of the 'Israelised' Magrehbi tzaddikim (saints) is Rabbi David u-Moshe, who is now 'relocated' in a small room in a modest apartment in a working-class neighbourhood of Safed, following a dream by the flat-owner Avraham that the Saint wished to reside with him. The room has now become the focus of a mass celebration in which some fifteen to twenty thousand people take part in an atmosphere of fervour and ecstasy.[78]

At first sight, the re-emergence of Saint-cults and other 'indigenous' practices could be interpreted as a process of 'demodernisation' of Israel, or of the immigrant groups being unable to let go of their practices and modernise. In fact, these practices suggest that the immigrants in question have gained enough confidence to assert their ethnicity, and are therefore a manifestation of successful integration.[79]

A similar growth in confidence, and consequent aggrandisement of Ethiopian cultural practices, is evident among the Beta Israel. In the early eighties, when there were comparatively few in the country, they claimed to want to shed their Ethiopian heritage to integrate into Israeli society;[80] fifteen years later, while still maintaining their wish to integrate, they have also developed a forceful rhetoric of cultural preservation and have reinvigorated a number of Ethiopian customs – some of them with a large element of display. *Ethiopian Jewish Immigrants in Israel* show the dynamism of change in which some cultural practices are dropped, others retained and new ones taken on.

With a historical perspective, Hobsbawm (1983) has written of 'the invention of tradition' in modern societies, especially by dominant groups to justify social, economic and political advantage. The Beta Israel provide a remarkable example, less of invention, than of the recasting and recycling of tradition (certainly 'invented' originally)[81] by an underprivileged group which migrated from one set of painful circumstances to an entirely different one. Here, too, the advantage is obvious: 'tradition', in practice and rhetorical discourse, is a defiant defence against disorientation and perceived discrimination.

2 How does the fact that the Beta Israel are returning to a perceived homeland affect their immigration experience?

Most immigrants leave their countries for economic or/and political motives, to earn money, to flee a repressive regime,[82] and many plan to return home once the trouble is over. They maintain a strong ideology of return.[83] For example, a young Yemeni in New York says: 'Yemenites ... anywhere else other than Yemen, they're just halfway, half of them is there. Physically they are here. Mentally they're always back there. You rarely find Yemenis settled completely forever, no way. A person might stay here thirty, forty years, but he has to go back to Yemen, no matter what. Because it is the atmosphere, there is a magic in the air over there.'[84] Similarly for Brazilians in New York, the image and wish for an imminent departure is a vital aspect of immigrant life: it influences their self-perception (e.g. they are not bothered about their low status in America) and it inhibits the formation of formal communal groups since this would seem like laying down roots and thus relinquishing the desire to return to Brazil. They say 'We are here but our heads [or hearts] are in Brazil'.[85]

This image of a future back home is all the more potent given that in most cases it is no more than a dream, a 'myth of return'.[86] The hoped-for imminent departure becomes increasingly hard to effectuate as the years go by – children are in school, immigrants cannot yet 'afford' to return, grown children and their families have all decided to remain in the country, and elders do not want to leave their offspring. Imagining a bright future plays a central role in the immigrants' efforts to overcome the difficulties of the present and their low status in the host society, and what brighter image than 'back home' as a wealthy returnee? But as the years go by, the imagination of 'home' becomes brighter and brighter, just as the return becomes more and more mythical.

Jewish immigrants to Israel, on the other hand, envisage their future in their new homeland;[87] they have a prior sense of belonging to the host country, and imagine living there as Jews amongst Jews, in equality and peace. The final chapter in the book details how the Ethiopian Jews imagine the future – how they neither look back, not are they content with the present: they imagine a new homeland, the homeland postponed.

The way in which the future is imagined by immigrants affects the experience of immigration in more immediate ways too. Susan Jeffery's study of Muslim and Pakistani immigrants to Britain shows how visions of the future influenced the way in which they approached the conflict between integration and preservation of ethnic identity and traditions.[88] The Christians and Muslims were similar as immigrants in most respects except for the fact that the latter imagined their future back home in Pakistan and the former saw theirs in Britain. The Muslims strove hard to maintain as much of their cultural traditions as possible, and sought to bring up their children with their own society's norms and values so that the children could become good Pakistanis. Their prime concern was the cultural continuity of their children. Much debate was devoted to this issue, and many practical steps were taken to transmit Muslim religion and behaviour to their children and to counteract negative 'British' influences.[89] For example, women did not tend to work out of their homes, or when they did, in Pakistani-only work forces. Women did not attend English language classes because they saw no need for them; on the other hand, intensive religious classes were set up for the children.[90] All in all, Muslim Pakistanis built an 'encapsulated community'.[91]

Christian Pakistani immigrants, on the other hand, considered that they had joined their brethren in England, to which as Christians they felt a sense of belonging. Contrary to their Muslim counterparts, they adopted a positive orientation towards their host country, seeking to integrate as far as possible, and encouraging their children to do so. For instance, they did not criticise their children for listening to pop music or for dating members of the opposite sex. Adults joined British churches, and women sought to learn English. They still took pride in 'their own' culture, and maintained many ethnic characteristics (such as dress, speech, and food), but their primary ethnic marker was Christian – in common with British society – and second only were they Pakistani.[92] While the Muslims idealised Pakistan and despised British culture, the Christians spoke ill of Muslim Pakistanis (and Pakistan) and wanted to befriend British people.[93]

A firm intention to remain in the new country thus encourages integration into the host society. Jewish immigrants to Israel are consequently more orientated towards integration than immigrants who live according to a 'myth of return'. However, they too struggle to find a balance between their aspirations for integration into Israeli society and the preservation of their own cultural heritage; as recent commentators of Israeli society have noted, ethnicity is vibrant in Israel.[94] This study explores how Ethiopian Jewish immigrants play out this balance.

3 How do the Beta Israel respond to the ambivalence of a sense of belonging to Israel on the one hand, and feeling rejected by its population on the other? How, in particular, does the older generation react when their leadership role is doubly challenged – by Israeli religious and welfare institutions and also by the new models followed by their own children?

In Ethiopia, the Beta Israel survived as a 'despised' minority, with distinctive social, economic and religious traditions despite continuous pressure to convert to Christianity. In fact, together with other non-Christian Amhara groups, such as the Qemant,[95] the vast majority of Beta Israel did convert to Christianity, leaving the remaining Beta Israel with a particularly strong sense of cultural identity and an arduous task to maintain it.[96] As well as tightening their group boundaries, they ideologically subverted the negative ascriptions of the dominant Amhara society. They adhered to a rhetoric of communal purity which cast the Amhara as 'polluters';[97] they claimed to be the true Israelites, thus denying the Amhara claim to Israelite descent;[98] and they upheld a potent image of the future – a return to their Jewish homeland. Their dream finally came true and they reached Jerusalem. But once again they have been cast in an inferior position – as Blacks, 'improper' Jews, and uneducated 'primitive' people. They could have chosen to deal with such negative preconceptions by abandoning their native traditions and integrating as rapidly as possible. Instead, they have formed a proud self-confident *edah* (ethnic group, Hebrew), almost obsessively asserting the superiority of their traditions compared to those of other Israelis. Moreover, as in Ethiopia, they have created a potent image of the future: in what I have called 'the homeland postponed', all Jews will be colour-blind and will live in peace and purity.

The Bene Israel ('Sons of Israel'), the Indian Jews who migrated to Israel in the 1950s, offer a close parallel to the Beta Israel. They too have a darker skin than most of the host-population. The Rabbinate demanded from them a symbolic conversion to Judaism before marriage because of their prior ignorance of Halakkah law. Three decades later, the Beta Israel were faced with a similar request. To most Bene Israel however, just like the Beta Israel after them, the issue concerned race, caste and purity rather than abstract Halakkah law. The Bene Israel took this perceived threat to their sense of belonging to the Jewish brethren very seriously: they responded with demonstrations and hunger strikes until the Rabbinate reversed the directive, and they developed a strong ethnic identity, proudly maintaining social relations within the group and upholding many ethnic traditions.[99] The Beta Israel have adopted similar strategies.

The older generation of Beta Israel immigrants face an additional set of problems: their moral order is also threatened from within as the younger generation fast absorb new norms and modes of behaviour. How they experience this and try to deal with the problem is a central theme of their lives and of this book.

Cambodians refugees in the United States offer an interesting parallel and have adopted one of the strategies that the Beta Israel have developed: an elaborate discourse of unchanging traditions. They are forever debating issues such as 'Can we be Buddhists if we attend Christian churches? What will happen to Cambodians if our children do not observe the proper rituals?'[100] Cambodians cope with a culture that is rapidly changing by speaking of it as unchanging and unchangeable. What 'should be' becomes more rigid, and what 'really is' is often not seen, and imperfections and deviations from the 'ideal' are overlooked. For example, definitions of virtuous women and children remain as strict as ever, yet women go to work, girls to school, and children make decisions about their lives – practices which directly contravene the moral discourse.[101] Similarly, the Beta Israel often speak of their most cherished traditions as if they were unchanging and unchangeable, even when they are redundant in contemporary daily life.

4 How do they reconcile their often contradictory reactions to their new home – appreciation and disappointment?

Much of the ethnography presented in this book might appear contradictory: on the one hand, I describe deep contentment and appreciation of Israel and of new Ethiopian Jewish lifestyles, and on the other I write about malaise, anger and extreme disappointment; moreover, one chapter deals with successful efforts at integration, whilst many of the others depict the creation of ethnic separateness. While we all have contradictory experiences and evaluations of the present, the rapid changes that immigrants live through makes such contradictions all the more acute. Following Lisa Gilad's account of Yemeni Jewish immigrants, the book tells 'a story about contradictions and how people cope with them'.[102]

Plan of the book

Ethiopian Jewish Immigrants in Israel, the first published ethnography based on extensive field-work conducted in Amharic amongst Ethiopian Israelis living in permanent housing, aims to provide an intimate picture of Ethiopian Jewish life in Israel from their own perspective.

> Mama Fantae, Abba Negusse's younger sister: 'We are well in Israel. The young people work and we [elders] get help from the government. If the Christians that we grew up with were to ask me, I would tell them that I am happy here. But our Amharic and their Hebrew do not meet and we have 'become deaf' (*dinkoro*, lit. ignorant, stupid). This is our problem.'

Part One, *Living well and becoming deaf in the homeland*, elaborates on Mama Fantae's comments: how Ethiopian Israelis on the one hand appreciate their new country, and how on the other they are disappointed, and in particular feel that they are becoming 'deaf'. Ethiopian Israelis owe their wellbeing in the first instance to their successful recreation of communal life. Each day is structured in a tight web of social relations amongst Ethiopian neighbours and kin, punctuated by an endless cycle of celebrations and funerals – the subject of Chapter 3. Chapter 4 turns to Ethiopians' appreciation of Israel, both as a 'developed' country and as their 'homeland'. While these chapters, and indeed most of the book, focuses on the older generation of Ethiopian immigrants, Chapter 5 turns to the successful aspects of the younger generation's adaptation to Israel, at school, in the army and at work, as well as to the remarkable way in which they combine Ethiopian and Israeli norms of behaviour.

Chapters 6 to 8 turn to the difficulties Ethiopian Israelis encounter. Chapter 6 shows how and why they feel rejected by the host society – the threat to their sense of belonging to Israel as Jews is the hardest to bear. Chapter 7 elucidates the meaning of the expression 'becoming deaf': the older generation's frustration at their inability to understand and speak Hebrew and their ignorance about the ways of their new country. Chapter 8 argues that, for Beta Israel adults, difficulties with respect to Israelis are overshadowed by their new-found impotence and loss of authority within their own society. Ultimately, 'becoming deaf' is a metaphor for the loss of control Beta Israel adults experience over most aspects of their lives, and their children in particular.

If Ethiopian Israelis can confidently assert 'we are well in this country', it is because they have been able to cope successfully with their problems of immigration in the promised land – the subject of Part Two, *Overcoming difficulties*. Ethiopian Jewish immigrants have shaped their lives in Israel by resisting those aspects of dominant society which they dislike and reaffirming with pride their own distinctive heritage. Chapter 9 portrays the strong intra-group relations that Ethiopian Israelis have developed, particularly at Israeli-style weddings in hired halls and in Ethiopian synagogues. Chapters 10 to 12 turn to their affirmation of Ethiopian practices and norms of behaviour, which they differentiate from and raise above corresponding Israeli ones. Chapter 10 focuses on the maintenance of their cultural traditions as Ethiopians. Chapter 11 focuses on Beta Israel pride as the 'purest of all Jews'. Chapter 12 illustrates further the Ethiopian Jews' ability to subvert disparaging attitudes – the rhetorical device of speaking of traditions as unchanging, even when they are rapidly doing so. It also analyses one of the pervasive themes of the book: the tension between assimilation and the deliberate retention of their distinctiveness. The final chapter details another useful strategy for dealing with a difficult present: the imagination of an ideal future. Fighting against a sense of disparagement from dominant society is not new for the Beta Israel – Chapter 2 provides the historical context and briefly recounts their story from the first recorded sources in the fourteenth century to their settlement in permanent housing in Israel.

Additional notes

1 I have written the text in the present in order to give it more immediacy. Clearly the situation of new immigrants changes rapidly and the reader must bear in mind that the ethnography refers to the period of my fieldwork: 1995 and 1996.
2 This book concerns Beta Israel perceptions of immigrant life and not my own objectivist pronouncements on how they are doing. For example, when I discuss well-being and difficulties – particularly feelings of rejection – in Israel, I am describing Beta Israel experience as I understood it, not my own evaluation of the reception they receive in Israel.
3 Names of persons are fictive to protect the privacy of my informants and hosts.
4 I have transliterated Amharic words as they are pronounced. Foreign words are in Amharic, unless otherwise stated.

2

From Ethiopia to Israel

The Beta Israel's response to their experience in Israel needs to be understood in the context of a long history of struggle to forge a distinct identity whilst adapting to changes that lay outside their control. Over time, the Beta Israel faced discrimination, systematic attempts to convert, and economic hardship as well as periods of relative stability and prosperity. They developed a complex relation with their Christian and Muslim neighbours which was based on economic interdependence and ideological constructions of one another.[1] Later chapters show how these perceptions of their neighbours in Ethiopia are mirrored by their responses to their new neighbours in Israel. This chapter describes the process of the Beta Israel's struggle to define and retain their identity.

In Ethiopia: historical fragments

Origins

Given the lack of historical data, the origins of the Beta Israel remain 'shrouded in mystery'.[2] There are no sources prior to the fourteenth century. According to their own tradition, the Beta Israel are direct descendants of ancient Israelites. Some myths suggest that they are the children of the lost tribe of Dan which reached Ethiopia during the exodus following the destruction of the First Temple in 586 BCE. Others suggest that Israelites came to Ethiopia via Egypt after the destruction of the Second Temple in 76 AD.[3] A number of scholars[4] proposed instead that the Beta Israel are the descendants of the indigenous inhabitants of Ethiopia[5] who converted to Judaism, but never to Christianity. From this perspective, there was no large scale migration of ancient Israelites into Ethiopia; Judaism would have reached Ethiopia through a small number of emissaries. The debates have focused on when this infusion of Judaism occurred and from where: from Egypt or South Arabia, at any time from the desecration of the first temple to the early centuries of the common era.[6]

Following the pioneering historical work of Kay Shelemay, James Quirin and Steven Kapan in the 1970s and 1980s, most contemporary scholars have come to view the Beta Israel not so much a group apart from the rest of the Ethiopian Highlands population, but rather as one extreme of a continuum from Jews to Christians.[7] The Orthodox Christian Church in Ethiopia is indeed markedly Hebraic in form, with an Israelite self-identity,[8] the Saturday Sabbath,[9] circumcision, Biblical dietary laws, and a three-fold division of the houses of worship in imitation of the temple of Jerusalem.[10] After analysing the religious and cultural similarities between Beta Israel and Orthodox Christians, and other ethnic groups such as the Hebraic Qemant and the craftsmen of Shewa, Richard Pankhurst concludes that one has to think in terms of a 'Ethiopian Judaic-Christian continuum, in which most of the peoples of Northern Ethiopia had their place; i.e., a kind of gradation, in which the Beta Israel were important rather than unique'.[11]

Ironically, this recent scholarship which places the Beta Israel firmly in their Ethiopian context has coincided with the group's migration to Israel. This has led to a political conflict between the academic stand-point and the popular view, including that of the Ethiopian Israelis themselves. Steven Kaplan, the most prominent proponent of the modern approach, has become a *bête noire* amongst the Ethiopian community, and I soon learned not to mention his name in front of my informants. There has been at least one attempt to remove Kay Shelemay's book from a Jewish bookstore in the USA.[12]

Crystallisation of the group (15th–17th century)

Emperor Yeshaq's reign (1413 to1430) was a significant period in the history of the Beta Israel because it marked the beginning of their dislocation and loss of land-rights. The emperor is said to have decreed: 'He who is baptised in the Christian religion may inherit the land of his father, otherwise let him be a *Falasi* (a landless person, a wanderer)'. A later scribe added the comment: 'Since then, the Beta Israel have been called *falashoch* (exiles)'.[13] Most Beta Israel converted to Christianity; the others migrated to areas of poor quality farmland which were vacant or stayed on their lands, no longer as independent agriculturists, but as tenants to recently arrived colonists.[14] They sought ways to supplement their income from agriculture and turned to crafts such as pottery, weaving, building and black-smithing.

The early fifteenth century also marked major transformations in the religious sphere, and contemporary scholars believe that the ethno-religious identity of the Beta Israel was crystallised around this time. Ironically, their formal religious distinctiveness from the Ethiopian Orthodox Church evolved when renegade Christian monks joined their ranks and instituted monasticism among the Beta Israel. The monks soon came to acquire a central position in Beta Israel society; they provided religious leadership and an institutional basis for the creation of a more uniform identity.[15] A number of religious innovations followed: the introduction of new religious literature, the institution of new holy days, rules for conversion of outsiders, and the reinforcement of a distinct set of purity laws.[16] These purity laws became a central boundary marker for the Beta Israel. A number of rule were based on the Biblical laws of Leviticus: the seclusion and purification of women during menstruation and after child-birth, and the purification of persons who had touched a corpse or other impure object. The ritual purity of the group was ensured by a prohibition on touching non-Beta Israel, and ritual purification in the case of infringement.[17]

An 'infamous group' in Ethiopia[18] (18th–19th century)

The Beta Israel lived in hamlets within larger Christian villages in the Highlands of Gondar and Tigre.[19] Population estimates for the mid-nineteenth century range from 80,000 to 250,000. The Beta Israel population is thought to have decreased to approximately 50,000 in the early twentieth century.[20] Because of their association with the blacksmith craft, which was considered unclean, and their lack of land ownership, they were regarded as an inferior population without 'honour' (*kibur*).[21] They were also credited with a powerful threatening supernatural force: the evil eye (*buda*).[22] While the Beta Israel were viewed as threatening outsiders, they nonetheless held an essential position in the local social structure since they produced the tools and pots necessary for daily life.[23]

The Beta Israel, for their part, claimed to be the true Israelites – literally the 'House of Israel' (Beta Israel) – denying the Amhara claims to this title, as depicted in the national epic Kibra Nagast (the Glory of the Kings).[24] While the Christians, called Amhara in the Gondar region, regarded the Beta Israel as 'dirty', the Beta Israel turned their neighbours' ideology on its head and claimed that it was the Amhara who were polluting because of their disrespect for Biblical purity laws. Indeed, if a Beta Israel so much as touched a Christian, or food and drink prepared by him, he was obliged to wash clothes and body and ritually purify himself from the polluting contact before entering a Beta Israel home. Given economic interdependence with the Christians, with the exception of monks and priests, the rule of *atenkunye* ('do not touch me') was hard to respect, and in recent times, only the ban on eating meat from animals not slaughtered by a Beta Israel has been enforced.[25] But the rule remained a symbolic boundary-marker between the two culturally similar groups and, to this day, is central to Beta Israel discourse. With the exception of a small minority of urban dwellers and High School students, the Beta Israel did succeed in upholding their internal purity laws (particularly with respect to menstruant and post-partum women and persons who had come into contact with a corpse) right up to the departure for Israel.[26]

Protestant Missionaries (19th–20th century)

A Protestant mission under the auspices of the London Society for Promoting Christianity Among the Jews was established among the Beta Israel in the late 1850s. Beta Israel resisted the threat presented by the missionaries in a variety of ways. A number of leaders opted for political and judiciary means, such as challenging the missionary ban on animal sacrifices through the courts – the case was taken to Emperor Tewodros II in October 1862.[27] Other Beta Israel opted for migration. In a dramatic exodus, a group under the leadership of Abba Mahari set off on foot for Jerusalem. Unfortunately, the miracles which had aided Moses' flight from Egypt – such as the parting of the sea – did not materialise, and the expedition failed. Most of the group perished on the journey and the survivors returned home or settled in the Tigre region.[28] Other Beta Israel settled in less distant lands, but still beyond Missionary reach.[29] The missionary Flad described the situation in the 1870s:

> ... Beroo and our people told me that when the intelligence of my arrival reached him, Abba Maharee ordered special prayers to be

offered up in all their synagogues for our destruction ... Seeing that they were disappointed in their hopes, when they learned that we were in good health ... the Falasha priests took it as a bad omen, and resolved to emigrate to the low countries. The following is the proclamation which was read in the synagogues: 'Abba Maharee invites all those who wish to die as Falashas to leave West Abyssinia, and to follow him to a place of refuge. Those who do not care for their father's religion may remain; but let them remember that there is only one true religion – that of Moses.' This proclamation caused a great excitement in the Falasha villages.'[30]

Though the missionaries gained few converts, their impact on the Beta Israel was significant. They undermined the Beta Israel monastic clergy, provided educational opportunities for youngsters, and above all brought the Beta Israel to the attention of World Jewry.[31]

The Great Famine (1888–1892)

During the Great Famine of 1888–1892, a third to half the Beta Israel population perished. In times of extreme hardship, communal laws of purity and village life were largely abandoned as Beta Israel ate whatever food they could find, irrespective of its provenance, and mixed freely with Christians. A large number converted at this time to both the Protestant Church and to Ethiopian Orthodox Church. Beta Israel monks suffered their final blow as no-one could afford to support a class of clergy, and the monks which had survived the famine felt compelled to raise families to replenish the population.[32]

The involvement of World Jewry (1867–1970)

It was, ironically, the activities of Protestant missionaries which made the Beta Israel aware of a more universal Jewish identity and brought them to the attention of World Jewry.[33] In 1867, the French scholar Joseph Halévy travelled to their villages as an envoy of the Alliance Israélite Universelle.[34] Forty years later, his pupil Jacques Faitlovitch also travelled to Ethiopia and dedicated the rest of his life to bringing Ethiopian Jewry closer to world Jewry.[35] He wanted to establish a Western-educated elite,[36] to raise education standards in general and to reform Beta Israel religion to bring it closer to 'normative' Judaism.[37] He set up a network of village schools and health clinics, distributed religious literature, brought several Falasha youths to study in Palestine and Europe, and acted as an envoy for the Falashas to Ethiopian and European political leaders.[38]

After a careful appraisal of historical sources and interviews with Beta Israel informants, Danny Summerfield concludes that while Faitlovitch's political work may have advanced the cause of the Beta Israel, his impact on the Beta Israel was extremely limited. The booklets which were distributed had little effect given the high rates of illiteracy and his education programme 'can in many respects be considered a failure'.[39] Moreover, the Beta Israel resisted the religious reforms Faitlovitch tried to institute. Normative Jewish practices, such as celebrations of Talmudic Jewish holidays, were not espoused and they refused to accept the illegitimacy of their traditions which Faitlovitch considered to be 'unnecessary', such as monasticism, animal sacrifice and the seclusion of impure women.[40] This said, the Great Famine, prior to Faitlovitch's arrival, had already undermined Beta Israel monasteries and curtailed the practice of animal sacrifice.[41]

Faitlovitch's work among the Beta Israel was interrupted by the Italian Fascist occupation of Ethiopia (1935–1941). While the Jewish literature portrays the period as a time of persecution for the Beta Israel, given Fascist anti-Semitic politics,[42] Summerfield argues that the impact of the occupation on the Falashas was minimal – even positive.[43] Indeed, I found that the 'time of the Italians' was fondly recalled by many of my older informants. The Italians provided many of them with a market for their agricultural produce and opportunities to become soldiers, and thus earn both prestige and income.

Whatever the extent and nature of the impact of Faitlovitch and the Italian occupation on daily life and religious beliefs, both events have become significant historical markers for older Ethiopians. They are often referred to in the context of changing traditions.

> An old woman: 'Ah, our religion before the Italians came! You should have seen it! If you touched a woman who was in the menstrual hut you had to go in yourself and stay there till the following evening, and only after washing could you go home. You could not as much as touch an Amhara. But after the Italians, things changed.'

Abba Negusse: 'Mrmr Yaacov ['teacher' Faitlovitch] said: "Do not make the *kurban* (meat sacrifice) because the temple in Jerusalem has been destroyed." I still remember the time when a goat was slaughtered and the meat was burned and thrown away. But that was before the Italians.'

If Faitlovitch's direct impact on the Beta Israel was limited, his advocacy on their behalf to Western Jewish communities paved the way for their eventual emigration to Israel. He portrayed the Beta Israel as an alien Jewish element, out of place in their strange African environment. In his report to Baron Edmond de Rothschild after his first visit to Ethiopia he wrote:

> Lorsque je me suis trouvé en Afrique parmi ces Falachas entourés de peuplades à demi-sauvages, j'ai ressenti une joie indicibe en constatant leur énergie, leur intelligence, les hautes qualités morales qui les distinguent. Nous pouvons être fiers de compter parmi les notres ces nobles enfants de l'Ethiopie, qui, avec un non moins legitime orgueil, se glorifient de remonter à nos origines, adorent notre Dieu, pratiquent notre culte. L'ardeur avec laquelle ils cherchent à se regénérer, à sortir de cette barbarie africaine qui les enveloppe et les étouffe, prouve qu'en eux persiste le caractere instinctif de la race [...] combien différents en cela des autre Abyssiniens, si refractaires aux études, au progrés et à la civilisation des Européens auxquels ils se croient naivement supérieurs!'[44]

This mythic image of the Falasha as a pre-talmudic lost tribe, out of place in Africa, was accepted in the Jewish world with 'remarkable readiness'.[45] Jewish religious bodies eagerly followed Faitlovitch's call to 'bring [the heritage of the Beta Israel community] into line with the general tradition of Israel'.[46] From 1953, representatives of Israel's Jewish Agency's Department for Torah Education in the Diaspora and the Israeli aid organisation ORT were active in Ethiopia. A further network of clinics and schools was established throughout the Gondar region. Twelve Ethiopian youngsters were also brought to study in an Israeli Youth village in 1955, in order to acquire the necessary skills and knowledge to return to Ethiopia as teachers and leaders of the Falashas. In 1961 the Jewish Agency distributed 1,500 copies of a booklet in Amharic on Jewish holy days and Sabbath observance.

A Jewish Agency report on their first representatives in Ethiopia notes in a chapter entitled 'Corrections in Religious life according to Halakkha' that 'crucial progress was made towards returning them [the Ethiopians] to Judaism'.[47] Wolf Leslau, who had first visited Falasha villages in 1946, commented on a return visit sixteen years later:

> The situation was not the same when I visited the same village in 1962. Several young Falashas now spoke Hebrew and some elders knew how to read Hebrew. Unlike the practice of former days, the Feast of Hanukkah was celebrated and candles were lit in the synagogue. During the Feast of the Tabernacles, a booth was built in the compound of a synagogue, a practice not known previously. As for the two young teachers of the village, they wore the prayer shawl during worship.[48]

While the Jewish Agency's programme in Ethiopia had a significant impact on the Beta Israel, it was not evenly felt throughout the villages, with those closest to Gondar town most exposed and remoter ones the least.[49] Beta Israel from the Tigre region in particular complained that fewer resources were reaching them.[50] The influx of resources and externally appointed leaders caused other divisions within the Beta Israel community. Traditional leaders, the priests and elders, disputed the new-found status of the educated young elite.

> In the words of a leading priest (in the 1970s): 'The young teachers want to lead the people, but the priests and elders don't want to surrender their leadership ... but, because the young teachers have access to the government, Falasha follow them, and only adults and the elderly continue to obey the priests of old.[51]

The main effect of the Jewish Agency's programme was to transform Jerusalem into a living reality and emigration to the golden city, a goal for which to strive.[52]

Modernisation and the Ethiopian revolution (1960s and 1970s)

Transformations in Beta Israel society were also brought about by the general processes of change and modernisation in Ethiopia. From the 1960s, their economic position worsened because both land availability and the profitability of their handicrafts decreased due to Amhara population growth and the increased availability of cheap factory produced tools.[53]

The 1974 Ethiopian revolution led to the establishment of a military Marxist regime. Some observers and commentators report a negative impact on the lives of the Beta Israel. Although some gained land in the land-reform programmes, the old landlords often organised raids to evict them or destroy crops. Moreover, together with the rest of the local population, the Beta Israel fell victim to the counter-revolutionary guerrilla groups fighting in the area.[54] Other observers claim that the position of the Beta Israel improved after the revolution. The head of the Israeli ORT aid programme, for example, commented that 'Discrimination against the Falashas has abated radically in the last five years. (...) The revolution has given the Falashas their freedom'.[55] Many of my informants spoke of Haile Mariam, the head of the revolutionary government, in enthusiastic terms, and recalled land reform and literacy campaigns positively. Clearly, further research is required to ascertain better the impact of the revolution on the lives of the Beta Israel.

Young people became much more exposed to secular education and contacts with non-Beta Israel as they were conscripted into the armed forces or sought job opportunities in urban areas.[56] All in all, the community's poor socio-economic position, their long-standing dream of a return to Jerusalem, and the increased presence of Israelis, Jewish tourists and Jewish projects in Beta Israel villages, fermented the idea of wholesale migration to Israel.[57]

Migration to Israel

Waves of immigration

Fantanesh describes her migration to Israel: 'We were on our way from our village near Ambover, after my mother who was rich had sold all her animals, when we were stopped by police. The Amhara policeman/judge (*dagna*) said: "Go back! Where are you going? To Jerusalem? That is not your country, that is the country of the *farenj* (White people)! Go back home!" He took our money, leaving us just a little. Tsega and Birtukan [her sisters who had reached Israel in 1984] sent money to my Mum and Tsega some to me. My husband Birre's brother sent him money. It was hard. Then we heard that people were reaching Israel from Addis

Abeba. Birre went there and with 100 Birr (Ethiopian currency) he called his brother in Israel:

– This is Birre!
– Birre?!
– Yes, we are coming!

We went to Addis by plane from Gondar, it took just an hour. [Fantanesh spent one year in Addis Abeba before migrating.] Then, we went to the airport, and we landed in Rome five hours later. They were nice people in Rome, just like you [and she put her hand to her face, indicating that she meant "like me" in terms of skin colour]. We reached Israel at eleven o'clock. People had masks, they were at war [the Gulf war]! We first went to Ma'alot absorption centre and then thank God we reached here in Afula.'

Migration prior to Operation Moses (before 1984)

During the first decades of Israeli statehood, the idea of Ethiopian Jewish immigration was rather abstract, on both sides. While Jewish Agency immigration envoys were actively preparing for the emigration of Jews from Iraq, North Africa and Yemen in the 1950s, the first Jewish Israeli missions in Ethiopia were aimed at 'reform and rehabilitation' within Ethiopia. In the 1960s and early seventies, small groups of Beta Israel, about two hundred and seventy in total, emigrated on their own accord. Most of them were young and had already left their villages for education and work prior to migration. Their motives were as much economic and adventurous, wanting to discover and work in a developed country, as religious. They either raised money for the journey themselves or found a 'sponsor', often a visiting Jewish American tourist.[58]

In 1973, the Sephardi Chief Rabbi of Israel issued a religious ruling recognising the Falashas as Jews. Citing rabbinical opinion from four hundred years earlier, he stated that they were descendants of the lost tribe of Dan. Two years later, the Ashkenazi Chief Rabbi accepted the ruling and eventually the government of Israel granted rights to Ethiopian Jews to immigrate to Israel under the Law of Return and, like other Jews, receive full Israeli citizenship on arrival. In 1977, a group of one hundred and twenty one Ethiopian Jews was the first to reach Israel legally as Jews. Many more Beta Israel were scheduled to follow, but in February 1978, Ethiopia closed its doors.[59]

From 1979, fleeing the conflict between government forces and guerrillas, large groups of Beta Israel from the Northern regions of Tigre left their homesteads (together with many Amhara villagers) for refugee camps in the Sudan. In the Gondar area, where Government forces were in stronger control, mass movements were inhibited, although intrepid youngsters braved the journey – a long walk on foot, beset by armed bandits (*shiftas*).[60] The refugee camps were no better, with overcrowded conditions, little money, the need to conceal Jewish identity from authorities and the necessity to forgo purity laws and other religious customs, illness, and high death rates.[61] Throughout the early 1980s, Israeli agents and an American Jewish organisation (the American Association for Ethiopian Jewry) succeeded in clandestinely evacuating small groups of Beta Israel.[62]

Operation Moses (1984)

By the end of 1983, over four thousand Beta Israel, virtually the entire Jewish population of Tigre and Walqayit, had reached Israel via the Sudan. As news spread of their successful emigration, and conditions on the ground improved a little, Beta Israel from the Gondar region began to make the arduous journey. By the middle of 1984, close to ten thousand had reached the Sudanese refugee camps. As the situation in the refugee camps became worse and the mortality rate rose, and the pressure from pro-Falasha groups – including Ethiopian Jewish Israeli citizens – increased, the Israeli government decided to mount a large-scale immigration operation. After a complex process of negotiations with Sudanese rebel forces and the Sudanese government, involving millions of dollars[63] and high level US intervention, Operation Moses was staged. In less than two months, starting in mid-November 1984, more than six thousand five hundred Ethiopian Jews were airlifted to Israel.[64] The several hundred Beta Israel which were left in Sudan following the suspension of the airlift[65] were brought in another CIA-sponsored airlift a few months later.[66]

Operation Solomon and beyond (1991 to 1997)

Between August 1985 and the end of 1989, a further two thousand Beta Israel succeeded one way or another in reaching Israel. When diplomatic relations were re-established between Israel and Ethiopia at the end of 1989, the Ethiopian government permitted a slow rate of emigration, and departures from the capital Addis Abeba were authorised. With the help of Israeli agencies, by the summer of 1990, over twenty thousand Ethiopian Jews[67] had travelled to the Ethiopian capital, ready for emigration to Israel. Despite assistance from international Jewish organisation and the Israeli Embassy, conditions in Addis Abeba were harsh – malnutrition, inadequate housing, diseases including HIV, and the unfamiliarity of a new urban environment. By March 1991, with the progress of the Ethiopian rebels, the Israelis were concerned that a new regime would suspend Ethiopian Jewish emigration. More drastic measure were needed. With the help of the USA, and a thirty-five million dollar grant paid to the Ethiopian government, Operation Solomon was set in motion. In just thirty-six hours, between May 24 and May 25 1991, over fourteen thousand Ethiopian Jews were airlifted to Tel Aviv.[68]

With few exceptions, Operation Solomon brought to a close Beta Israel emigration. From that time, however, a second emigration from Ethiopia started – that of Christian Ethiopians of Jewish descent, generally referred to as 'Falas Mura'. During their long stay in Addis Abeba awaiting emigration to Israel, they have been exposed to Israelis and Rabbinical Judaism, and a number made formal conversions to Judaism. Many members of this group have close relatives in Israel and can apply for emigration under the Law of Entry, that is as part of family reunification, rather than as Jews under the Law of Return.[69] Despite fierce debates on the question, Israel has admitted between 1,300 and 1,660 Falas Mura per year from 1994 to 1997.[70]

Ethiopian Jewish immigration to Israel can be summarised in the following table.[71]

1948–71	1970–72	1980–89	1990–92	1993	1994	1995	1996	1997	**Total**
167	306	16,965	27,803	863	1,192	1,312	1,361	1,660	51,629

According to the Ministry of Immigrant Absorption,[72] the total number of Ethiopian Israelis at the time of fieldwork in 1995 was 57,000. This figure is approximate: strangely, as Steven Kaplan pointed out to me, it does not include deaths in Israel and births are not always reported. Salamon & Kaplan estimate that over 16,000 Ethiopian Israeli children were born by 1997.[73]

Reaching Israel

When immigrants from Ethiopia first arrived in Israel, they were housed, alongside other new immigrants (which were mainly from the former USSR) in temporary accommodation all over the country. This accommodation included: 'karavanim', large expanses on the edge of towns or in rural areas in which hundreds of mobile homes were erected; absorption centres, usually large apartment blocks in urban centres; and during the peak influx of Operation Solomon, in hotels. In these centres, Ethiopian immigrants were under the care of the Ministry of Absorption, which provided them with basic furniture and essentials, a lump sum for initial expenses (e.g. for clothes), a monthly stipend, Hebrew classes (ulpan), and vocational training courses.[74]

After a period ranging from a few months to several years, Ethiopian immigrants acquired permanent housing. Most moved to council housing in towns throughout the country. Towns which are home to more than one thousand Ethiopians include Haifa, Hadera, Netanya, Ashqelon, Rehovot, Ashdod, Ramle, Beersheva, Kiryat Malachi, Yavne, Afula, Kiryat Gat and Kiryat Yam.[75] Ethiopian preferred towns and neighbourhoods in which they already had a number of close relatives. However, Ministry of Absorption officials sought to limit a 'ghettoisation' effect;[76] moreover they wanted Ethiopians to settle in areas with strong education and employment opportunities. To this end, in 1993, the Ministry of Absorption initiated a special mortgage programme for Ethiopian immigrants to help them purchase their own homes in fifty-two authorised locations. It consisted of a grant equivalent to ninety per cent of the price of the apartment (up to a maximum of $120,000). For a variety of reasons, the Ministry has not been overly successful in housing Ethiopian Israelis in economically strong neighbourhoods, and the majority live in poor neighbourhoods.[77]

Within this new urban setting, the Beta Israel's history of cultural adaptation and innovation continues.

PART ONE

Living Well and Becoming Deaf in the Homeland

This section describes how new Ethiopian immigrants feel in their new country and what leads them to assert on the one hand "we are well in this country" and on the other "we have become deaf".

Ethiopian Israelis have successfully recreated communal life reminiscent of their former villages. Daily life is structured around a tight web of social relations amongst Ethiopian neighbours and kin and an endless cycle of celebrations and funerals (Chapter Three). Chapter Four turns to Ethiopians' appreciation of their new country, both as a "developed" country and as their "homeland". While these chapters, and indeed most of the book, focuses on the older generation of Ethiopian immigrants, Chapter Five turns to the successful aspects of the younger generation's adaptation to Israel.

Chapters Six to Eight turn to Ethiopian Israelis' perceptions of the difficulties they face in Israel. Chapter Six shows how and why they feel rejected by the host society, and illustrates these feelings with a discussion of the world-famous Blood Crisis. Chapter Seven elucidates the meaning of the expression "becoming deaf"; the phrase denotes the older generation's frustration at their inability to understand and speak Hebrew, their ignorance about the ways of their new country, and their feeling of being excluded by dominant society. Chapter Eight argues that, ultimately, "becoming deaf" is a metaphor for the loss of control Beta Israel adults experience over most aspects of their lives – livelihood, work, health, children, religion and the social order.

Part One

Living Well and
Becoming Great in
the Everyday

3

An Ethiopian Village in Urban Israel

An Ethiopian Jewish priest blesses the holy bread at the celebration of a boy's circumcision: 'May He enable us to eat and may He not separate us from one another.'

Being together is second only to eating, and on arrival in Israel, Ethiopian Jews immediately recreate the social life of their former Ethiopian villages. This chapter describes the dense web of social relations that Ethiopian Israelis have formed amongst themselves as neighbours and kin. Their success in this venture accounts to a large extent for their well-being in Israel.

An Ethiopian neighbourhood

Afula Tse'era, where I conducted my fieldwork, is a newly-built suburb of the town of Afula in Northern Israel. It is home to new Russian immigrants, veteran Israelis and to the highest concentration of Ethiopian immigrants in the country. Of the five hundred households in the immediate vicinity of my adopted home, ninety-six were Ethiopian. Moreover, after a twenty minute walk, one reached the neighbourhood of Givat Hamore with several hundred more Ethiopian households, and a ten minute walk in the opposite direction led to Afula Tse'era B, home to another Ethiopian neighbourhood. The town of Afula as a whole (with a population of approximately 24,000) had about a 10 per cent Ethiopian population in 1993.[1]

The main street of my neighbourhood, Rehov Ha'Erez, was lined on one side by small two-storey apartment buildings, behind which stretched the older neighbourhood of Afula Elite, with its detached villas and high-raised apartment blocks. Newly built semi-detached red-roofed bungalows lined the other side of the main street and the other streets of Afula Tse'era. The neighbourhood was bordered by cultivated fields which stretched out to the hills of Nazareth.

Ethiopian Israelis who have settled in other towns do not have so many Ethiopian neighbours, although I rarely visited an Ethiopian household which did not have at least a handful of Ethiopian neighbours within walking distance.

Outside: street life

In the winter sunshine and after the heat of the day in the summer, the streets come alive as Ethiopians come out to *'tetchawot'*. *'Tetchawot'* is a beautiful Amharic word without a precise translation in English; it means 'to chat', 'to play', 'to converse' – 'to chat playfully'.

Three men stroll down the street, chatting and laughing together. The younger one wears a Panama hat, the others, woolly hats. The older of the three is wrapped in his thick white cotton shawl (*gabi*), and leans on the walking stick he brought with him from his former village. As each Ethiopian home is passed, the men interrupt their chatter to call out greetings. Their greetings are returned, sometimes from third floor apartments, and they are invariably invited in, especially by those households who are hosting a coffee session. But after brief conversations, they promise to return later and move on. They greet a group of women sitting together in a front garden on an old sofa and on the low garden wall. They are draped in white Ethiopian shawls over colourful dresses. While they embroider small pieces of clothes and de-husk Ethiopian spices, they gossip in quiet high-pitched voices and often burst into shrieks of laughter. Young mothers watch over their toddlers, and run screaming after them when the children venture out of their reach.

The men eventually settle on the benches under the shade of the trees in the square by the supermarket. They continue there to *tetchawot* amongst themselves and are soon joined by other men. Near them, little Ethiopian children, with a few non-Ethiopian playmates, play on the swings and climbing frames. Older children gather in small groups and chat or play ball in the near-empty car parks by the side of the road.

On the wide steps leading up to the supermarket, the trendy teenagers, with their Rastafarian hair-dos and Bob Marley T-shirts, make merry together. They return the greetings of a group of women with white shawls wrapped around their colourful clothes, who make their way slowly towards the house of a neighbour who has recently given birth, carrying offerings of milk, *muk* (a hot broth which helps convalesce), and *injera* (Ethiopian pancakes) with meat stew.

White neighbours also walk to and fro. However, they remain outside the warm communality; in some respects, they are invisible.

I remember once walking down the street with a couple of Ethiopian women. We stopped to greet some Ethiopian women on a bench, and only after a while did I notice two Russian immigrants sitting there: my companions and I had failed to even register their presence, let alone greet them.

Inside the home

While Ethiopian Israelis enjoy street life together, proper social intercourse happens inside the home (*bewust*), and the border between inside and 'outside' (*bewuch*) is firmly controlled. In the quiet neighbourhood in which I lived, I never heard of a burglary taking place. Yet Ethiopian houses are locked carefully at all times, irrespective of the number of people inside the house and the volume of too-ing and fro-ing in and out, and windows and blinds are shut most of the time. Houses are closed, people say, for fear of harmful intruders such as 'Arabs' or thieves. In fact any person, until proven to the contrary, is potentially harmful.

When a knock at the door is heard, even though non-Ethiopians rarely knock at the door (Israelis ring the door bell), the master of the house or, if absent or busy, someone else, growls in Hebrew: 'Who is it?' or 'What?' Once a voice has been recognised, the door is unlocked and the visitor warmly invited in.

When the door is wide-open, it is still treated as 'closed', and even a household member knocks first on the open door before making an entry into the house. Nobody, not even a close relative, ever enters a house without first being invited to do so. The stress on the invitation to enter the house accentuates the gesture of opening the door and receiving a guest inside the house.

One day, Abba Negusse began to construct a fence around his front garden. I was perplexed, because he seemed to enjoy his front wall being used as a place to sit and chat, transforming his garden into a social meeting place for elders. The ostensible reason he gave was to prevent 'the children coming and spoiling things', but, since there was nothing to be spoiled in the garden. I pressed further, and pointed out that the fence would prevent neighbours from coming to chat by sitting on the wall. 'Well, now they will come in and sit on chairs [in the garden]'. In other words, he wanted his garden to become an extension of his house, where neighbours would be 'inside' his garden, rather than merely sitting at the frontier of his home.

Thus, neighbours sitting on the wall and in Abba Negusse's 'open' garden, were transgressing the border between 'inside' and 'outside' the house and so the garden had to be fenced 'in'.

Ethiopian Israelis usually live in two-three bedroom flats or small semi-detached houses.[2] The striking aspect of Ethiopian Israeli household decoration is its uniformity – few houses deviate from the standard decor. The living room is equipped with a sofa, a matching armchair, additional chairs, a display cabinet, a TV and a radio. Size and finances allowing, the living room also comprises additional sofas or armchairs, a spare bed, and a dining table with six matching chairs and a video. The sofa and armchair is covered in a flowery patterned cotton cloth. The display cabinet exhibits china, unopened sets of glasses and coffee cups, new pans, and a range of brightly coloured decorative objects such as china figurines and plastic flower arrangements, as well as unopened bottles of alcohol, preferably with colourful labels. Many cabinets also display a number of religious objects: Hanukkah and Sabbath candles and religious books in Hebrew and Amharic. Plastic flowers and bright decorations adorn the room, hanging from the ceilings and the walls. Walls are densely covered. One large area boasts a wall hanging, such as a fake tapestry of a medieval scene, and the rest of the walls are covered with brightly coloured framed pictures, family photos, and traditional Ethiopian basket work, as well as an elaborately decorated wall clock. The overall effect is colourful and ornate with family photos and Ethiopian handicrafts on display giving it an Ethiopian flavour.[3]

In contrast, the kitchen, bathroom and adult bedroom are bare with little decoration. The kitchen has basic amenities: a cooker, large fridge, coffee grinder and pots and pans. The master bedroom in most homes has a double bed with matching dressing table, and a clothes cupboard. Younger Ethiopians, on the other hand, decorate their bedrooms with posters of their favourite stars (e.g. Black Americans such as Whitney Houston and Michael Jackson, as well as Ethiopian stars), advertisements for clothes and cars, school photos, photos of themselves (especially in the army), and a number of Ethiopian decorations (e.g. handicrafts, the Ethiopian flag, cloth, and hand-written Ethiopian verses).

Receiving a guest

Once a person has crossed the threshold of the door, she becomes a guest. Both she and her hosts greet each other in the prescribed manner. The form of the greetings depend on the relative seniority of the two parties, as well as the length of time which has elapsed since their last meeting. Seniority is a function of both gender and age, with the oldest male ranking highest. Persons senior to an arriving guest generally remain seated, and the guest goes to each in turn, bending right down, making as if to kiss the feet of her senior. The seated person catches her head before it reaches too low and kisses each cheek at least twice. Junior persons rise at the entrance of the guest and the guest kisses their cheeks. When a pair are equal in status, they play-fight as each one offers their cheek to the other to kiss, and each tries to bend lower than the other. The 'loser', that is the one who has accepted the superior role, tends to make the other one repeat the whole process in reverse, forcing him to take the superior position. Both parties laugh, as do the seated persons, especially, when as each tries to bend lower, the two end up bent-double, with their backsides sticking out.

Warm effusive clicking sounds and verbal greetings, often in a sing-song, accompany the physical gestures: 'How are you (you, singular)?'(repeated by each at least three times) 'How are you (you, plural)?' 'How is your health?' 'How are your children/husband/parents?', 'Oh you, where were you lost to? It has been so long!', 'Welcome! Welcome! (*inkwan dehna metah* Lit: Thank God you arrived well)', 'Thank you for your welcome! (*inkwan dehna koyachuh* Lit: Thank God you remained here/waited well)', 'Sit down! Sit down!'. The longer the time-lapse since the previous greeting the more elaborate the greetings.

Eventually, the guests sit down. Another ritual now begins over the offering and accepting of food and drink. The guests refuse all offers of food and drink at least twice before reluctantly accepting. Once the host has succeeded in placing food in front of the guests, the former has to encourage the guests to eat, repeatedly, and often resorts to placing food directly in the guests' mouths.

> Ethiopians from the Gondar region, the Christian Amharas as well as the Beta Israel and the Muslims, are well known for accepting food only on the third offer. Thus, in Addis Abeba, when I declined food, and my hosts knew of my acquaintance with people from Gondar, I was asked 'is that a real 'no' or an 'Amhara' no?'

Conversation begins in a mundane fashion. If the TV is not already on, it is switched on at the arrival of the guests, and remains the focus of attention at first. The atmosphere slowly warms up and conversation becomes more intimate. In-depth inquiries are made about the guests' and hosts' kin and neighbours; daily news, especially pertaining to Ethiopians, is discussed, and anecdotes of the past and present are shared and laughed over.

> Two former neighbours, meeting in Israel for the first time, amused the coffee drinkers with stories of old times. Once, they recounted, at the end of their sojourn in the menstrual hut, they went to wash in the river. One was carrying a child on her back, while the other was young and beautiful. An Italian soldier saw them and tried to court the youngest woman, but she clung onto her friend's dress. Luckily, the Italian did not get her or she may have ended up with an Italian baby! The company roared with laughter and the two old ladies smiled coyly.

'Being together' as neighbours

Ethiopian Neighbours

For Ethiopian Israelis, the term 'neighbour' (*gworabet*) is resonant; it involves a specific set of obligations between people who live within walking distance of one another. These obligations include the exchange of greetings and conviviality (no mean task given the density of neighbours in some neighbourhoods), reciprocal invitations to celebrations and gatherings, visits to neighbours who are in difficulty or joy (e.g. illness, bereavement, child birth), and the exchange of labour and money.

Circles of neighbours

Like ripples in a pond, social relations in the neighbourhood extend into ever-widening circles. Next-door neighbours are at the centre,

The next-door neighbour is the everyday coffee partner, and the first call for any assistance required, such as loan of money, child care, and cooking and cleaning in the case of illness or childbirth. Next-door neighbours spend a lot of time together: partaking in coffee ceremonies once or twice a day, shopping, visiting other neighbours, chatting outside in the garden, and attending celebrations and funerals together. Next-door neighbours are often relatives, but when they are not, they acquire kin status, and are referred to in kin terms.

The next circle of neighbours comprises the households in the immediate vicinity. The vicinity is usually bounded by a road, a shop or a stretch of *farenj* (white people) houses. Such a circle of neighbours is sometimes referred to as a 'hamlet' (*mander*). For example, my adoptive mother used to inform me that her husband had gone over to Addissu's *mander* – which I knew referred to the houses near Addissu's house the other side of the supermarket. My household's immediate neighbours comprised some eight households, the next door neighbour to our left, three houses to our right, and the four flats directly opposite. The other houses were inhabited by non-Ethiopians. These immediate neighbours were the people we sat around with outside, the core invitees for a small gathering and a pool of potential coffee partners. This neighbourhood group tended, as far as possible, to go together to funerals and celebrations held in other parts of the neighbourhood. Women arranged to go to the market in twos' and threes' and to purchase together sacs of *teff* flour (imported from Ethiopia) from itinerant traders; men often formed a small party to buy a goat or cow together and shared out the meat (called in this instance *frida*).

The outer circle of neighbours includes the whole neighbourhood. My neighbourhood comprised ninety-six houses. Whenever a large celebration was held, a cow was killed and all these ninety-six households were systematically invited, together with selected neighbours from other suburbs of the town and the hosts' close kin from other parts of the country. This group of neighbours offer each other mutual assistance, but more haphazardously than the core group of neighbours. Strong social relations within this wider circle are formed on the basis of friendship and kinship, with particularly strong bonds between members of a rotating credit society. The widest circle comprises all Ethiopians living in a given town. Strong bonds within this circle occur on a voluntary individual basis, usually due to kinship or prior neighbourhood ties. The only morally binding commitment within this circle is to attend funerals.

Becoming a neighbour

The principal criterion for becoming a neighbour is residential proximity. All Ethiopians who lived in the neighbourhood of Afula Tse'era, an area with definite physical boundaries (the older neighbourhood of Afula Elite with its older housing stock on one side, and fields to the other), were automatically part of the community of neighbours, and were bound by its social obligations.

When households are situated on the boundary of two distinct neighbourhoods, each with its own group of Ethiopian neighbours, they choose which neighbourhood to be most closely associated with, usually on the basis of kin ties, and maintain minimal relations with the other. For example, there are four Ethiopian households situated in the area between Afula Tse'era and Afula Tse'era B. Two of these households are part of the Afula Tse'era community of neighbours: both households are related – the women are first cousins – and one of them has her father in Afula Tse'era and the other her brother. They attend all Afula Tse'era celebrations and mourning rituals, and also maintain relations, albeit less pronounced, with the other neighbourhood of Afula Tse'era B. The other two households joined the community of Afula Tse'era B (one of them had two children living there), and come to Afula Tse'era only for special occasions.

The community of neighbours is also delimited by less tangible boundary markers, such as years of residence in Israel and former ethnic origin (i.e. Tigre or Gondar region). For example, Afula Tse'era, home to new Ethiopian immigrants, is adjacent to Afula Elite, an older neighbourhood home to many Ethiopian immigrants from an earlier wave of immigration (known in Israel as 'veterans'). Most Ethiopian households in Afula Elite are minutes away from Afula Tse'era, separated on the main road only by a stretch of grass. Yet Ethiopians from Afula Elite and Afula Tse'era maintain their own separate communal relations, and join each other regularly only for large celebrations and mourning gatherings.

> Rachel, the Ethiopian woman who cleaned the centre in which Afula Tse'era Hebrew classes were held, gave birth. She lived in Afula Elite and had been in the country several years longer than

the Ethiopian women students. The Israeli teacher suggested visiting her after class with a gift. The Afula Tse'era women agreed, but it took a while to locate the apartment for none of them had ever been to her building, three minutes away from theirs.

Another Ethiopian neighbourhood I knew well, a twenty minute walk from Afula Tse'era, is home to immigrants from both the Gondar region and the Tigre region. Though there is no spatial separation between the two groups, who often share the same apartment blocks, two clearly demarcated community of neighbours were formed.

Once an Ethiopian family moves into an area, it automatically becomes 'neighbour' to other Ethiopians in the neighbourhood (within the visible or invisible boundary markers noted above).

A young family moved into our street. During the first few days, the wife was rather despondent and spoke with regret of her last home fondly recalling her former neighbours. But she felt confident that she would soon get to know her new neighbours, who were coming to visit her in small groups, bringing offerings of drinks and *injera*. Within a few weeks, she was going to the shops with her downstairs neighbour, had gained coffee partners, and attended celebrations with her closest neighbours.

Avi became head of his household at twenty-two after his widowed mother died. He was one of the 'trendy' lads and had rarely attended neighbourhood celebrations since he was away at the army in Eilat (eight hours away) and in any case he found such gatherings 'primitive'. At his mother's death, he left the army to live full-time at home and look after his younger siblings. He became a 'neighbour' overnight. He attended all neighbourhood celebrations, often taking on a prominent role such as collecting money offerings. At the anniversary of his mother's death, he himself organised a large funerary gathering at his house, hosting the whole neighbourhood and feeding them six goats. Avi did not stop criticising Ethiopian neighbourhood life, but he nonetheless accepted his new role and appeared to enjoy it more than he admitted.

*Gomange Mariam, Gondar, Ethiopia, 1995.
The village in which Abba Negusse lived until 1990.*

White neighbours

After two years in her new neighbourhood, Aveva told me that she continued to be too shy to visit her new Ethiopian neighbours. The latter had all visited her, bearing gifts, to welcome her in her new dwelling and soon they began to reprimand her: 'Why do you not visit Ethiopian houses? Are you a *farenj*?'

Non-Ethiopians, referred to as *farenj* (white, foreigner) or *russit* (Russian, Hebrew) when specifically referring to Russian immigrants, are not considered 'neighbours'. In terms of the social network described above, they are invisible. Indeed, when a family has the misfortune not to have any Ethiopian households living within a five minutes walk, they complain that they have 'no neighbours'. Ethiopians and *farenj* neighbours rarely exchange greetings, and greetings are the foundation of neighbourly relations. In fact, the lack of basic relations with non-Ethiopian neighbours reinforces the closeness between Ethiopians.

An Ethiopian is shopping in town. A sea of foreign (*farenj*) faces pass him by, until suddenly an Ethiopian neighbour appears in the crowd. The two greet each other warmly, a moment all the more intimate given the multitude of 'others' all around.

If non-Ethiopian households are invisible in terms of the social world of neighbourhood relations, their presence is felt, not least because of the animosity which sometimes erupts. White neighbours frequently complain about the smell of Ethiopian cooking and coffee and about the noise when a household hosts a party.

Mulualem's first child's *cristenna* celebration and purification ceremony to mark the eightieth day after the birth of his baby-girl was a raging success. The tables outside his house at the end of his street (a cul-de-sac) were full with hundreds of relatives. Youths and adults were dancing to the disco sound-system, alternating popular Western hits and Amharic music. But at 11.30 p.m. the party was brought to an abrupt close by the arrival of the police. I was not surprised, given the comments made to me earlier in the day by the Israeli neighbour, a recent immigrant from Brazil: 'You work with Ethiopians, perhaps you can help us. We are getting fed up, every month there is something. That woman from across the road died and for seven days, all night, until five a.m., there was noise. Then they had that wedding in the house next-door. For three days, until five a.m., noise. Now this today for the birth of a child. They are always having children, will this happen each time? We are going to call the police. The street is not just theirs, it is ours too. If they come to Israel, they must learn Israeli ways. Otherwise, they should stay in Ethiopia! They cannot be primitive here. They should hire a hall, like normal people'.[4]

While most Ethiopians' relations with their *farenj* neighbours are neutral and some are hostile, a minority of *farenj* neighbours are positively valued, at least enough to invite to celebrations at home. As expected, younger couples, who speak Hebrew and are prepared to comply to Israeli norms of social behaviour, entertain better relations with their non-Ethiopian neighbours.

Lea, a bubbly young woman: 'The *farenj* like me. I speak Hebrew. I am quiet at home and my garden and house are well-kept. I know how to speak to them, and I dress like them.'

Social relations among neighbours

Visiting neighbours

A dense network of visits creates and upholds neighbourly relations on a daily basis. A day rarely passes without each person making at least one visit to a neighbour, and conversely receiving at least one in turn, in addition to daily coffee sessions with the next-door neighbour. When the person being visited is ill, grieving, or has given birth, a small offering of food or money is taken. The receiving party offers a drink and, depending on other factors, coffee and food. Such visits are motivated by sociability and by a desire to offer assistance to a neighbour in difficulty.

Gifts and money are bestowed in a casual manner, but the exact nature and value of the gift as well as the precise amount of money given is registered by both parties, and an equivalent return is expected at a later date. Whenever I gave a standard NIS 20 (£4) to a woman who had given birth, she would say something like 'but you mustn't – how can I return it to you when you give birth? You will be in England!' In other words, giving to a neighbour with no expectation of return was anathema.

Celebrations and mourning

The idiom of 'being together' is most forcefully enacted when neighbours gather to celebrate, mourn and pray. In my neighbourhood, there are approximately three large celebrations (two to six hundred persons) per month during the summer season, and one per month during the winter. Such celebrations mark life events such as weddings, Bar Mitzvah, and *cristenna* (the purification ritual after the birth of a child). Moreover, a week rarely passes without a small celebration (thirty to fifty persons) for a boy's circumcision, for the send-off to the army of a son, or for a myriad of other events such as the purchase of a car and the visit from a relative from afar. In addition, groups of neighbours gather to attend funerals (four hundred to one thousand persons) or smaller local mourning sessions (approximately one hundred to five hundred persons), at least once a month. All gatherings to mourn the deceased are called by the generic term '*lkso*', which is a noun derived from the verb 'to cry'. These are held for funerals, at various set days after the funeral (such as the seventh, the thirtieth, and annually), and to mourn locally with a neighbour whose close relative was mourned in another town.[5]

Celebrations and mourning rituals are a prominent feature of daily life, given their frequency, their financial cost and the labour involved in hosting them. They cement bonds between neighbours and kin. The surest way to display animosity towards a neighbour or relative is to fail to attend his celebration without a valid reason. The requirement to attend the funerals (or one of the subsequent mourning sessions, such as the seventh day after the funeral) of relative and neighbours is stronger still, and however vehement a dispute between neighbours or kin, this obligation is always fulfilled.

A well-known saying goes: better be seen with unwashed feet or bedding an in-law, than miss a relative's funeral.

At celebrations and *lkso*, neighbours display their commitment to one another in three ways: they celebrate or mourn with the host according to proper custom, they help to organise the event by contributing both cash and labour, and they socialise and eat together.

Communal labour

The day after the week-end celebration of his son's Bar Mitzvah, Melash invited his close neighbours for a final serving of food and drink. He explained to me why: 'The relatives who live far away have gone home. The close neighbours helped me with the preparations, the men with the meat, and the women with the *injera*, so now I say to them: "Come and eat and drink!"'

Each large event requires a phenomenal amount of preparation: food, drink, seating and music (for celebrations) for up to a thousand persons. 'Hamlet' women, i.e. the closest neighbours, get together weeks in advance to prepare the spices for the stew and batter for the *injera* pancakes. The day before the event, each close neighbour comes to collect a small bucket of fermented batter and returns in the early morning with between ten and twenty prepared *injera* pancakes. 'Hamlet' men set off to slaughter a cow (or a number of goats) and return several hours later with large plastic bags full of meat. Men from the whole neighbourhood come during the day, carrying their own carving knife, to help cut up the meat into small bite-sized portions. The celebration (or mourning) house is turned into a temporary butchery as meat and meat cutters fill most rooms. The meat is cooked in large pots on an outdoor fire. The men enjoy chatting together and drink plenty of beer in the process. Tables and chairs are set up in an empty space near the receiving house, such as the building's parking lot, which is enclosed as far as possible with sheets of green plastic. During the celebration, the hamlet men seat the guests, serve food, collect money donations, and in the early hours of the morning, when the other guests have left, they clear up.

Communal financing

As well as providing labour, neighbours provide cash for celebrations and mourning events. Every guest gives a contribution which is marked into a notebook alongside his or her name. When the recipient himself goes to a party, he verifies in his notebook the amount that the present party giver gave him (although he tends to remember the sum in his head anyway), and he gives an equal amount of money, or a little bit more. The total sum obtained at these parties is usually considerably more than the expenses, and, in my experience, profits range from between NIS 1,000 (£200) to NIS 25,000 (£5,000).[6] The money is spent on household goods or put away in a savings account for future use – for example, a child's education, a trip to Ethiopia, or furniture.

People are often quite cynical about this money, complaining that they will have to give it back (at future celebrations) in any case so it is not really theirs. The frequency of parties are also cause for complaint, and people are accused of holding large parties 'just to get money'. The sums given are indeed large – between NIS 50 and NIS 200 (£10–£40) – and a significant percentage of monthly income is spent on celebration donations. Repaying a former debt is often given as *the* reason for attending a party.

> Alefash, whose husband is a member of one of the largest Beta Israel kin groups, complained that in just one week she and her husband spent NIS 1,300 on party donations. Alefash and Moshe got married the previous year and they were now in the business of repaying their debts to over a thousand wedding guests. She explained that she had given a particularly large sum to her elder brother for his house warming (NIS 900) because the latter had given them NIS 700 for their wedding, and he probably would not have any more parties now since all his children were

married, but that she and Moshe would have lots coming, God willing. In other words, she was consciously laying out money, in the form of a donation to her elder brother, for the celebrations she expected to hold for her unborn children.

Celebrating together: a local Bar Mitzvah

Fantanesh and Abuhay held a Bar Mitzvah celebration for their second son Moshe. At 8 p.m. on Thursday, all the food was cooked, the tables and chairs were set out in long rows in the open car-park closed off on three sides by large green plastic sheets, and the Israeli DJ and video-men were ready. Fantanesh, Abuhay, their children and one of Abuhay's elder brothers stood in line at the entrance of the space. The elder brother guarded the home-made donation box. The video camera was switched on, the Israeli DJ played Israeli traditional melodies and neighbours began to arrive in small groups. After placing their donations in envelopes distributed by young boys on which they wrote their name (or got a literate person to do so), they greeted in turn all the standing hosts and placed their envelopes in the box. They wore bright new clothes or clean white Ethiopian dresses, wrapped in white shawls. They were invited to sit by members of the helping group of men and were served beer and soft drinks. Seated guests chatted quietly or remained in silence as they watched the newcomers arrive. Dozens of children ran around, sometimes begging their parents for soft drinks. By the time a few hundred seats were full, young men served plates of *injera* with meat stew. Other than myself, the only non-Ethiopians present were a couple of community workers, the DJ and video-men. Curious neighbours came to watch from time to time, or peered from their windows.

At 10 p.m. the Bar Mitzvah candle ceremony, led by the Israeli DJ, was performed without much emotion and a little difficulty, given the novelty of the custom for Beta Israel. But as soon as it was over, the atmosphere livened up. The DJ played a traditional Hebrew '*mazel tov*' song, and the Bar Mitzvah boy and his father were hoisted onto shoulders and paraded around the assembly. Around them, guests broke into dance and clapped. Soon, an Ethiopian youth helped the DJ to select and play Amharic music, and the dancing group grew rapidly. Pairs of dancers stood facing one another, eyes interlocked, gyrating their shoulders energetically in traditional

North Ethiopian style. Others stood around them in a large circle several layers deep, clapping and swaying to the sound of the music. The hosts danced most of the evening. Their guests stuck bank notes on their sweaty foreheads (in total NIS 1,250 on the boy's forehead, NIS 400 on the mother and NIS 350 on the father, i.e. a total of NIS 2,000 (approximately £ 400)).

At midnight, the police van drove past slowly, and the hosts took the hint. The music was immediately turned off, and most of the guests left. After clearing up, kin and close neighbours continued the party at home until the early hours of the morning. For the whole week-end, Abuhay and Fantanesh held open house. Kin stayed over and neighbours came and went, drinking, chatting and eating. A little dancing resumed on Saturday evening, after Sabbath. Visiting kin left on Saturday night or Sunday morning. On Sunday, Abuhay sent his son around to invite the close neighbours at 5 p.m. to finish the *injera*. A small cheerful reunion of intimates took place, and the party was much praised.

Beta Israel stress the importance of eating and drinking with kin and neighbours at celebrations. Whenever I asked anybody 'how was the party?', they invariably answered: 'It was good, there was lots of *injera*, meat, and beer'.

As a vegetarian, I could not eat at celebrations, where meat is always served. More than once I was asked by a neighbour: 'What is the point of going, since you cannot eat?'

Celebrations provide hosts with the opportunity to demonstrate their hospitality and commitment to the group. The event in honour of which a celebration is held, such as a Bar Mitzvah or a wedding, remains in the background and appears to be little more than an excuse to invite neighbours and kin. Indeed, after the occasion is marked with the appropriate blessings and other ceremonies, the Bar Mitzvah boy or the wedding couple assume junior roles more or less as they would on any other occasion. It is their parents who are at the centre of attention. It is their chance to affirm themselves as proud Beta Israel. In the process, they reaffirm the idiom of 'being together' as neighbours, kin and Ethiopian Israelis.

Credit societies

As well as visiting, celebrating, mourning, and praying together, neighbours 'drink together' (*abran tatan*) at their rotating credit society (*kuvie*).

I joined one of the two women's *kuvie* in my neighbourhood. The twenty-two women met every two weeks in alternate members' houses to consume food and drink and to pay the due NIS 100 (approx. £20). Each woman received her turn of the total (NIS 2100, £420) approximately every eleven months (depending on new entries and exits to the group). The sessions were jolly affairs as the group of women chatted, drank Ethiopian coffee, soft drinks and beer, and their children played.

The men's *kuvie* group that I sometimes attended as a guest was more gregarious. The sessions, held every three weeks, started late afternoon on Saturday, and continued for a good three hours. The men drank much alcohol and enjoyed joking: 'A man 'did not know how to', and asked his friend to show him; the latter was delighted and did 'it' with the man's wife!'; 'A couple were watching an Ethiopian video. The man said that he wanted to go to Ethiopia to 'have' the girl who was dancing; his wife was not amused and threw a bottle into the TV!'

The *kuvie* provides a means of saving so that 'you get lots of money and can buy something big', such as a large refrigerator, household furniture, and, more recently, the air-fare to Ethiopia for a holiday or health cure.[7] Like celebrations, it rests on commitment and trust, sociability and economic exchange between neighbours.

The use of the expression 'to drink together' to refer to *kuvie* membership shows the importance of the social nature of the gatherings. As Kanubesh put it: 'The *kuvie* is to chat (*tetchawot*). For saving, I can put money in the bank, where it can earn interest.' The sharing of money is a means to socialise. Educated women, slightly embarrassed by their membership of such an apparently un-modern institution, stressed this point: 'The money makes us get together regularly, otherwise, when would we meet?'

The *kuvie* is a means to socialise and to pool resources; it also cements trust and commitment between neighbours. Each member pays out a significant amount of cash every month, with trust the only guarantee of return.

When I joined the *kuvie*, my standing as 'a neighbour' rose significantly, because by giving my NIS 100 every fortnight, I was committing myself to my neighbours for a least a year (after which time I would recoup my savings) and I showed the women that I trusted them to pay me back.

The social cementing function of the *kuvie* was particularly evident in the case of working women members who were unable to attend sessions (therefore missing out on the sociability function) and usually held direct debit saving accounts (and therefore did not need the economic function of the *kuvie*). They joined the *kuvie* to reinforce their social bonds of commitment and trust with their neighbours, particularly given the fact that their paid employment often excluded them from daily social interaction. *Kuvie* members enjoy a certain 'group feeling', a special sort of communality, explicit in the following incident.

The son of a *kuvie* member died in the army. The *kuvie* members got together a small sum of money (approximately £2 each), and altogether went over to the grieving mother to donate the offering. This donation was over and above the women's previous contributions, as neighbours, to the funeral. They wanted to show the woman support as *kuvie* members.

Another type of association was created in my neighbourhood towards the end of my stay which illustrated well the neighbours' sense of 'being together'.

> The Chair Society' (*yewomber mahaver*) was born at a neighbourhood meeting called by two residents who had realised that they could dramatically cut the cost of neighbourhood events if they could rid themselves of the astronomical fee for hiring chairs and table. They worked out the cost of buying five hundred chairs and accompanying tables, and divided this sum between the neighbourhood's ninety-six Ethiopian households. They invited each household to join by paying their share of the total cost. This one-off payment worked out at about a third of the cost of renting chairs and tables for just one evening. It was therefore advantageous for any household which envisaged holding a celebration in the future: nearly all of them. Ninety-two households agreed to join, and within six months eighty-five had paid up and the chairs and tables were purchased. The members can use the equipment for free, but the Chair Society charges a fee to non-members, the income from which will go towards the purchase of large freezers for the storage of drink and meat.

Dissent amongst neighbours

The rosy picture of neighbourhood life that I have depicted does suffer from friction and quarrel. However, these are kept well beneath the smooth surface: quarrelling parties avoid each other to minimise disruption and a reconciliation is fast engineered.

A quarrel erupted between two next-door neighbours. Apparently one of them, for unknown motives, had told the social services that the other was lying about his poor health and consequent inability to work. The two men cut their neighbourly relations and ceased all contact. But this rupture in neighbourhood harmony was contained because their wives remained good neighbours, drinking coffee together and sharing labour, and other neighbours avoided taking sides. After about a year, when well-wishers' surreptitious attempts proved unable to break the dead-lock, elders stepped in, a reconciliation meeting was held, and peace established. From one day to the next the two men became inseparable, drank coffee together, and set off together for social outings and shopping expeditions.

Abba Makwanent wanted to boycott Mama Wuvenesh's celebration of her daughter's wedding because the latter was marrying a relative, which is forbidden by Ethiopian Jewish custom. More lenient elders stepped in and pleaded with him to join the party: better transgress a cherished custom than threaten the unity of the neighbourhood.

As well as such open quarrels, even the most dedicated neighbours sometimes complain about the rigorous demands of neighbourhood sociability and economic exchange.

Fantanesh, one of the most popular women in the neighbourhood, occasionally became weary: 'It is good to have a job in this country. Because when you are at home all the time, guests come continuously and you have to serve them coffee and *injera*. It is expensive!' But her words nearly amounted to blasphemy, and she quickly reiterated the standard rhetoric: 'If you provide for a guest, God will give back double in return. You are happy when a guest comes whom you can feed and give drink to.'

The constant requirement of sociability and good humour can be wearing. A neighbour takes back streets in order to avoid having to extend greetings to all and sundry, another stays indoors with the express purpose of not seeing anyone, another still complains of the 'blah blah blah blah' to which he is subjected to all day, wishing people would just stay quiet sometimes.

For young people, growing up in Israel with notions of personal freedom, the ever watchful eyes of neighbours is resented because any suspicious movement on their part will instantaneously become the talk of the neighbourhood.

> Alemwork, a twenty-five-year-old who immigrated at the age of sixteen, wishes her husband and his family would be less 'Ethiopian' sometimes. 'If I want to study in evening classes, his mother comes by and asks him where I am and he says 'studying' and she says 'oh yes?' He cares about what people say. He says that he will not walk with me if I wear trousers.'

'Being together' as kin

> A 25 year-old man tries to persuade a girl towards whom he is romantically inclined to make a trip with him to Netanya. He suggested what might tempt her most: 'We could visit all my relatives there!'

> One young woman did not enjoy visiting kin. Her kin complained: 'In Ethiopia, she was nice. Here it seems like she has no relatives!'

Defining kin

The term *zamad*

On the one hand, *zamad* includes a finite, albeit huge, group of blood relatives; on the other, *zamad* is used loosely to refer to anyone one wishes to express closeness towards. Being kin, in the latter all-inclusive sense, is essentially about feeling close 'like a brother and sister'; anybody one feels close to becomes 'kin' and calling someone with a kin term is a way of honouring a particular individual.

> A close neighbour who is not a relative by blood is referred to as *yinne zamad* 'my relative' and addressed with a kin term such as 'sister', 'father' or 'aunty'.

A man recalls with affection a former Christian neighbour in Ethiopia: 'He was our *zamad*!'

The term *zamad* in this wide sense, is also used as a boundary marker to enforce a sentiment of group identity beyond the circle of blood relatives. For example, Beta Israel assert that 'we are all kin' when they seek to contrast the Beta Israel to other groups, such as their former Ethiopian Christian neighbours.[8] Broader still, the term can be even more inclusive and refer to Jews as a whole, i.e. Ethiopian Jews and other Israelis, in contrast to Arabs. Occasionally, even Arabs are included in the category *zamad* because they are 'our cousins, the descendants of Avraham'. In this latter context, most of the world becomes kin.

As well as this inclusive sense, *zamad* has an extremely specific meaning, and includes a finite group of people: blood relatives related to each other within seven generations on both maternal and paternal side[9]

> My neighbour Fantanesh Yalew returns home from a visit to a post-partum woman, Adisye. Her elderly mother Tarikye Melash wants to know who the woman is. 'Adisye is Taye Ayelign's granddaughter, daughter of Belaynesh Taye'. 'Ah, I know who she is!', said Fantanesh's mother, predictably. Explaining to me: 'Ayelign Alemu, who is Taye Ayelign's father, and Turuwork Alemu were brother and sister. Turuwork [begat] Melash Turuneh, and Melash Turuneh begat Tarikye Melash, and then [Tarikye begat] Fantanesh Yalew. Do you understand?', she asks me. 'Well, I am not sure ...' 'OK, Turuwork and Ayelign are siblings, so that is one [generation], then Melash is two, then Tarikye – that is me – three, then Fantanesh four [generations]. On her side, Ayelign one, Taye two, Belaynesh three, Adisye four. Fantanesh and Adisye are related four and four. It is close – she is a sister! Understand?' Fantanesh came to my rescue: 'My grandfather and Adisye's grandfather were first cousins'.

Counting kin tends to start, as in this example, with the joint sibling pair counted as 'One', a short hand term for 'one generation'.[10] Counting generations of kin is a common activity, particularly enjoyed by elders.

> Most visitors to Fantanesh's house have to sit through the 'finding the common ancestor' ritual with Fantanesh's mother,

They are amused if they have already been through the process several times, or show genuine interest if their memory needs refreshing. Fantànesh often smiled at me at such occasions, knowing that I was taking mental note of the proceedings. My interest in kinship was easily understood by my informants, since it is a chief interest of theirs.

Generally, people love to count generations and when youngsters meet outside of kin circles, such as at school, army or work, they try themselves to work out their exact kin connection, and failing this, ask an elder on their next visit home. When youngsters want to marry, the counting of generations becomes crucial.

Close kin are thought of as descendants, called 'children', of one ancestor a few generations back.

At a house warming party, I ask a middle-aged daughter of late Abba Desta how many children he had. She waves her hand to include all two hundred and fifty guests: 'Lots! They are all his children!' She included in 'his children' (of which he had at least fifteen to my knowledge) all Abba Desta's living relatives – his natural children, step-children and their offspring, and the offspring of all his junior relatives.

The most intimate circle of kin is composed of first and second degree relatives and more distant relatives who have become friends, often as a result of neighbourhood bonds. The next circle comprises 'close' kin (*kirb zamad*), who are related up to about three or four generations. The widest circle includes all other blood relatives. Few individuals even know the names of their most distant kin and precise kin relations can be ascertained only with the help of kinship specialists, older priests and old people who are well versed in Beta Israel lines of descent. Circles of relatives are drawn from both maternal and paternal kin, although individuals are often drawn towards one set of relatives more than the other.

Alefash was having a rant while she cleaned the house. Her children, she decided, do not love her. Recalling the displays of affection between her and her eight children, and the abundance of love between them, I expressed my surprise. She continued defiantly: 'They like their father, not me; they only visit his kin!'

The 'feel' of kin

As I was leaving for Abba Negusse's home, after visiting kin in another town, Abba Brhan, Abba Negusse's uncle, said to me: 'Say hello to all of them. They are my relatives (*zamad*), my elder brother's children!' As he contemplated the image of his brother's 'children' – ranging from eighty years to three weeks old – his voice filled with warmth and pride, and a radiant smile spread across his face.

At the other extremity of the kin group, twenty-one year-old Solomon, grandson to Abba Turuneh, announced to his twenty-five-year-old cousin Worku the birth of his first child. Worku, himself a father of four, exclaimed: 'Ah, Abba Turuneh's *zer* (seed)!' His tone combined jest, pride and a sense of awe at the fresh realisation of the great size of his close kin group, the ever growing number of his grandfather's 'children'.

As the above examples illustrate, individuals have a strong sense of being part of a group of kin, and they derive pride and satisfaction from this constant awareness. Having kin involves feelings of inclusion, protection, safety and 'oneness'.

A young friend was explaining to me the differences between the various terms used to denote 'kin': '*Yigna saw*' (lit: our people) denotes people whom you would protect if someone wanted to do them harm.' In other words, he chose the image of protection to define kinship.

Relatives are those people one feels very close to – that one cannot live without.

Since the Beta Israel migrated to Israel in two waves, most close kin groups were split for several years. Family reunification was invariably listed as one of the best things about Israel. In fact, many Ethiopians, who arrived during the second wave, stated that 'to be with kin' was their main motivation for migration.

Kin often exclaim: 'We are one!' According to Beta Israel ideology, kin *should* feel close to one another and in practice they are, as the following account illustrates.

When the Israeli-style Bar Mitzvah celebrations at a hired hall (*oulam*) were over, at around two a.m. on Friday, close relatives converged at the local *moadon* (community club). Young men galvanised to serve *injera* and meat stew, which was much enjoyed by the older guests, who had only picked at the four course Israeli catered meal. After eating and drinking, men sang Ethiopian folk tunes with improvised verse, using the table as a drum for accompaniment. Relatives danced together. In a small annexe, young teenagers made their own party, dancing to modern Western music (especially 'house' and 'techno'). Neither group was apparently perturbed by the other, even though the singers had to sing over the sound of the taped music coming in from the other room.

Workie's three bedroom flat, the closest home to the party, soon filled as relatives came for coffee and rest. By about four a.m., there were at least three bodies on each mattress and rows of children slept side by side on the floor, with one blanket covering them all. Around seven a.m., elders rose for coffee, leaving their mattresses for the next shift of sleepers.

For forty-eight hours, relatives laughed, chatted, drank and eat, with only the odd hour of stolen sleep here and there, in any Ethiopian house which had some floor space. Saturday morning, after synagogue, close kin congregated at the hosts' house. All nine siblings of the Bar Mitzvah boy's father were present together with their partners, most of their children and grandchildren, as well as a few cousins. The Sabbath home-made bread was blessed and cut by the eldest brother and prayers recited in Amharic and Hebrew.

Cousins of both sexes lay on each other's laps, touching each other affectionately. They teased each other about their looks and personal characteristics. Courtesy towards others was pronounced. Whenever someone got up to get a drink, for example, he or she offered a drink to everyone assembled and elders were bestowed even more respect than usual. There was continuous coming and going, as individuals moved from one house to another or small groups went for short strolls. As soon as Sabbath ended, at around seven p.m. on Saturday, the party, although reduced in size, resumed in the *moadon* and dancing continued until the early hours.

Social relations among relatives

Kin (*zamad*) is 'the most important thing' (*yewanaw neger naw*) and success at maintaining social relations with kin is the main factor which accounts for Beta Israel well-being in Israel. Conversely, failure to do is said to lead to tragedy.

> Daniel, twenty-three years old, explained why an eighteen-year-old soldier committed suicide: 'The boy asked for leave to attend his cousin's funeral. He was not granted permission because for an Israeli, a cousin is not so important. But for us, a cousin is a brother, a father. So the boy killed himself.'

I am sure that the soldier's motives were more complex, but for Daniel, frustration at being unable to fulfil a duty towards kin was a valid reason to account for a young man's suicide.

Visiting kin

It is Saturday eight a.m. Abba Negusse's two-bedroom house is full. His eldest son is staying, with his wife and four children. His younest son and one of his grandson's from Haifa University are also visiting for the weekend. A few youngsters still sleep curled up in their white sheets. Worku, Abba Negusse's nephew who lives down the road, arrives with his little boy dressed in his Sabbath green suit. We sit outside and Abba Negusse teases his great-nephew affectionately. A party of young men, siblings and cousins, wander off slowly to Abba Negusse's daughter Dege's house, chatting and laughing gaily. Later, some of the women go over to Worku's home to visit his wife who is heavily pregnant, while the others eventually make their way to Dege's, stopping over at the house of a distant kin on the way. At Dege's, a group play cards, others sleep in corners. Children play outside. Cousins remember stories of life in Ethiopia and laugh merrily.

With the exception of the next-door neighbour, the people most often visited and received are kin who live close by. They meet several times a week, or at the very least on Saturdays. Leaving the house to visit kin in other towns[11] is usually precipitated by a particular event – a religious holiday, a celebration, a bereavement, a sickness, the birth of a child. Once in the neighbourhood, all kin in that area are visited, even just to say hello if there is no time or appetite left to consume food and drink. Whenever I heard complaints about kin uttered openly, they were complaints that the relative(s) in question had not visited recently enough. Visiting kin is imperative, but as imperatives go, it is on the whole a pleasurable one.

> Workie, Abba Negusse's eldest daughter, comes to visit because her father is unwell. She brings home-made bread and raw coffee beans which she presents to her mother-in-law and a small bag of sweets for her nieces and nephews. She spends her first evening chatting over coffee and *injera* at home. The following morning, she cleans the house. After a coffee session and *injera*, about noon, she wraps herself in her white shawl and goes out. She starts with her sister and spends most of the day there. Her cousin Asrebav, who lives next-door comes to drink coffee, as does her husband, but no sooner is the session over that Asrebav insists Workie come to her house for another coffee session. The next day, she goes to her brother, visiting another cousin on the way. They watch together the video of a recent family wedding, catching up on the latest gossip about their relatives when they appear on screen, and saying out loud their names for the benefit of the children. Next, she does the 'rounds', visiting briefly all other close kin in the neighbourhood, including her deceased mother's kin.

The telephone

The phone rings frequently in Ethiopian Israeli households, and other than the youngsters' friends, it is a relative calling. The caller speaks to the person who answers the phone and then speaks to every member of the household who is present, sending greetings to absent household members. The form of telephone conversations are similar to face-to-face meetings. Most contain little more than standard greetings: 'How are you? How is your wife? How is son X? How is son Y? How is that sick neighbour of yours?' More substantial conversations concern family affairs such as a marriage break-up, the purchase of a house, or wedding plans. Unsurprisingly, youngsters chat on the phone the most, and they often take the phone into their own room to gossip with their cousins and other friends.

Ethiopian Israelis praise the telephone because it enables them to be in constant touch with close kin. Women commented that after they got married in Ethiopia and moved to their husband's village, they saw their parents and former close neighbours only a few times a year at most. Now, they can chat whenever they want, or at least within the limitations of cost. In fact, the telephone plays an integral role in maintaining social relations between kin. As Ethiopian Israelis often say: 'In this country you do not need to go and visit your relatives: you can just telephone!'

Mutual help

For the Beta Israel, a loving relationship is expressed by giving and receiving. As with neighbours, kin express their affection and consideration by helping one another. The idiom of reciprocity is fundamental to Ethiopian social interaction; it even defines relations between parent and child.

> A woman laments that her aged sister Worku is unsupported by her children: 'She carried them in her tummy nine months, fed them with milk from her breast, carried them on her back, and now look, she is all alone and they are far away!'

> Mama Zaudie wails when she hears that her husband refuses to buy a goat for his daughter's engagement: 'Ah! Just one daughter [living at home], she cleans the house and does this and that, and he cannot even buy her one goat!'

Cash circulates between kin as it does between neighbours. Relatives give large cash donations at celebrations, funerals and when a relative is sick, has given birth or is embarking on a journey to Ethiopia. Like neighbourhood *kuvie* (rotating credit societies), groups of close relatives form small *kuvie*. In addition, relatives lend each other money in times of need and parents try to contribute to their children's large purchases, such as a car or a flat.

Young people help elders in non-monetary ways, namely in dealing with difficult aspects of Israeli society, such as acquiring benefits and housing. The obligation to help kin in this respect can become difficult to fulfil for educated Ethiopians who work in government welfare jobs, given the consequent constant demands placed on them.

> I often heard about a particular cousin who was 'not a good person'. When I eventually met the man in question, he

explained to me that because he works in an office which gives mortgages for Ethiopian Israelis to buy houses, all his relatives approached him for help when they were considering house purchase. Given the size of his kin group, it would be impossible to get any work done if he helped them all, and worst still, it would look to others like he was favouring his own kin.

Quarrels and reconciliation

Given the intensity of social relations between relatives and the high expectations placed on such relations, it is unsurprising that feuds and quarrels rage under the surface. Thanks to a number of internal mechanisms, quarrels and animosities do not endanger the ideal image of kin 'being together' and their impact is reduced. First, kin who are not directly involved in a specific quarrel avoid taking sides openly, thus limiting the spread of animosity. Also, given the large numbers of people present for family occasions, it is easy for quarrelling individuals to avoid each other. Moreover, kin exert pressure on both sides until a public reconciliation is achieved.

Mulugeta and his father and sister quarrelled badly one day, and the physical fighting was terminated by neighbours only after Mulugeta had broken the phone, beat up his sister, hit his father (which is one of the worst thing an Ethiopian can do) and received his father's walking stick across his back. For over nine months, Mulugeta refused to enter the house, and put the phone down on his mother when she tried to call him. Although relatives varied in the versions of the story they believed, they unanimously urged Mulugeta to come and apologise to his parents. Eventually, when plenty of close kin were in the neighbourhood, attending the Bar Mitzvah of a close relative, Mulugeta was finally persuaded. About two dozen relatives escorted him to his father's house, the group growing as curious neighbours joined in, and after several attempted retreats from both sides (e.g. Mulugeta's father: 'How can we reconcile today, it is Sabbath?'), Mulugeta bent down in front of his father and asked forgiveness, which was granted, albeit reluctantly.

Difficulties in social relations in Israel

Following Beta Israel's own discourse, I have presented an idyllic image of relations between kin and neighbours. But it is not infrequent to hear an Ethiopian Israeli complain about these relations in Israel. Women in particular bemoan former times when neighbours 'helped each other', when a woman could, according to Beta Israel custom, sojourn in the menstrual hut for seven days during her periods because her neighbour cooked all the required *injera* for her household. Now, they say, they can no longer seclude themselves during their times of impurity: 'Who would look after the children? In Ethiopia, we had neighbours, here we are alone!' Or: 'Who is there to cook *injera* for a woman now? There we lived together, here we are separate.' Similarly, with kin: 'In Ethiopia, we all lived together, but here in Israel, it is so difficult because one brother lives in Beersheva, my sister lives in Haifa, my mother is in Holon ... all over the place!'

How can we understand such statements given that most Ethiopians, and certainly the women who made such claims to me, *do* live surrounded by Ethiopian neighbours, who *do* cook *injera* for them and help in other ways, and they *do* have frequent contact with kin?

First, given that neighbourhood and kin relations are central to Beta Israel social life, I suspect that even in Ethiopia, it was the chief focus for complaints.[12] Given that expectations of social relations between kin and neighbours are based on an *ideal* set of norms, it is impossible for them to be met in practice. This is not only because of human frailty. But also, since marriage partners in Ethiopia were usually chosen from other villages, one of the two partners, usually the woman, was forced to live away from close kin. Thanks to the telephone and public transport, the frequency of contact between kin living apart has actually increased in Israel.

Second, for Beta Israel, the quality of neighbourhood relations does appear to them to have decreased in Israel compared to Ethiopia, even if the above statements are exaggerations. There is a tendency to romanticise the past and to create an image of Ethiopian village life which was idyllic, and therefore by comparison contemporary life appears to fall short. Moreover, many women now go to work, with inflexible working days and hours, and it is therefore hard for them to take care of a neighbour's household as well as their own. Furthermore, although I have stressed the strength of the neighbour bond, it remains inferior in terms of expectations and obligations to that of the kin bond. In Ethiopia, this difference was merely theoretical since in most cases a next-door neighbour was also a close kin or in-law, and a strong kin relationship was superimposed onto the neighbour one. Fantanesh once made this point with reference to running out of a kitchen ingredient, explaining that 'there' it was easy, since she could pop into her mother's or sister's house to borrow something. I have seen her do the same with her neighbour in Israel, but she *feels* less free to do so. Although many Ethiopians do live in close proximity to kin, for many of them, kin neighbours are more scarce than in the Ethiopian village.[13]

Third, given the prominence of social relations between neighbours and kin, these relations are a good scapegoat for less tangible problems. For example, when a woman complains that she cannot maintain purity laws because of a lack of good neighbours, she might actually be speaking about her difficulties with changing purity customs rather than with her neighbours. Given that there is so much flux in Israel, and that so many traditions, customs and aspects of daily life are changing, the one discernible issue – relations with kin and neighbours – comes to the fore. It is easier to bemoan lack of living close to kin – when in fact contact with kin is very frequent – than it is to air grievances such as loss of productive activity or loss of a common language with which to talk to one's children.

Finally, Ethiopian complaints about kin and neighbourly relations actually add weight to their prominence by keeping them at centre stage of daily conversations: if one is not with relatives at a given moment, one can still complain about not being them, and thereby strengthen the cultural expectation of 'being together'. Similarly, Moshe Shokeid vividly portrays an impassioned quarrel at a gathering of Moroccan Israeli relatives over unmet expectations. This conflict between kin was itself an innovative way in which these immigrants expressed the strength of their bonds of kinship: by arguing about the transgression of obligations towards kin, the obligations are reinforced.[14]

Conclusion: Being together in Israel

Asras Mulugeta found himself heavily in debt after the social services asked him to reimburse the NIS 40,000 (£8,000) he had received on false claims or face a prison sentence. Asras did not despair – he knew that help was at hand, and he knew the form in which it must be solicited. He invited his close kin, all the Ethiopians in his neighbourhood, and a good proportion from adjacent neighbourhoods to come drink beer and eat *injera* on a specific day so that everyone could make a small donation towards the sum of money he urgently needed. Neighbours disapproved of Asras' way of life (he was reputed to have two wives) and his dishonesty with the social services. Still, they came, contributed between £10 and £30 each, and had a thoroughly enjoyable afternoon.

Asras Mulugeta's plea illustrates the idiom of being together as neighbours and kin in Israel. His guests all gave him money because a neighbour and/or relative of theirs was in need. By hosting a party, Asras not only raised the required money, but also, just like a credit society, socialised the process. In fact, socialising the request for cash not only succeeded in legitimising the demand, but also, the party reinforced the communality which makes such demands legitimate in the first place.

Ethiopian Jewish immigrants have succeeded in recreating strong social bonds between neighbours and kin in their new environment. They come together through sociability and economic exchange. The humanising function of these social relations is most evident among men and women who go to work; as soon as they return home, they resume their cycle of visiting and receiving Ethiopian guests, and their day begins in earnest.

If social relations amongst themselves is the foundation upon which the well-being of Ethiopian Israelis rest, a second factor is their arrival in, and appreciation of, the Promised Land.

4

Israel the Homeland

In his book 'From Falasha to Freedom', Ethiopian Israeli Shmuel Yilma describes his first day in Israel and the 'dream of families reuniting on the holy soil of Jerusalem':

We had abandoned our village and all that we had there, we passed through fire and water, jungle and desert, we climbed heights, forded rivers and crossed seas, we outwitted the powers-that-be, deceived neighbours and bandits, overcame wild beasts, conquered disease and affliction. We had traversed foreign states, dry land, sea and sky, *to bring to pass the ancient dream that we held in our hearts*. Grandmother raised her arms up high, gazed into the heavens, and declared, 'In this moment *we make real the small dream of reuniting our families*. This small dream was brought about by the great and ancient dream of two thousand years of exile – *to go up to the Land of Zion, to Jerusalem*. I said to you a few months ago when I set out: 'We shall meet again in Jerusalem. And here by the grace of God we are in Jerusalem!' The women set up their shrill ululation, customary when celebrating a joyous event.[1]

Given the importance of 'being together', illustrated in the previous chapter, it is unsurprising that accounts of arrival in Israel focus on family reunification. A close second, however, is the joy of reaching Jerusalem. Jerusalem is a short-hand for Israel, the Holy Land, the Promised Land – our homeland (*agerachin*). For the Beta Israel, arriving in Israel was, quite literally, a dream come true.

While subsequent chapters discuss the many disappointments the new immigrants soon experienced, this chapter details those aspects of the country which Ethiopian Israelis appreciate. Foremost, is a sense of belonging which they feel as Jews in the Land of Zion, the

Jewish Homeland. But also, as former village dwellers, they enjoy their new-found material wealth and free access to education for their children. This chapter focuses on the older generation of immigrants, postponing till the next chapter the experiences of integration of younger Ethiopian Israelis.

Our Homeland Israel

The descendants of ancient Israelites

The Beta Israel myths of origin are numerous. A number refer back to the story of the Queen of Sheba, who by means fair or foul, was impregnated by King Solomon and gave birth to a son called Menelik, the founder of the Ethiopian dynasty. The Beta Israel are said to either be the descendants of Israelite courtiers who accompanied the Queen of Sheba on her return journey home to Ethiopia, or those that accompanied Menelik on his return home to Ethiopia, after paying a visit to his father. Another set of stories suggest that the Beta Israel are descendants of Israelites who migrated to Ethiopia after the destruction of the First Temple in the sixth century BC and/or after the destruction of the Second Temple in the first century AD.[2]

Given the variety of stories of origin, many Beta Israel remain confused and different stories of origin were mixed together, and single accounts often detailed several waves of migration.

> A young priest assured me that Jews came to Ethiopia in three stages. He first told me the story of the Queen of Sheba and finished by saying that King Solomon sent back to Ethiopia with their son Menelik one member of each of the twelve tribes (Reuvel, Joshua, Dan, etc.), and these are the ancestors of the Beta Israel. Afterwards, following the destruction of the First Temple, when Jews went to Babylon, some came down to Ethiopia. Then later, others came from Yemen. All of these Jews reproduced and stuck to their faith.

> I asked an old man about the origin of the Beta Israel. A young man answered in his place. He first said that the Beta Israel are from the 'seed' (*zer*) of one of Jacob's twelve children; his wife completed: Dan's seed. Then he told me his version of the Queen of Sheba and Solomon story: when the Queen of Sheba returned from Israel, she was accompanied by a group of Israelites. They

had children and remained faithful to their faith, and never converted to Christianity. I asked which of the two stories he believed in. He was hesitant and his wife answered that she believes that they are descendants of the tribe of Dan because it says in the Bible that Israelites went to Havesh (Ethiopia) via Qwara (a region in North West Ethiopia). The other story however is not in the Bible, and Queen Sheba was not Israelite herself. Her husband agreed, and concluded: the Dan story is religion and the Sheba story is a 'people's story'. The old man apologised for his ignorance and suggested I ask a priest.

The important point about these myths of origin is that they all claim that the Beta Israel are descendants of the original Israelites who inhabited the land of Israel. In fact, the notion of direct descent is imagined quite literally.

An elder: 'Our ancestor is Gideon.[3] The last Gideon – there were seven of them – had seven children, who were all rulers. One of them was Shashura, who married Kantiva Herui (the mayor Herui), and they gave birth to Kantiva Gebru and Tesfu. Gebru was mayor of Gondar, and his daughter was Wayzero Tsayveva (Mrs Tsayveva). She married Khaled and gave birth to Atarshign. She married Atila and gave birth to Biterf. Biterf had Wuvenesh and Wuvenesh gave birth to my father. So there are ten generations from the last Gideon to me.'

Given that the Beta Israel think of themselves as direct descendants from Israelites, they imagine that their emigration to Israel is quite literally a return to their former homeland and that they share the same ancestry as all other Jews. These notions are fundamental to Ethiopian Jews' sense of legitimacy and belonging in Israel. It is therefore unsurprising that educated Ethiopian Jews vociferously reject current historical theories about their origins, which question a direct link with ancient Israelites. The Israeli historian Steven Kaplan, the principal proponent of this view, regularly suffered verbal abuse and threats from Ethiopian Jews.[4]

After accounting for their common origin with other Jews, a basic problem remains for the Beta Israel: how to explain the darkness of their skin colour compared to other Jews? Originally, I was told, the Beta Israel were white like the *farenj*. Sometimes, intermarriage with the host population is given as a 'reason' for their dark skin, although this is not a popular explanation since it threatens the image of the religious purity of the Beta Israel. More often, they blame the effect of Ethiopia's hot sun. In any case, the Beta Israel do not consider themselves 'black' (*tiqur*) like 'Africans': they are 'red' (*qay*). Non-slave (*chewa*) Beta Israel do consider Beta Israel slaves (*barya*) black, and I was told on several occasions a separate myth of origin for the 'black' *barya*. The *barya* are descendants of Cain, who was cursed by his father Noah that all his children should become black and become slave to his (good) brother Yafet's children. A man whom I knew was *barya* himself, also told me the story of the cursed son of Noah, Cain, but he included all Beta Israel as descendants of his children.

Returning home

During the general election campaign in May 1995, Ethiopian supporters of the Labour party, however secular, sought voters with comments such as: 'It was not Likud [the party in power at the time of the airlifts of the Beta Israel] which brought us here, but God who brought us back to our homeland!'

When Ethiopian Israelis speak of their homeland (*agerachin*, lit.: our country), they may be referring to one of three places: Israel, Ethiopia or the specific Ethiopian locality they used to live in. Ethiopia is the homeland because it was the Beta Israel's country of birth and they grew up there, acquiring Ethiopian customs and Ethiopian appearance; Israel is the homeland because it is the country of Jews.

Israel is the land which God promised (*calkidane*) to the Jews, and since the Beta Israel are Jews, it is therefore their country. Given their Israelite ancestry, Ethiopian Jewish immigrants speak not of 'coming' to Israel, but of 'returning' to Israel after thousands of years of exile (*sedet*). They often mention their former prayers for the 'return to Jerusalem' – Jerusalem was the name by which Beta Israel in Ethiopia called the Holy Land – as if the image of the golden land had sparkled before their eyes for generations. The youngsters that Gadi Ben Ezer (mns) interviewed in the mid-1980s illustrate the power and vividness of the dream of Jerusalem. They said that they were propelled to Israel by 'a dream' and a sense that it was their destiny – 'in our blood' – to 'return' to Jerusalem.

I was sitting on the beach with young Avi watching the sun setting over the Mediterranean. I asked him for a memory of village life as a small boy. He recalled a song his grandmother used to sing while grinding grain which spoke of the return to Jerusalem. Wistfully, Avi said how much she would have liked to have come here, if only to die.

Avi deliberately chose a romantic image to accompany the sun as it disappeared behind the horizon, but I did not doubt the accuracy of his memory nor the sincerity of the accompanying emotion of regret that his grandmother's most fervent dream was not realised in her lifetime.

An elder, Abba Fikadu: 'Jerusalem was promised to us by God, it is our *erest* (land right). We waited for thousands of years to come here. We left our motherland Ethiopia, a country which our ancestors had developed with spear and shield. We came here on God's command. We did not even eat the food which was ready, and we did not wait for our cattle to come home, we just left everything and came to Israel. God flew us in the skies to the land which he promised us.'

Abba Fikadu's words express a range of sentiments about the homeland that is Israel. As a Jew, he has God-given rights of possession of its land. Ever since they arrived in Ethiopia, thousands of years ago, his forefathers have yearned to return. In fact, even if they had *not* wanted to leave the country they had 'developed with spear and shield', they were 'commanded' by God to do so. Moreover with his details of the hasty departure, Abba Fikadu illustrates the sense of inevitability of the migration. It was destiny — the time to regain the mystical land of their forefathers had arrived, and so they departed.

Falagu, a young woman: 'This is our country, it says so in the Bible. Before the First Temple was destroyed we were all here. It is in the Bible that all Jews must return to their country. We *had* to come. You think we came because we were poor and needy but we had plenty – there was no famine in Ambover!'

Falagu stresses that the God-ordained religious obligation to come to Israel overrode all other motivations. In fact, like most other Ethiopian Israelis, she denies economic factors altogether. This denial serves to reinforce the image of the religious fervour which drove the Beta Israel to leave their homes to regain the promised land, without even finishing the prepared food – thus recalling the ancient Israelites hasty departure from Egypt with unleavened bread.

The Golden Country: Israel

I was chatting to Turunesh, a young and forthright mother of three, telling her that many Ethiopians complain about Israel to me. Turunesh's response was adamant: 'Hah! They eat and eat and eat and speak only of Ethiopia! They had nothing there – those that tell you that they did are lying! Israel is gold! Without doing any work, you get money. There we worked so hard – old women fetching water on their backs – here everything is in the house, water, food, the toilet. Here you sit, go to the bank and eat! It is great (*alem naw*)!'

Ethiopian immigrants are particularly aware of living in a new country and of having travelled from one country to another. For example, they often identified with my position as a foreigner in Israel, and asked me about practical details of travel to England (e.g. flight times, currencies, the weather) and my evaluations of Israel. They also asked about the life of Ethiopian immigrants in London (e.g. in terms of housing, education, and government welfare provision).

Ethiopian Israelis like their new land and they say that 'it is a good country'. This section briefly describes facets of Israeli life which the Beta Israel particularly enjoy.

Israel as a country of knowledge

Ethiopian immigrants appreciate Israel as a developed country – a place of roads, elections, schools and modern health care.

A young man: 'This country has a lot of knowledge. That was the problem of Ethiopia, the land had many riches – the air and grain were good, but there was no knowledge of how to use them. Here there are many factories.'

While Ethiopian Israelis often reminisce about Ethiopia, they rarely mention in positive terms aspects of daily life such as grinding grain, fetching water, tending cattle instead of going to school, and if one was lucky enough to go to school, walking over an hour to get there. Israel's modernity – roads, infrastructure, TV, material goods, technology – is a definite improvement in daily life. In fact, these aspects of modernity have been rapidly assimilated into Ethiopian Israeli life, and they rarely discuss them as such. Modern society has become 'normal' to them.

> Fantanesh: 'There our children looked after cattle, here they go to school.'

Children's education is perhaps the most highly valued aspects of Israeli life. Several adults even stated that while they themselves preferred life in Ethiopia, they had come to Israel primarily for the education of their children. Education is the vehicle through which Ethiopian children will gain good jobs and become respectable members of society.

> Solomon, a twenty-five year-old father of five, bears a grudge against his parents for sending him to herd cattle and for marrying him off as a teenager rather than sending him to school. He would have been a wealthy man by now had he received an education, he often told me. I loved to watch the pleasure he took in involving himself in his children's schooling – trying to help with homework, buying essential equipment, complimenting them on pieces of schoolwork. 'He,' he said pointing to his three-year-old son, 'will go to university one day, you will see!'

Although Beta Israel have imported their own forms of health care, modern Israeli health care is much in demand. Ethiopians go to the doctor for the smallest physical problem and demand full treatment, preferably an injection.

> Kanubesh values the maternity services in Israel: 'In Ethiopia, while you give birth, the women drink coffee, chat and eat *injera*. If a problem arises, how can they help you? In the village the hospital is far away. You just die! Here if you have a problem they give you an operation.'

Educated Ethiopians also appreciate the Israeli political system: democratic elections, freedom of speech and movement, and the judicial system.

> A middle-aged man: 'In this country, there is democracy, that is good. Everybody has rights and they can do as they please. For example, if the demonstration [against the discarding of

Ethiopian blood] had been held in Ethiopia, the police would have shot real bullets not plastic ones!'

Educated Ethiopians value the government's favourable policies towards immigrants from poor socio-economic backgrounds – such as providing grants to purchase houses, and subsidising the first years of university education.

Moshe, who lived in Canada for eight years before coming to Israel, says that he and all Ethiopian Jews in Israel feel more connection here than in Canada. There, they are always strangers, even after decades. There, it would be inconceivable to have an Ethiopian Member of Parliament after just twelve years. And there no Ethiopian can own his own house like they all can here.

Moshe speaks of the sense of connection Ethiopian immigrants feel in Israel thanks to positive state efforts at inclusion such as policies that allow for positive discrimination in the electoral system and subsidy for house purchase.

An easy life

As he pointed to his full glass, old Abba Brhan said merrily: 'Jerusalem is a good country: beer in plenty and lots of food. There, in Ethiopia, you had to seed, plough, harvest, and grind grain for your food. Here you eat, drink and sit!'

Unemployed Ethiopian men and most women enjoy an easier lifestyle in Israel thanks to a reduction of household chores for women, increased leisure time for unemployed men, easier transport, and plenty of food and drink.

'There it was so hard to receive guests! You had to fetch water and wood on your back, and make a fire. Here you just light a match and you have your coffee and you just light a match and your stew (*wot*) cooks! There you had to grind the grain, here we buy ready-made flour. There you had to pound the coffee beans, here you whiz them in the machine. If you run out of stew, you can pop out to the shop and buy some yoghurt [to accompany *injera*]. There you had to make *talla* (alcoholic beverage made from barley), here you buy beer. Here everything is easy.'

Women enjoy their new-found ease at, running the household and adapted extremely quickly to modern household appliances. Given that men play a secondary role in household chores, they have been little affected by such changes within the house. Only five years in the county, at the time of my fieldwork, I rarely heard these former village dwellers comment about such novelties as running water, electric coffee grinders, electric gadgets – all are taken for granted and have become incorporated into ordinary daily life.

Affordable public transport is another wide-reaching innovation in daily life. Buses did operate in the region in which the Beta Israel lived in Ethiopia, but these were rarely used by villagers. Buses which operated only on roads, often a thirty to ninety minute walk from the village, were always full, and usually too expensive to afford. In Ethiopia, therefore, heavy loads were carried to and from the market by back or on a donkey, and long walks, lasting one or more days, with little food, were frequently undertaken to visit relatives. In Israel, by contrast, the bus is rarely further than a few minutes walk away, and it is affordable. When neighbours attend funerals and celebrations together, they organise the hire of a private bus and divide the cost between the travellers.

> Abba Negusse spoke about the regular long journeys on foot under the sun to attend funerals in Ethiopia, with only a snack of roasted chick peas to eat on the way. 'Here though, you go by bus.' I asked him which he prefers: 'The bus is better!'

Ethiopian Israelis appreciate the ready availability of food. They rarely admit this, because it goes against the rhetoric of the wealthy Beta Israel who emigrated for purely religious reasons. But off-guard, I often heard comments such as 'in this country, you never go to bed fasting!'

Material goods

Ethiopians love to spend their new-found wealth on large household goods and gold jewellery and watches. They spend minimal amounts on food, clothes, and children's pocket-money, and splash out on a new bedroom suite worth NIS 2,500 (approx. £500) – well over the household monthly income for welfare recipients.

Buying an object

One morning, Abba Negusse set off to town to buy a refrigerator. His first task was to find an interpreter and advisor. In the market, he soon found a Hebrew speaking nephew. Addissu delayed his own shopping plans to guide his uncle. They started in a shop where a neighbour had recently bought a good fridge, and toured a few others for the sake of comparison. The shop-keepers did not hide their dislike of Ethiopian customers, but the two men were not perturbed by the rudeness showed them: they were used to the exasperated looks, sighs, and gruff tones of voice. Abba Negusse sought a shop which gave credit, even though he had more cash than the total cost of the fridge hidden away in a pillow case in his bedroom. Eventually, Abba Negusse chose the cheapest of the large-size fridges, buying an Israeli make so that, as his nephew told him, spare parts would be readily available.

Ethiopians choose the shops according to word of mouth, and are particularly drawn to places which offer discounts or where they can bargain.

On one shopping trip, Fantanesh succeeded in paying just NIS 410 for a NIS 450 necklace, and Asresie NIS 100 for a NIS 125 watch.

When Ethiopian immigrants first arrived, the Absorption Agency provided them with the basic household goods such as beds, a large display cabinet, a sofa and armchair set, a fridge, a TV, cooker, blankets, and money for clothes. Gradually, as savings grew, and immigrants settled into permanent housing, the original donated goods, even when in perfect condition, were replaced by bought items.[5] There was a definite order of acquisition in my neighbourhood: a large fridge first, then a new display cabinet, a video, a bedroom set (double bed and dressing table), new cooker, a dining room set (table and six chairs), a new sofa and armchair, and finally children's' bunk beds. Then the cycle began again, as each of the above is replaced. Small items were also acquired regularly, but with a less discernible pattern: clothes, ornaments, wall-hangings, plastic flowers, pots and pans, coffee cups, glasses, cutlery, gold jewellery and watches. Since Ethiopians in my neighbourhood arrived in the country at the same time and have more or less the same income, the rate of acquiring new large objects was more or less identical. Although enterprising heads of households and/or those with a higher income were well ahead and other households lagged far behind.

When I first arrived in December 1994, most houses had already bought their replacement fridge and were onto replacement cookers. Then the bedroom suite phase arrived, and in a few months, many houses in my neighbourhood had beautiful new double beds to show off to their neighbours. When I left, in August 1996, the craze was dining room table and chairs.

Keeping up with the Alemus

Household goods are valued because they have become important status markers. Buying household goods demonstrates to neighbours and kin, and to oneself, that one is doing well and adapting successfully to modern life. Neighbours love to inspect each others' new items, to compare them with their own (and inwardly chuckle at the better deal they got), or to seek inspiration for their forthcoming purchase.

> Avraham sought to explain why my co-Godfather had insisted on buying everything new for the new-born baby (push-chair, baby mattress, etc.) even though his sister had recently acquired, but no longer required, such items: 'Ethiopians want everything new so that the neighbours do not think that they have no money!'

> When I asked Fantanesh why she bought a new sofa shortly before the large celebration for her son's *Bar Mitzvah*, when her old one was in excellent condition, she said: 'Why, people would say 'they have a *Bar Mitzvah* and did not buy a new sofa!'

Ethiopian consumerism is all the more striking when the cost of purchased items is compared to monthly income and when the frugal lifestyle adopted to afford the goods is considered. Fantanesh's new sofa cost her about NIS 2,000 (£400), roughly equivalent to her household's monthly income. Yet, she often complained of poverty, of being unable to buy basic necessities for the house at the end of the month. Indeed, I witnessed the decline in quality and quantity of food in her house, as in other households, towards the end of the month.

> When her elderly mother's welfare money came through, Fantanesh bought herself a necklace for NIS 410. The following

day, she told me that she could not afford the extra three shekels for a taxi from the hospital, opting instead for the arduous task of getting her frail blind mother on and off the bus.

Buying household goods reinforces social relations between neighbours. While the acquisition of household goods includes an element of competition, given that most households proceed at a similar pace and that household goods are remarkably uniform, communality between Ethiopian Israelis is reinforced. Moreover, many goods are purchased with the proceeds of rotating credit society savings, that is with pooled and socialised neighbourhood money. Members of credit societies love to inspect the items bought from their co-members' savings for they feel involved in the process of acquisition. In this way, by using pooled funds and by conforming to Ethiopian Israeli tastes and priorities, the act of purchasing an object moves from a private individual affair to a social activity.

Financial dealings

Most Ethiopians have adapted rapidly to financial dealings with banks, Israeli money, and household bills, even if many remain distrustful of government and financial institutions.

> Solomon was laughing at his cousin Fantaun because the latter gave money to an individual to safeguard: 'Money in this country goes in banks – giving to a person is what we did in Ethiopia!'

Ethiopians all have bank accounts, and couples hold joint accounts, into which wages, benefits and pension are paid. Most younger Ethiopians hold savings accounts and use cheque cards and cheque books. Older Ethiopians go to the bank once a month, on the day that their income arrives, and take out what they want for the month, which is usually the whole amount. They prefer to keep their money and savings hidden in their bedroom.

> Abba Negusse would always say 'the bank is a thief' and explain, in a fashion incomprehensible to me, how the bank had kept some of his money. He therefore withdraws all the money on the day it arrives and keeps his savings under his bed. When he dies, he added, the children will come to find it.

For Avi too, a young Ethiopian worker, banks are thieves. He found that his mother was not receiving the correct amount of monthly income. He took the matter up with the bank, who at first denied any problem. However when he threatened to go to the newspapers, they made an investigation and agreed that there was a fault and his mother was given NIS 7000 in arrears payment. He believes that banks try to rob but if found out quickly by a clever Ethiopian such as himself, they give the money back.

Such statements reveal that Ethiopians, of all ages, feel that they understand the system, even if they decide that it is untrustworthy.

On the day a bill arrives (usually the same day for neighbouring houses), Ethiopian Israelis sit together on benches, the literate ones reading the bills of their illiterate neighbours, and together they lament the high cost of living in Israel.

Bills are one of the most heated topics of daily conversation and many new immigrants have not quite go used to the idea of having to pay for water and heat and rent.

Some people associate bills with former taxes: 'In Ethiopia we paid *asrat*, *mengist-geber* and *anfo* (local and government taxes). Here it is electricity and telephone!'

Employed Ethiopian Israelis have adapted quickly to wage earnings, and they frequently check their monthly salary against their log-in statement which shows the total number of hours worked.

Worku was very pleased with himself when he succeeded in proving to his employer that a mistake was made to his payment one month and that he was NIS 250 short. Even though Worku has never received any formal education, he managed to work out the sums involved, including allowances for over-time.

Social security

'Government money'

A middle-aged woman: 'This government is very good. It helps the poor people and gives them money – even if they do no work! In Ethiopia, it was the poor who gave money to the government!'

Abba Wandu, a neighbourhood elder, asked me to compare my country with Ethiopia and Israel. When I said that my country was the richest of the three, he was perplexed that any country could possibly be richer than Israel. He enquired whether my country was 'good like Israel' and gives money to single mothers and to people who are too old to work.

Thanks to the state welfare system, the government is regarded as a benefactor who gives a salary and a house to Ethiopians 'who are so poor and who know nothing in this country'. Sometimes the government is spoken of as a 'breast' which feeds the needy.

Mama Fantae is a single mother of six. In Ethiopia, after her divorce, she went to live with her brother who supported her and her uncle gave her a cow, so that she 'brought up [her] children on milk'. In Israel, 'the government gives money, like a breast. You feed the child with a bottle which is bought by the government. We cannot bring up children alone, we just see the hands of the government!'

Mama Fantae's youngest child was already fifteen when she arrived in Israel, which implies that she is using 'breast', 'milk' and 'bottle' as symbols to connote the magnanimous nature of the government, and its role as ultimate provider, comparable only to a parent. Her account draws a direct parallel between kin and government as providers. When Rabin was assassinated, he was ardently mourned by Ethiopian Jewish immigrants because 'The president dying is like your own father dying!'

Fantanesh speaking about newly orphaned children: 'They are OK. The government will bring them up, giving them much money every month. If no relatives take them, then the government will – they have special homes.'

Government financial support is taken for granted; it is a given in the land of Israel. For example, a young woman, who lives in a small flat with her parents, bemoans that she is single because, as she says, 'if I had two children now, I would have my own house'. She does not mention that the house would be a council house (i.e. 'from the government'), because that is obvious to her and to her interlocutors. Similarly, on seeing a bulging purse, a man jokingly asked for cash. The response, which might have been 'go out and work for money!', was: 'Why, is there no government here?'

In a matter of fact fashion, a few neighbours discussed their relative social security incomes over coffee. I was struck by how rapidly such a source of income had become 'normal' for them and I could picture them, only a few years ago, speaking in just the same way about relative grain prices and yields.

Knowing the system

Many Ethiopian immigrants may not have a well-developed conceptual understanding of the welfare state, but they soon learn to get the most out of the system.

> Worku wants to move house to live closer to his mother so he wants another child (a fourth) because with four children he can say that his two-bedroom council house is too small and that he therefore needs to move house.

> Agarnesh kept her forthcoming marriage secret from the social services in order not to dash her hopes of obtaining 'a house and a fridge and everything'.

> One neighbour told me about another neighbour living off social security: 'He could work, he is pretending not to see well enough, because he just likes to sleep and eat the money of the government.'

Ethiopian immigrants also succeed in using the system to their own advantage during personal disputes amongst themselves.

> Two neighbours were engaged in a long standing feud (which began in Ethiopia). One day one used the ultimate weapon: on pretext that the other had hit a grand-daughter of his, he called the police. His neighbour received a caution.

While Ethiopians appreciate welfare payments and have rapidly learned to get the most from the social security system, they are also deeply mistrustful of it. They often question the motivations of government personnel, arguing that the latter make decisions for their own personal benefit, rather than that of the Ethiopian immigrants. Charges of embezzlement, corruption, lies and dishonesty were frequent.[6]

As a foretaste to Chapter Eight, I end this section with the nostalgic words of an elder, who, though appreciating the generosity of the government, bemoans his loss of control over his livelihood and daily consumption:

'There I had a cow; here, the government gives me money. There I had milk and made *agwot* (curdled milk) and butter; here I have to go to the supermarket and buy it with money. There, I had everything at home myself; here, everything is brought with money, from the government.'

A desire to integrate

Ethiopian Jews live in Israel, and intend to do so for evermore, and their identity as Israeli citizens is orientated to this unalterable fact. This makes Ethiopian Jews different from most immigrants to other countries because the latter maintain an ideology of return to their country of origin. Ethiopian immigrants' positive outlook towards their new homeland is reflected in their desire to integrate into Israeli society. At the same time as maintaining their 'tough traditions', they seek to participate in civil life, relate socially with other Israelis, and to adapt, to an extent, to Israeli cultural patterns.

Rhetoric of integration

In a Bar Mitzvah blessing, the priest said 'let him [the Bar Mitzvah boy] be an important person for the country'.

The prayer asks for this boy to contribute to 'the country', which testifies to a sense of allegiance to Israel. When young Ethiopian leaders or elders speak publicly, they espouse an ethic of integration.

At a hearing of the governmental commission to investigate the blood donation affair, an elder priest speaks: 'The horn and the ear live side by side. We came here wanting to live together.' Likewise, Ethiopians expressing their anger and hurt at the policy of discarding Ethiopian blood donations frequently asserted: 'Our skin colour is different but we are one people.'

Such statements suggesting a unity between Ethiopians and other Israelis are rhetorical in the sense that they are usually said in public when Ethiopians engage in a particular mode of discourse. Ethiopians expound well-rehearsed statements which follow a set pattern, in this case that of integration; the very same persons at another moment express themselves with equal vehemence to argue the exact opposite. Alternatively, they express one view-point, perceived to be the 'correct' one, publicly, while adopting an alternative position in private. For example, former government policies which led to large groups of Ethiopian Jewish immigrants living together in one neighbourhood are publicly denounced by young leaders, even though the latter acknowledge that most Ethiopians actually *want* to live in close proximity to many Ethiopian neighbours. Unsurprisingly, younger Ethiopian immigrants adopt a stronger rhetoric of integration than their parents' generation. They argue that Ethiopians must acquire an 'Israeli' (*farenj*) way of life: Israeli food, dress, religious customs, and social behaviour, should be adopted, even if some Ethiopian 'customs' are simultaneously maintained.

Participation in civil life

The rhetoric of integration is complemented by attempts to participate in civil life and relate to other Israelis. Ethiopians pre-date their allegiance to Israel to their time in Ethiopia before emigration.

> A learned old man, speaking of his past in Ethiopia, said that he did not sleep for ten days during the Yom Kippur war, listening to the events on radio. Then he sent his son to Israel to fight for the country, and he was proud that his son fought the next war for Israel.

Joining the army is the clearest manifestation of Ethiopians' desire to participate in their new country. Older Ethiopians express great pride when their youngsters enlist in the army. Photos of the youngsters in uniform adorn living room walls, large communal send-off parties are organised for the soldier-to-be, soldiers remain in uniform for large neighbourhood and kin celebrations, and an air of importance surrounds mention and conversations about soldiers.

Ethiopians' civic feelings were also evident in the high level of participation in the 1995 general elections. Several politically active young men joined their respective parties and canvassed the community for weeks beforehand. They worked non-stop on the day to drive elders to the booths, and instructed them on which candidate to vote for. Ethiopians voted because 'this is what you do here', it was a way for them to feel part of the country, to join in an activity alongside other citizens.

Ethiopians expressed their political preference – for the overwhelming majority, the Likud party and Benjamin Netanyahu – in patriotic terms. Most claimed that Simon Peres and the Labour Party wanted to divide up the country, and Jerusalem in particular, and give half away to the Arabs. 'But', they would exclaim, 'Israel is the country God promised to the Jews, not the Arabs!' They also resented the Labour party for refusing to bring Ethiopian Jews to Israel when it was in power. They often, mistakenly, quote Golda Meir, a former Israeli Prime Minister, as saying: 'Ethiopian Jews do not exist. Better bring Russian dogs than Ethiopians!'.

Melissu explained why she voted for Likud party leader Benyamin Netanyahu. She came here to the land of Israel. She did not lack grain and did not come for a holiday but to live and give birth. 'Peres [the Labour leader] wants to give the land away: He has already given Hebron and Jenin and that place by the Dead Sea [Jericho], now he wants to give Jerusalem and the Golan Heights. Then the Arabs will ask for still more! Also, it was the Likud Party that brought us here.'

Ethiopians are saddened when Israeli servicemen die in battle. They partook fully in the national mourning for assassinated Prime Minister Yitsak Rabin, even if they did not support his party: tears flowed, long telephone calls were made to relatives about the tragedy. Many stayed up into the early hours of the tragic night watching the news, and the funeral was watched on television all day. It was very much *their* Head of State that had died, not just the Head of State of 'this country'; they identified fully.

Around 10 p.m. on the fateful night of the assassination of Rabin, I heard on the BBC World Service that Rabin had been wounded. Abba Negusse had just gone to bed, but when I called out to him with the news, he immediately got up and turned the TV back on. About one hour later, he went back to bed and, from my room, I asked for the latest news. 'Rabin is fine', he said, 'I saw him sitting in a chair.' The BBC midnight news bulletin, five minutes later, announced Rabin's death – Abba Negusse must have seen archive footage of Rabin, and concluded from that that he was alive and well! I called out with the news and both he and his wife got out of bed to watch TV into the early hours, not understanding a word of it, but finding it the best way to relate to this tragedy.

Social integration

Ethiopians on Israelis

For Ethiopians, Israel is a country which belongs to Jews from all over the world and which they all co-habit. They usually think of Israelis as a whole, referring to them all as *farenj* (Whites). However when specifically asked, they distinguish, as is common in Israel, between Ashkenazi Jews of European and Anglo-Saxon heritage, and the Sephardi population of Middle Eastern and North African extraction. They do not place themselves in either category, although they do feel closer to the latter group. They say that they dislike the Ashkenazi because 'they do not like Ethiopians'. The Ashkenazi are associated with the *datii* (Orthodox religious Jews) 'all dressed in black' who are to blame for the Rabbinate's rejection of Ethiopian Judaism. The Sephardi are said to be 'dark' (*quay* lit: red) like Ethiopians. A particular rapprochement was felt after the demonstration which Ethiopian Israelis held in protest at the Blood Bank's policy of discarding the blood that Ethiopians had donated. Groups of Moroccans and Yemenis voiced their support for Ethiopians, taking the 'mistreatment' of Ethiopian immigrants as further evidence of the discriminatory dominance of Ashkenazi Jews.[7]

Ethiopians love to mock Israeli behaviour given that typical traits such as loudness, brashness and openness are diametrically opposed to Ethiopian decorum.[8]

> Moshe, a veteran immigrant (he arrived in Israel in the mid-seventies) spoke about a holiday he had in England with a group of Israelis. He recalled their visit to an East London market where his fellow travellers thought they were still in Israel and shouted around at everybody.

There is little consistency in any one individual's remarks about other Israelis, let alone in the remarks of Ethiopians as a whole. The same person one moment will say how 'good' (*turu*) Israelis are because 'they look after Ethiopians', 'they chat', 'White skin is beautiful', yet the next moment that same person will speak vehemently against Israelis, 'they brought us here, but now look how they treat us?', 'they have no religion', 'they do not talk to us'. These opposing view-points voiced more or less simultaneously express Ethiopian Israelis' ambivalent feelings towards other Israelis.

I think that the Beta Israel arrived in the country positively disposed towards their fellow Jews, but then as many began to feel rejected by their new neighbours, these 'proud Ethiopians' began to alter their opinion of other Israelis. Put simply, rather than risk the hurt of being rebuffed, many took the attitude 'I do not like you anyway!'

Ethiopians also interact with Israeli Arabs, at work, in hospital, or during the purchase of cows and goats for meat consumption.[9] They tend to speak extremely badly of Arabs, telling me for instance: 'Do not take a shared [Arab] taxi from Haifa, the Arabs will kill you!' and 'be careful of the Arabs, they want to kill all Jews!' However, when Ethiopians actually came into contact with Israeli Arabs, relations appear friendly.

> Worku, a young manual labourer, speaks positively of his Arab work mates, and has learned a couple of Arab songs.

> Abba Negusse while sipping strong coffee from a small cup ('just like Ethiopian coffee') in the backyard of an Arab farm after the purchase, slaughter and carving of two goats, watches the multitude of children and says 'the Arabs are just like us: strong coffee and lots of children!'

Palestinian Arabs (that is without Israeli citizenship, living in Gaza and the West Bank) are universally hated by the Beta Israel, and are apparently fit only to be killed.

> A young woman, member of a far right political party says: 'Gaza should be closed – let them starve to death! If they are going to come to kill us, let them die!'

> A young man: 'The Arabs want to kill the Jews and destroy Israel. I do not want them to have Hebron, they just want to kill Jews there. We came here for Jerusalem, it must be kept, all of it! We were here first, how many thousands of years ago? Three thousand years ago!'

Socialising with Israelis

Social integration with Israelis is sought to a considerable extent.[10] Israeli colleagues, community workers and friendly neighbours are invited for celebrations, such as weddings and Bar Mitzvah. If a household has developed a friendly relationship with Israeli neighbours, they are often invited to more intimate celebrations such as a circumcision or a child's birthday. Parents approve of their children playing with Israeli children.[11] Hebrew classes are attended so that Ethiopians can 'talk with and understand the *farenj*'. I sense that many Ethiopians would like more contact with their White neighbours, but with language problems, cultural differences, and mistrust on both sides, a wide gap separates them: in eighteen months, I rarely saw Ethiopians and non-Ethiopians visiting each other socially.

Cultural adaptation

Beta Israel efforts

Many Ethiopians make conscious efforts to adapt culturally to Israel and praise their children for doing so.

> When I first met my Ethiopian neighbours during an elders' social club, they tried to introduce themselves Israeli-style by giving their surname before their Christian name. Clearly, despite plenty of criticism for this naming system – in Ethiopia, Christian name comes first – they had accepted it, and used it when faced with a new *farenj*. However, in fact, they were being over-zealous since in Israel the surname-first custom is generally only applied in writing and Israelis introduce themselves with their Christian name first.

The television is a medium through which Ethiopians try to understand their new society. Ethiopians of all ages love to watch television, and indeed it is rarely switched off, and has become a backdrop to all other social activities in the home. Adults understand little of the dialogue, but they try to make as much sense of what they see as possible. They enjoy in particular seeing 'dreadful' things like a soap opera star divorce her husband and marry his son, thus contravening the fundamental Beta Israel ban on sexual relations with in-laws. Nature programmes are a favourite, as are films which feature black people. When the news comes on – which most households watch daily – a teenager is asked to translate the essential. Usually though, having heard the news on the Amharic radio a couple of hours earlier, and recognising names, they can often guess what the image refers to.

> As well as for enjoyment, Telahun, a young educated Ethiopian, watches TV to be involved in Israeli society. He recalled a recent

conversation with Israelis about TV personalities; they were amazed about how much he knew – a knowledge which served him well to quickly make friends in the army too. 'We are newcomers and so we have to learn the ways of the country', he concluded.

Ethiopians are concerned about their image in front of 'the Whites'.

Samagn comes into the house beaming: he is wearing the new jumper he just bought himself. His wife laughs and chaffs him for wearing what she sees as a woman's jumper because of the V-neck. Him: 'So what, if I like it?' She: 'But the *farenj* will laugh at you!'.

Often, an Ethiopian criticises an Israeli practice but then says that since this is the country's traditions, it must be followed.

Turunesh told me that Israeli women did not know the love of a child, compared to Ethiopians who carry their babies on their back, sleep with them, and breast-feed them for three years. When I pointed out that Ethiopians do not do this anymore in Israel, she said, laughing, that Ethiopians were now becoming *farenj*. She said, in a resigned tone of voice, that this was a positive change because 'we have to behave according to the country'.

Changes in behaviour are attempted specifically to better suit Israeli norms. For example, although Ethiopians are extremely proud of their soft-spoken manners, they realise that to succeed in Israel, new behaviour is required, and they must learn to become more assertive. Sometimes, young men go too far and become even more loud, pushy, and rude than those they seek to emulate.

On the religious front, a growing number of Ethiopian Jewish households of young adults who attended religious boarding school, adopt standard Jewish religious practice. Others attempt to conform, if only partially, to Israeli norms. A large proportion of Ethiopian immigrants who arrived in the 1970s and 1980s attend non-Ethiopian synagogues, and carry out there their sons' Bar Mitzvah and other rites of passage. In one Ethiopian synagogue, home to the only surviving Beta Israel monk, most prayers are recited in Hebrew. During *Succoth* holiday the appropriate hut is constructed according to Jewish custom outside a number of Ethiopian homes, and parents encourage their children to dress up for *Purim*, buying them expensive Power Rangers costumes.

Moreover, a number of former cultural practices which Israelis deem offensive have been abandoned. For example, both the practice of and discourse about female circumcision[12] have been discontinued: female circumcision has become taboo.[13] Many educated Beta Israel have even attempted to eradicate the practice from recent history. I was often told that the practice ended generations ago while more reliable informants assured me that it continued to be practised until departure to Israel. Some elderly informants have gone as far as disclaiming their own words on the topic, collected by earlier researchers in Ethiopia decades ago, and accusing the researchers of 'lies'.[14] When I raised the subject, I was either curtly answered that it is not practised because 'it is forbidden here' or the question was turned into a joke. As Abba Negusse aptly put it: 'The hole remains the same!'

> One woman tried to rationalise the issue: 'In our country, we had no underwear, so 'it' could protrude and be seen. But here since people wear underwear, it does not matter.' I should add that the times when I did successfully raise the issue was at considerable personal cost. One day, after hearing about the repugnance of uncircumcised women, I had to admit that women were not circumcised in my country... As I blushed further, a young man stuck out his index finger, wiggled it about, and asked me whether 'it' did not grow and become very long ...

Finally, Ethiopian's positive attitude towards Israeli norms is apparent in the way they sometimes self-consciously cloak Ethiopian practices with Israeli notions.

> Qes Admass and his family are crumbling the Sabbath bread into a large communal bowl. He looks at me and says, laughing: 'You see, we have democracy in this country!' In other words, he was justifying an Ethiopian practice by an Israeli concept.

Beta Israel's experience of cultural change

Despite obvious embarrassment and displeasure, most women and men accept cultural changes as inevitable, and do not appear to undergo undue stress as a consequence.

Abeba was cooking *injera* during her periods. I asked if this was not forbidden. 'Yes, but what can I do?' Her nephew Alemayo added: 'It is forbidden to even be in the house or to touch people!' He brought the conversation to a close with a joke: 'But as long as she washes her hands, it is OK!'

The changes were necessary in the new context, and 'that is that'. I often felt that the change in location per se was enough to account for, and accept, cultural change.

I asked Fantanesh about how she felt shaking a post-partum (impure) woman's hand. 'Oh here it is not forbidden!', she answered gaily.

Often a question of mine about a contemporary practice was met by a blank expression and a muffled answer such as 'in our country, it is forbidden, but here ... I do not know.' Many Beta Israel affected a sort of denial of knowledge, and a denial of responsibility, which seemed to pave the way for acceptance of radical changes in tradition and concepts of purity in particular. By changing location, previous hard and fast injunctions were suddenly annulled. Purity laws were a basic tenet of daily life in the Ethiopian village, and now in the Israeli environment they are no longer obligatory. The previous set of rules and beliefs is not brought into question – they are just no longer applicable in the new context. What was appropriate in one context is no longer so in another.

Alemwork, a twenty-five year-old educated young woman, who arrived in Israel at the age of sixteen, spoke of *astasreyo* (the Day of Atonement) in Ethiopia as the day to beat all days. She smiled longingly as I described the traditional style in which it had been celebrated in my neighbourhood, a twenty minute walk from her home. I asked her why if she enjoyed Beta Israel *Astasreyo* observance so much, she did not attend an Ethiopian Prayer House on that day, rather than an Israeli synagogue: 'Ah, I would not do it here! I would be like a *farenj*', she responded. In another words, in this context, it would feel false to her, she would feel like a spectator, an outsider, as if she were a *farenj* trying out a primitive custom. She felt nostalgia, but had also apparently made a candid appraisal of the fact that she is no longer the girl doing *zelen* (the Day of Atonement chanting) in Ambover (her village in Ethiopia). She is now a *datii* (religious, Hebrew) girl in Afula who observes Yom Kippur solemnly in the synagogue in keeping with other Israelis.

This acceptance of change due to a new location is also apparent in the frequent assertion 'this is the way here because this is the country's traditions'.

> During the state elections, Alequa Telahun complained that voting was done by men in Israel, while in Ethiopia, the king was anointed by God. On reflection, he said that he liked this new way because 'it is the country's traditions'.

Sometimes new norms and Beta Israel custom come into conflict:

> Young Avi: 'The *farenj* say that it is bad to drink beer at funerals and laugh at us saying 'Ethiopians cry but make a party of the funeral by getting drunk on beer!" At his own mother's funeral, he did not serve beer. However, after complaints from elder relatives, he served beer at the seventh day *teskar* mourning gathering. The Ethiopian viewpoint is expressed by Tsay who did not go to her cousin's wedding because 'in this country you have to wait a year after the death of a close kin before attending celebrations ... But we Ethiopians, we cry so much at the funeral that we do not need to wait a year! *Farenj*, they do not cry at all! And they say that Ethiopians just drink beer!'

Often, the Beta Israel deal with such conflicts with humour:

> Qes Admass amused the coffee drinkers with the following tale: 'I was walking down the street with my wife when a *farenj* at the bus stop said that it was not good for my wife to walk behind me like that: a couple should walk arm in arm. So, taking my wife's arm, we set off again. But as soon as we were out of sight ...' His wife completed the story: 'He said "Get off me! Get off me!" (*Woredge*). And when we returned to the bus stop, he said to me "Come come! Walk by me!"'

Conclusion

Alemwork concluded her account of her first few days in Israel: 'And then we ate food that was brought to us in a truck'.

Alemwork's recollection exemplifies the large cultural and social jump which Ethiopian immigrants have made in coming from their former villages, where food was harvested from the field, to urban Israel where it is delivered in a lorry. But Ethiopian Israelis adapted rapidly to their new Western urban lifestyle – the trappings of modern life have proved largely intelligible. Lisa Anteby reaches a similar conclusion: Ethiopian adults have had little problem in adapting to daily life in Israel and soon found versatile ways to cope without a knowledge of Hebrew.[15] Likewise, Marilyn Herman, who carried out fieldwork in the early 1990s, concluded that the Beta Israel had 'no culture shock in dealing with technological society'. She explains that Ethiopian immigrants who arrived with Operation Solomon spent time in Addis Abeba, an urban environment, before reaching Israel and that it is not in fact that hard to learn to turn on an electric switch.[16] Ethiopian immigrants appreciate their new country precisely because it is modern and 'developed' and their children can become educated. Moreover, they soon learned to manipulate to their advantage elements of their new environment such as the social services and national political discourse.

Ethiopian Israelis feel that they belong to their new country, the land that God promised to the Jews from the four corners of the world, and this chapter has described their consequent efforts at participating in the affairs of the country and to effect necessary cultural changes. However, this sense of belonging is extremely fragile and later chapters reveal that these efforts at integration, on the part of the older generation at least, are actually minimal. First though, I turn to the positive aspects of younger Ethiopian Israelis' efforts at integration, which unsurprisingly, far surpass that of their parents and grandparents.

5

Young Ethiopian Israelis

Introduction

The drop-in centre for young Ethiopian Israelis in Tel Aviv's new bus station provides a glimpse of Ethiopian youth: side by side, the successful well-adjusted Ethiopian volunteers and staff members, and the street youths. The former are proud of their Ethiopian heritage, ambitious in their career plans, and keen to assist the well-being and integration of less successful Ethiopian youngsters, not least by setting them a good example. They are confident, cheerful, beautifully dressed, and they seem to enjoy life and their University studies. They have succeeded in accepting themselves as Ethiopians and make their way in Israeli society, as Israelis, at the same time. They claim to experience racism (*zeregnett*), but refuse to be defeated by it. The teenagers, clad in their Rasta colours, were also cheerful, but their laughter betrayed a sense of feeling lost in the world around them. Many are drop-outs from school and the army, and they couldn't find or stick to a job. A few are said to be homeless after quarrels with families. One of the workers explained: 'They assume that everything will be hard for them because of racism. If they want to join Israeli society, they think "Oh but the *farenj* see us as Black! How can we fit in?"' So they identify instead with Blacks from Jamaica and America.'

Young Ethiopian Israelis require a separate discussion because their experience of Israel is, predictably, much different to that of their elders: younger people adapt faster to changed circumstances and learn spoken Hebrew rapidly. This chapter introduces Ethiopian Israeli teenagers and young persons in their twenties who arrived in Israel as teenagers and have benefited from the Israeli education system – at school and university or in full-time vocational training and from service in the army.

Ethiopian young people are generally cheerful and sociable – they wander in pairs or small groups, chatting and laughing quietly. In a group, they speak in Hebrew most of the time, although they often switch to Amharic when they speak about Ethiopian matters, such as family. In my neighbourhood, the boys tend to congregate on the steps by the supermarket. One or two carry walkmans which are shared amongst the group, so that everyone can listen to Bob Marley or the latest Michael Jackson hit. Sometimes, one or two non-Ethiopian youths join the group. On a Saturday, they climb over the school fence to play football on the playing field. Girls tend to meet inside their homes, and they too stroll down the streets slowly, arm in arm. Ethiopian youths who live in large urban centres such as Tel Aviv enjoy a more urban social life. They congregate in the corners of the Tel Aviv bus centre, or in the Ethiopian music shops, and dance to Reggae and disco at the Ethiopian night-club.[1]

Ethiopian young people tend to dress similarly to their non-Ethiopian peers: the latest (affordable) fashion in jeans and trainers, sweatshirts, T-shirts, and mini-skirts. Boys tend to base their hairstyle on Black American crew cuts. Girls plait theirs in a variety of elegant styles. A growing section of teenagers adopt a 'Rasta'[2] image. They wear Bob Marley T-shirts, and adorn their clothes and jewellery with the emblematic red-yellow-green stripes. The boys also grow dreadlocks. At the other extreme from the trendy Rasta youths, the religious minority dress in conventional style. Religious boys wear a *kippa* (a cloth cap worn by religious Jews) and straight trousers and shirt. Religious girls dress modestly with long skirts reaching the ground and baggy tops. Less religious girls still wear modest clothes at home, keeping their mini-skirts and more tight-fitting clothes for evenings out of sight of their Ethiopian elders.

Students

Most Ethiopian children attend state religious primary schools and secondary boarding schools. 'Youth Aliya' boarding schools, set up for young immigrants, particularly those who arrived in Israel without their families, have become predominantly Ethiopian. In 1993, Ethiopians accounted for thirty seven per cent of the total Youth Aliya student population and sixty seven percent of the student population in religious boarding schools.[3] I knew many boarders, and with the exception of a few individuals, they loved their schools. Years after their school days, former class-mates remain in touch by phone, and invite each other to their respective weddings and subsequent celebrations. School photos adorn bedroom walls. Day-school children also enjoy their school days, walking home or jumping off the bus cheerfully. These youngsters say that they prefer living at home with their family than going to boarding school and that educational standards are higher than at boarding school.[4]

Most Ethiopian students are streamed into vocational studies at high school. A recent study by the Israel Association for Ethiopian Jews asserted that 85 per cent of high school age youths have been sent to vocational track programmes in boarding schools.[5] Although some youngsters are happy to leave school with technical knowledge, others resent this streaming and fight against it.

> Ronit is a bright Bar Ilan University student: 'I know the problems of the young. I was at boarding school. They do not let you study what you want. When I was entering the 10th grade, they told me to study infant care or sewing, but I did not want that. Some class-mates and I staged a protest and we got what we wanted [entry into the academic stream].'

After school, most young people attend further vocational training courses. Special courses were also designed for young new immigrants who were too old to attend school.[6] Even if many alumni of these courses failed to gain employment in their area of training, the courses achieved good results in helping those young immigrants who did not benefit from Israeli school education prepare for the Israeli job market.[7] A growing minority enrol at University and a handful of graduates have pursued their studies to MA and PhD level.[8]

Soldiers

> A young soldier: 'Everyone's experience at the army is different, depending on their type of work and their officer. At first, I had a bad officer, but I complained and got transferred, and then it was good. When my mother died for example, my officer gave me two months leave. Tadesse [whose mother also died] however had to go back to work immediately. I learned a lot in the army, especially time keeping – you have to do things exactly on time.

Some of the *farenj* were fine, others not. They try to cheat you with guard duty [i.e. try to get you to do more] and if you say nothing they go off blowing a kiss and saying '*etiopit tov*!' (Hebrew: Ethiopians are good). If you stand up for yourself it is OK because in this country, you have to speak up, you cannot stay quiet. After the army I stopped being scared in front of officials in offices and now I can go there and ask for whatever I want. In the army everyone is equal – all can be killed the same!'

After school, like every other Israeli, Ethiopians are drafted into the army, three years and the annual four-week reserve service for men, and two years for women. Religious girls can obtain exemption and undertake community service instead, an option chosen by a majority of Ethiopian girls. A number of Ethiopian girls told me that they would have liked to have attended the army, but their parents forbade them on religious grounds, since army service involves living in close quarters with members of the opposite sex.

Ethiopians are reputed to be keen and excellent soldiers, and a sizeable proportion achieve officer status.[9] Ethiopian youths carry their uniform and gun with great pride. Photos clad in their army gear adorn bedroom and living room walls.

After visiting the parental home of a young University student, the first question he asked me was: 'Did you see the photo of me in the army?'

In April 1996, during a period of intense conflict in Lebanon, young Dodu confides with an air of wonder and excitement: 'I cannot leave the house for long because I am on the reserve list to go to Lebanon – they could call me at any moment!'

Etan, a University educated young man, smiles as he explains in fluent English: 'There is this Ethiopian notion of The Gun. In Ethiopia, someone who goes out with a gun is someone with power ... Here, you see a lot of young people with guns at weddings. It makes them feel good, powerful and more secure – secure from what, I do not know. The desire to serve in the army, besides the desire to serve the country, is the desire to 'look good'. More than anything else, the uniform and the gun say a lot. People go around in uniform carrying their guns – it is like carrying a mobile phone!'

School leavers generally look forward to their service very much and spend hours thinking and discussing which units to apply for.

Telahun, a twelfth grade student, often spoke to me about his quandaries regarding the army. He wanted to enter a combat unit because that was the best way to serve the country and one of the most prestigious units, but his mother was too frightened, lest he be killed in battle. The trouble, Telahun said, was that she did not understand the importance for later life of being in a prestigious unit. He was also considering parachuting and in third choice driving, because, he chuckled, he could then learn to drive without having to pay for lessons.

The experience in the army varies, depending on both the youngster in question, and the nature of his work.

Moshe, an Ethiopian Israeli who works at the Absorption Ministry, told me that he had a wonderful time at the army, and became an officer in charge of the initiation of new Ethiopian and Russian immigrants into the army. He suggested that soldiers who were in low-status positions, working in the kitchen for example, tended to have a negative experience, and did not feel that the army contributed to their integration in the country.

Negative army experiences

Elan had just completed his army service: 'I did not like the army. My officer did not like Ethiopians. We did not like him either because once my friend wanted permission to go to his uncle's funeral and he was not granted it. I was in jail for a month because my officer insulted me about being Ethiopian and I hit him ... I do not get on with my step-father, it is hard, and I received no support about this problem in the army.'

Elan's negative experience is not unique and a number of Ethiopian soldiers have committed suicide while in service. The main problems are apparent from Elan's words: 'racial' abuse, lack of understanding and tolerance for Ethiopian customs, unfair treatment and lack of compassion for personal problems. Out of the dozen or so Ethiopian soldiers or ex-soldiers that I spoke to at length, nearly all had stories which depicted discrimination in terms of the 'colour of their skin'. In particular, they suffered from racial jokes which referred to their background, customs, or skin colour.

Samagn, an Ethiopian who runs training programmes for Israeli officers to deal with Ethiopian soldiers, explains the problem: 'Ethiopians cannot take insults, even little things like table manners, or being called '*kushi*' ('black', 'nigger'). More than once, an enraged Ethiopian soldier threatened at gun point an Israeli soldier after an insult. But such joking is the way that Israelis interact – they do it to themselves too.'

Most Ethiopian soldiers soon learn to deal with such humour. A more difficult problem – which Ethiopian workers also complain of – is the lack of leave of absence to attend weddings and funerals in particular.

I witnessed Turuneh's quandary early one Sunday morning. He was expected back at the barracks at ten am, yet his great-aunt, who lives in his mother's neighbourhood, was holding a *teskar* (the seventh day memorial) for her deceased husband, a four-hour bus journey away. After changing his mind several times, he finally decided to attend the *teskar*, even though he knew that he would be disciplined on return to the army.

Cultural differences also affect Ethiopian soldiers in more subtle ways.

Samagn, the Ethiopian cultural advisor to Israeli officers, explains: 'We are used to answering any request by 'yes, OK (*ishi*)'. But this is no good in the army because officers abuse Ethiopian traditions of quietness and good manners. They ask Ethiopian soldiers to do the hardest work and the worst guard duty shifts (i.e. at night) because they know that Ethiopians will not refuse. But [the anger and frustration] builds up inside their tummies.'

An Israeli waiter told me about Ethiopians: 'Ah the Ethiopians, I love them so much! They are so good to work with. They are so quiet and say 'yes' to everything. When I was a border watchman at the army, if there was an extra eight hour shift to do, the Ethiopian would do it, and if I wanted someone to swap a shift with, he would say 'yes!' Ah the Ethiopians, I love them!'

A further problem is caused by Ethiopians' unrealistic expectations and consequent disappointment.

Samagn explains: 'Ethiopians do not have the same basis as the others [i.e. education and cultural background] and so they do not normally succeed as well as the Whites in the army. They want the best jobs and to become officers, but most of them do not achieve this. Then they get depressed.'

Positive experiences in the army

Fortunately, negative accounts of the army are far outweighed by positive experiences and the army is usually spoken of as a positive life changing experience.[10]

Etan: 'The army makes you stronger. Physical and mental endurance – walking at night with a 70 kg backpack, facing Arabs in the West Bank – is such an intense experience, that you feel you could do anything afterwards'.

Ethiopian soldiers learn about other Israelis – 'their customs and behaviour' and how to interact with them.

Moshe: 'You learn to be punctual: 6.30 am in the army means 6.30 am, and not 7 am or even 6.35 am!'

Rachamin remembers that at first he always ended up doing the worst night duty shifts. 'In Ethiopia, it is not good to refuse what your friends or your officer asks of you. That is our tradition.' Once he learned to say 'no', Rachamin told me proudly that the Israeli soldiers praised him, telling him that now he was learning to be truly Israeli!

Etan: 'In the army, you learn to be with the Israelis – how not to feel insulted at their jokes and how to laugh with them. We learned to chat and play with them. You learn to be less quiet and to speak out.'

The army increased Ethiopians' sense of belonging to Israel and of equality with other Israelis.[11]

Aviva: 'Psychologically, when you give to your country, serve your country, give three years of your life, you feel nice, as if you are part of the people. I went and gave the same as the others, there is no black and white there, so I thought afterwards: we are equal.'

Taddesse: 'You eat, sleep and joke with them. You are equal to them – the same food, the same exercises, the same clothes, the same guns, the same work.'

Conversely, when Ethiopians' sense of belonging was threatened their enthusiasm for the army dropped accordingly. As Kaplan & Salamon note: 'While it is generally denied by military sources, some observers claim the Ethiopian community's general difficulties and particularly the 'blood scandal' have resulted in a lessening of motivation among Ethiopian inductees'.[12]

Workers

Young Ethiopian Israelis work in a variety of jobs.[13] University graduates enter white collar professions and often work in the public or voluntary sector on Ethiopian-related issues. They tend to be well integrated and successful. As Moshe, an Ethiopian who lived in Canada for eight years before recently immigrating to Israel, put it: 'They act Israeli but think like Ethiopians. They have their Ethiopian style with an Israeli coating.' A large number of youngsters from the earlier wave of immigration worked with the social services and absorption workers to help the integration of the new immigrants, although by 1995, many were losing these jobs as the new immigrants were settling in, and their services were no longer required. They acted as translators, community workers, assistance welfare officers, housing officers, and so on. The act of translation involved more than merely vocabulary since the youngsters had to translate and make intelligible foreign concepts and modes of thought to both sides.

> Moshe, who worked for a while at a caravan site to encourage dwellers to buy homes, explained that he had to explain the terms and conditions as told by his Israeli boss, and also to explain in terms by which Ethiopians could understand why it was in their advantage to buy a house – the Israeli discourse would be largely meaningless to them.

> Aster told me of her difficulties in the other direction: trying to make the Israeli social workers understand Ethiopian ways of speaking. For example, if a man says 'there is no more *injera* (Ethiopian pancake) in the house', she will not translate literally

because the social worker will think that financial difficulties are the problem, instead she will say 'he is having marital problems'.

The majority of Ethiopian youngsters are employed in manual work. The Israeli bosses I spoke to praised their young Ethiopian workers for their diligence, dexterity and respectful attitude towards their boss and their work. Despite apparent success, young manual workers, like their elders, do not tend to speak much about their work. They assert proudly that they have a job, and the story ends there. This silence, I believe, is due to a disdain for manual work, characteristic of Ethiopian Highland societies and well expressed in the proverb 'the mouth's wisdom [leads to] leadership; the hand's wisdom [leads to] slavery' (*yeaf bilhat getnet; yeijj bilhat baryenet*).[14] Young Ethiopians who emigrated to Israel dreamed of social advancement in a country in which they could excel themselves and rise above the former Beta Israel status of despised artisan. Working in factories, alongside low-status Arab workers, is a disappointment and humiliation.[15]

Identity

The search for identity is a preoccupation for all young people, but for immigrants, the search is all the more difficult as the range of choices is dramatically increased. However Ethiopian youngsters who arrived in Israel after the age of about ten or so are on the whole remarkably successful at combining dual identities.[16] As Malka Shaptay concludes on her exhaustive study of Ethiopian soldiers: 'The research findings show that close to the termination of their military service most of the Ethiopian soldiers were found to have developed an Israeli identity, and there was a great degree of continuity in their identification with Ethiopian culture.'[17]

> A young twenty-three-year-old electrical engineering student at one of Israel's most prestigious university, who lived in Canada for eight years and who speaks fluent Hebrew, Amharic and English affirmed: 'I am Ethiopian in everything! I hope that I have not changed and that I am Ethiopian like any other even though I have learned the Western way.'

Israeli citizenship and Ethiopian identity

Young Ethiopians seek to integrate into their new society while preserving aspects of ethnic identity. On the one hand, they want to become fully fledged Israeli citizens and progress socially and economically as equals in their new country. They seek good jobs and an Israeli lifestyle. Many youths learn Israeli religious practice,[18] dress in fashionable styles, learn to cook Israeli dishes, seek the company of non-Ethiopians, watch TV, read newspapers, become keen soldiers, and a few individuals have non-Ethiopian boy/girl-friends and spouses. Moreover, in this 'integrating' mode, they often appear to reject elements of past Ethiopian practice when these appear 'primitive', for they are 'modern' citizens like other Israelis.

> After being shown a picture of women cooking *injera* pancakes in Ethiopia on a large platter on a fire outside, I asked why *injera* is no longer cooked in this way, given that Ethiopian immigrants often complain that *injera* pancakes are too small in Israel. Abba Negusse replied 'I do not know'. My neighbour Kanu suggested a utilitarian reason: wood cannot easily be found. Her younger sister retorted rather angrily: 'We are now in the twentieth century!'

> Whenever I was walking barefoot, even around the house, Ethiopians always noticed and told me that 'in this country you wear shoes'.

At the same time, young people affirm proudly that they are Ethiopian, and seek to maintain a strong Ethiopian identity. Their social life is almost exclusively in the company of kin and Ethiopian neighbours and they maintain numerous Ethiopian traditions (e.g. food, social behaviour, and religious practice).

> Workie is a young married woman who immigrated eleven years ago, aged sixteen: 'I am born Ethiopian but my citizenship (*zegenet*) has changed and now I am Israeli. I am Israeli on paper, but not by all things – I do not eat the same as Yemeni Israelis for example. My traditions have not changed: Weddings, funerals, food, receiving guests, drinking [Ethiopian style] coffee …'

Why a desire to maintain Ethiopian identity whilst seeking to integrate? Creating an ethnic identity is one means of dealing with perceived discrimination. Young Ethiopians feel that they are viewed by Israelis as Blacks before all else, and worse still as 'primitive Ethiopians'. As illustrated in the following chapter, they think that however much they succeed, they will always be considered 'lower' than other Israelis because of the colour of their skin. Given that Ethiopian youths remain 'Ethiopian' in the eyes of other Israelis, they prefer to be seen, or at least to think of themselves, as 'proud' Ethiopians rather than 'primitive' shameless ones who are willing to forego their rich heritage for the sake of conformity.

Ethnic pride: Ethiopian friends and spouses

Ethnic pride is manifest in young people's tendency to socialise and marry amongst themselves. Several young Ethiopians I knew had romantic relationships with non-Ethiopians, but eventually opted for an Ethiopian spouse. Their choice, they told me, was based on the 'black/white question', a strong sense of cultural differences, and a desire to reaffirm their Ethiopian heritage. One man said that it is good to be out in the world of Whites by day and to return to an Ethiopian household – and Ethiopian spouse – at night. Men had more incentive to marry Ethiopian since they are privileged in Ethiopian households – whether the wife works outside the home or not, she is solely in charge of housekeeping and child care. Educated Ethiopian women have more incentive to marry out since many Ethiopian husbands find the notion of a high-achieving wife difficult to accept and they are aware of the better deal for women in non-Ethiopian households. Whatever the complex web of motivations for choosing a marriage partner, many young Ethiopians explained their choice in terms of a political statement, a reaffirmation of Ethiopian identity.

Young Ethiopians seek out the company of other young Ethiopians for their social life.[19] Although Ethiopian youths are popular at work, in the army and at college with other Israelis, such friendships do not usually extend beyond the work place. It is in the company of other young Ethiopians, that they can relax and 'be themselves', without needing to conform to either their elders' expectations or to adopt Israeli social behaviour.

> Etan explains that Ethiopians are better for friends, they are easier for Israelis do not know their customs: 'With Ethiopians, it is close, we meet at weddings and funerals, we know each others'

relatives. Whites can easily insult you, not intentionally but because of their way of speaking. They say for instance, to each other too, 'your mother is *tebeda* (a whore)'. For us respect is the most important thing. We have patience, and they have none. With Ethiopians it is 'tight' (*thek*).'

Tadesse: 'My best friends at school are Ethiopians. I know their life better and I understand what they think of me and they know what I think of them.'

Combining Israeli and Ethiopian identities

The pride young people have in their culture does not immune them from condemning aspects of Ethiopian culture. Marriage rules, codes of dress, and other constraining cultural practices are criticised and openly broken by a large segment of the youth – who continue nonetheless to proudly affirm their Ethiopian identity.

Solomon was telling me about the thousands of people at a funeral he attended in Jerusalem and burst forth: 'I hate Ethiopian culture!' Noting the strength of his outburst, he checked himself and explained: He does not hate the fact that there are such large gatherings, although he himself does not enjoy them, but 'the culture is not compatible with life here'. People cannot hold jobs as they get fired after they keep on taking days off work for funerals. 'They spend all their money on funerals and weddings and do not buy books for their children!'

Moshe complained of the high cost and frequency of Ethiopian celebrations: 'They have no head! How much does a cow cost [for the feast marking the birth of a daughter]? They could put that money in the bank and when the child is older use it for her education.' Me: 'But don't they recoup the expenses with the donations, and get a profit?' Moshe: 'Maybe, but they have to return it all at future celebrations. I had to put aside the profits of my wedding to pay it back now'.

Even when Ethiopian practices are not criticised, as Solomon says, they often come into conflict with newly adopted Israeli ways. The most evocative way to describe this intertwining of two cultures is to give a portrait of two youngsters I knew well, Efrat and Addissu.

Efrat, an animated twenty-six-year-old, has well-formed ideas about what integration means, and does not mean. 'I am Israeli by citizenship, but I am Ethiopian by birth. I grew up there and I want to maintain our traditions: The religious holidays, weddings, music, food ...' She mixes both Ethiopian and Israeli ways, consciously. She wears Jeans, but covers herself with a white shawl to go to drink coffee or to attend a funeral gathering. When her child was born she said that she would speak both Hebrew and Amharic to him (although the latter lapsed as the months went by). She is temporarily living at her parental home so that her parents and younger siblings can take care of the baby while she works. Her husband joins her at week-ends. She would not leave her child however at her mother's house, as the latter has requested, when she returns to her own home because she wants to bring him up 'her way'. She will buy him a computer. She works as a receptionist and speaks fluent Hebrew. Her social life revolves around her family and kin and she disapproves of her younger sister's immodest dress. She accords her parents all the traditional forms of respect, but disobeyed them in her marriage because she refused to abide by Ethiopian 'bad' traditions. Her parents did not want her to marry her husband but 'we wanted each other and that is what counts'.

Addissu, a twenty-five-year-old student in acting school, epitomised dual identity. Addissu quickly adapted to Israeli way of life and 'culture'. His Hebrew is perfect and when he speaks it, he adds all the appropriate mannerisms such as shoulder slapping, short interjections such as 'nu', and a raised voice. He is ambitious and doubtlessly will succeed in the Israeli world – he has already starred in a TV drama about the Ethiopian journey to Sudan. At the same time, Addissu is a proud Ethiopian. He has returned to Ethiopia several times in the last few years, and thinks of himself as part of the 'Ethiopian Diaspora'. His walls are adorned with Ethiopian artefacts, brought back from his two trips to Ethiopia. He works for the Ethiopian radio station, performs Ethiopian music at weddings and has brought out two CDs. His radio programmes are about 'our culture in Israel. To be Israeli, you do not need to forget your culture. If you have a second child, you do not have to forget your first born.' He is courteous and respectful towards his parents and maintains close relations with his siblings. He loves to amuse people by mimicking the way of speaking of the elders, getting their intonation just perfect and mixing in their Hebrew words pronounced incorrectly. He remains acutely aware of his colour and calls himself 'a little black man'.

Youngsters delicately weave together strands of two opposing cultures. Ethiopian young immigrants are developing an Ethiopian-Israeli social manner. It is marked by Ethiopian courtesy, cheerfulness, respect, and contains elements of Israeli individualism and strong will as well as Hebrew language. Another example of cultural mixing is the style in which Ethiopian youths organise their weddings; they combine Ethiopian requirements and taste (e.g. all kin are invited, Ethiopian music and dance, money donations) with Israeli practice (e.g. the venue is a rented hall, Israeli food, Western disco music, an Israeli Master of Ceremonies).

Sometimes, they have to choose which of two sets of norms to apply to the given moment, switching from one to another, more or less consciously. They are chameleons, adopting one behaviour pattern in the company of Israelis and young Ethiopians and another in the company of their elders. For example, as Israelis, in the presence of Israelis, they dress Israeli, speak Hebrew, smoke cigarettes, dance disco, eat Israeli food, and some even desecrate the Sabbath. The same individuals in front of their elders dress modestly, speak Amharic, never smoke, dance Ethiopian style, eat Ethiopian food and respect the Sabbath. There is no element of deceit: abiding by Ethiopian ways with elders is a mark of respect, and is on the whole enjoyable, albeit not always.

> Telahun hated being summoned by his grandfather to clean his back in the shower, but he never refused him.

> Young sixteen-year-old Ester had been looking forward all month to her cousin's wedding. She was dressed in new clothes and jewellery purchased for the occasion. As the hired mini-bus was about to leave, an elderly relative decided at the last minute that he wanted to go. Without a word of complaint, as the youngest in the party, Ester gave him her seat, and watched the mini-bus leave without her.

Amongst themselves, youngsters' behaviour is eclectic. Ethiopian youths take the best from both sets of norms – mixing languages according to the topic of conversation, smoking, greeting each other in full Ethiopian style, discussing family issues, watching TV, listening to Amharic music alongside Reggae and Israeli and Western disco music ...

Difficulties arise when new Israeli norms are in conflict with Ethiopian ones. Marriage is a chief problem in this respect. Many youngsters were in a state of turmoil because they had fallen in love with someone whom they later found out was a relative, and thus forbidden for them. In my experience, about half the youngsters in this situation went ahead with the marriage and half renounced their love. The former category did not make this decision lightly: they felt no allegiance to the marriage rule, but the marriage went against the wishes of their families and therefore forced them to infringe an Ethiopian norm which they do wish to hold onto, namely respect for elders. Sometimes conflict ensues between youngsters over correct behaviour since its boundaries have been pushed to extremes.

> Fanta, a young woman positioned on the 'traditional' extreme of the spectrum was in conflict with a suitor. She refused to spend time with him until they were officially engaged, with parental approval. He, having developed Israeli standards, thought this a premature step before they had spent time together to see if they got on.

Such conflict is also experienced by individuals, who are unsure which codes to adopt, and they battle with contradictory feelings.

> Alemwork, a twenty-five-year old who immigrated aged sixteen, wishes her husband and his family would be less 'Ethiopian' sometimes. He cares about what people say. He says that he will not walk with me if I wear trousers.' Although Alemwork complains about her husband's strict adherence to Ethiopian norms of behaviour, she herself is just as traditional, if not more so. I remember a trip she made to Tel Aviv to buy hair cream. She had wanted a companion so that she could 'wander' a little in town. However, since she went alone, she came straight back, because there were many Ethiopians about, and they would have 'thought things'. Alemwork feels that such thinking is 'backward' and she wants to break free, but she cannot escape the norms, which are prevalent in her society and, above all, in herself.

Conclusion

Beta Israel youth fast learn the host country's language and social norms. I never ceased to admire young Ethiopians' ability to oscillate relatively effortlessly between two cultures, adopting Ethiopian social norms in the company of their relatives and Israeli ones with non-Ethiopians. They switch from Amharic to Hebrew, from modest clothing to a mini-skirt, from quiet tones to brash conversation. Amongst themselves, they blend their favourite elements of each – a conversation in Hebrew about work and college, switching to Amharic when family matters are discussed, a feast of *injera* some days, with rice and pasta enjoyed at other times, full participation in daily Israeli life, while maintaining Ethiopian decorum and hospitality in their homes and proper respect towards their relatives.[20]

It seems to me that Ethiopian Jewish youngsters' ability to juggle with different cultural codes is a manifestation of peoples' ability to simultaneously hold apparently contradictory beliefs without ending up in some sort of mental confusion.[21] Lisa Gilad who studied Yemeni Israelis suggests that 'contradiction has become a 'normal' part of the routine cognitive efforts and social actions of the immigrant generation'.[22] She suggests that given the multitude of norms and expectations individuals face, they 'pick and chose' (*ibid*) and as a result, within any immigrant group there is enormous variety. Although, as Chapter Eight shows, former status holders do suffer from the resulting loss of control as new norms, which reduce their authority, are adopted.[23] I have shown in this chapter and the preceding ones why Ethiopians Israelis confidently assert 'we are well in this country'. But unfortunately, this well-being and sense of belonging to Israel is often overshadowed by feelings of rejection and discrimination.

6

Rejected

A young woman said to me: 'I like chatting with you. I do not normally chat with *farenj* (Israelis), but you are not like a *farenj*.' She explained further: I chat with them, and then they say something not nice, something like "you came here because you were hungry". Also, if they are alone with you, they are your best friend. But as soon as another *farenj* comes along, then they stick together and you are left aside.'

Soon after the initial euphoria at the arrival in Israel and reunification with lost family members, Ethiopian Jewish immigrants felt rejected in their homeland. At the immediate level, Ethiopian Jews complain that their Israeli neighbours 'don't even say hello'. They feel that they are looked down upon as primitive people who know nothing. Worse, the basis of their identity and sense of belonging to Israel – their Judaism – is doubted. Such feelings became head-line news when the international media reported the huge demonstration held by Ethiopian Israelis on 28 January 1996.

Feeling rejected in the homeland

Daily affronts

Ethiopian Israeli adults experience other Israelis' negativity on a daily basis: in the derogatory eyes of impatient officials; at the shops when a cashier barely in her teens growls to an elder that he has given a wrong amount of money; in the silence of their non-Ethiopian neighbours. They also complain that Israelis, especially Russians, pass in front of them at queues. This is the case in hospitals in particular, they say, because the staff are Russian and hate Ethiopians.[1]

Mama Turuwork describes her daily humiliation: 'One of my neighbours says "hello" but the others, when I walk out [of the apartment block], move aside without a word. They think that I am deaf, like a donkey. They do not even say '*shalom*' or '*boker tov*' (good morning, Hebrew) – I do understand that at least! It makes me very sad!

Smuel Yilma writes: 'The pangs of absorption in Ofakim hit us children particularly hard. Outside the class, the local children received us with clenched fists. Sneering insults and fists was our welcome if we ever tried to join in the games around the neighbourhood. Skin our colour they had never seen before and "Little Blacks!" was the first and last thing we heard from them.'[2]

Ethiopian Israelis bemoan the fact that other Israelis do not value their Ethiopian cultural heritage, and view Ethiopia merely as an underdeveloped poor country, where people go without clothes or food.

A man on an Amharic chat show on the radio: 'Israelis see us as people who have come from an undeveloped country and think: They are uneducated, they are *dinkoro* (ignorant), they are people who know only how to look after cattle.'

Mesganow, a young neighbour of mine, was speaking of the splendour of Ethiopian countryside after a return visit. 'The *farenj*', he added, 'think that there is nothing in Ethiopia – no trees, no water, just desert. Once one of them asked me if we had pens there!'

Ethiopian Israelis are particularly enraged and hurt that many Israelis perceive Ethiopians as ignorant about religion.

My young neighbour Avi: 'Our practices are different, but the *farenj* think that we do not know. We drink beer at funerals and they say that this is bad, that we do not care about our dead and are making merry!'

Ethiopian Jews recognise that aspects of their culture, namely their reserve and good manners are much admired in Israel. But, as the section on the army showed, many of them feel that these qualities are abused by Israelis who take advantage of Ethiopian meekness. Ethiopians also complain that appreciation for Ethiopian behaviour is superficial.

> As young Efrat put it: 'They [the Whites] do accept us, but it is only superficial, not in their heart.'

> Mesganow, a young man: 'Israelis say to us that the Ethiopians are *hamudi* (Hebrew: pretty, sweet, nice), they are courteous and nice. But they also think within themselves "Ethiopians know nothing!"'

> A seventeen-year-old girl: 'They look at us as stupid, people who do not understand, but we do understand, we just keep it inside!'

> A young woman: 'Some of our children are shy and when the teacher asks a question, they stay silent. The teacher then says: "These are stupid people who know nothing." They then place our children with Israeli mentally handicapped children. They impede the future of our children.'

Religious rejection

Most Beta Israel state that their chief problem in Israel is the religious question (*yehaymanot neger*). Following Rabbinical rulings in the mid-1970s stating that the Beta Israel were a Jewish community, the Ministry of the Interior decreed that Ethiopians were entitled to automatic citizenship under the law of Return, which declares that every Jew has the right to settle in Israel.[3] But despite the Rabbinate's acceptance of the *communal* status of the Beta Israel as Jews, there was ambiguity regarding *individuals'* personal status. This is because conversions and divorces in Ethiopia were not done in a manner consistent with *halakha* (post-biblical rabbinical law), resulting in the eyes of the Rabbinate in numerous non-Jews and *mamzerim* (illegitimate offspring) being included in the Beta Israel community.[4] In order to dispel these doubts and enable Ethiopian Jews to marry other Jews, the Israeli Chief Rabbinate adopted a policy requiring all new Ethiopian immigrants, and any resident Ethiopian Jew wishing to be married, to undergo a conversion ceremony of ritual immersion and symbolic circumcision, which involved taking a drop of blood from a man's penis.

In the early 1980s, Ethiopian Jewish immigrants submitted to the Rabbinical demands. However, they bitterly resented this practice since it negated their authenticity as Jews, and, as their numbers and confidence grew, they resisted. Marylin Herman, who conducted fieldwork amongst the Beta Israel in the early 1990s notes: 'The subject [of conversion, *giur*, Hebrew] invokes such strong feelings of anger and indignation that it is often accompanied by expressions of regret for ever having gone to Israel, and not having remained in Ethiopia'.[5] In September 1985, Ethiopian Jewish immigrants organised a forty day sit-in in front of the Rabbinate's office in Jerusalem.[6] Their demands were partially met: new immigrants no longer had to comply to the conversion process, but youngsters wishing to marry still required a symbolic conversion, albeit without the demand for a drop of blood.

More than ten years later, the fury about the original demands was not bated and campaigns to abolish the requirements for couples to be wed continues fiercely. However over the years, an increasing number of Rabbis are agreeing to marry Ethiopians without symbolic circumcision, as long as they get a written statement from a Beta Israel priest confirming the Judaism of the individual in question.[7]

> Old Mama Tarikye: 'We were never baptised, while the Christians went for *timquat* (baptism), we never did. [Mama Tarikye is equating ritual immersion with baptism[8]]. In this country too, we do not want to be baptised. Even for a marriage we do not want to do *temeqen*. The people [Beta Israel] who came before us, they were circumcised [symbolically] and 'baptised'. The *qes* [her son, the priest] said to them: "We were given the law by Moses. We will not circumcise like you do, we will not be baptised (*meteleq*). Even if you want to govern the country, so be it; we are better off losing the chance to govern the country than to be circumcised!"'

In Ethiopia, the Beta Israel thought of themselves as the true Israelites, the House of Israel (the literal translation of the term Beta Israel), as opposed to their Amhara neighbours who also lay claim to Israelite descent. In Israel now, they maintain that they are the purest and cleanest of all Jews, thanks to their purity laws, marriage rules, and, in their eyes, strict religious practice. By suggesting that the Beta Israel are not proper Jews, the conversion requirement amounts to a rejection of the essence of their identity – that part of themselves which kept them distinct from their neighbours in Ethiopia and which now provides them with legitimacy in Israel.

Discourse on racism

Young people complain not only of being looked down upon as primitive Ethiopians, but also of 'racism' (*zeregnet*).⁹ I put racism in inverted commas to stress that I am writing about how Ethiopians feel Israelis look at them, not my own interpretation of Israeli attitudes. By racism, Ethiopian Israelis mean that Israelis disparage them not only on account of their so-called primitive background, but also on account of the colour of their skin. They compare racism in Israel to racism in America and conceive the former as worse. Israel, as a country of Jews, should not have any racism at all (for Jews are all one people, they say), and, judging from MTV and American films, American Blacks are doing well, with jobs in high positions, and glamorous lifestyles.

Racism is increasingly taken as *the* cause for Ethiopian problems in Israel: lack of jobs, problems in education, in the army, poverty, unsuccessful medical treatments, the Rabbinical demands for religious conversion, failure to 'pull' a White girl ...

> I asked young Etan to explain to me where he sees the racism he was so vehemently denouncing: 'Everywhere! At work, if a Russian or Moroccan comes in, after two weeks, he is your boss. Yet he has the same education. That is how you know: is this not racism?'

> Fantaoun, a science graduate who speaks five languages fluently (Amharic, Tigrinia, Russian, English and Hebrew): 'The woman in the employment office had to convince the employer for half an hour to accept an Ethiopian applicant, saying that I was different to other Ethiopians. But I still did not get the job – they just did not want an Ethiopian.'

> A young woman died suddenly a few days after being admitted to hospital. As her family lamented her death, I heard an oft-repeated wail: 'They killed her! They killed her!' When I later inquired about this particular lament, the grieving relatives maintained: 'Yes, the doctors, they killed her. They killed her because she is black!'

I sensed that although Ethiopian Israelis vehemently denounce Israeli racism toward them, they hate to actually have to admit to the idea that their fellow Jews could look down on them on account of their colour. They prefer instead to try find reasons to account for Israeli racism: the reasons may not legitimise the racism experienced, but they can at least help to comprehend it.

The real issue, Taddesse, a leading Ethiopian political activist, explained to me, is the cultural and technological gap between Ethiopians and Israelis. Israelis look down on Ethiopians because of this rather than because they are Black – even if the Israelis, and thus the Ethiopians, think that colour is the issue. Therefore, once this gap is bridged, he argued, negativity towards Ethiopians will disappear: 'We need to work hard now so that colour does not become an issue for the future.' Moshe, the young Ethiopian who lived in Canada for eight years, lent support to this view. He stressed that Israeli racism is directed towards Ethiopian Jewish immigrants in particular, rather than to just any Black person. This suggests to him that Israelis are not racist per se but rather exasperated by the foreign ways of the Ethiopians.

> Moshe told me of a game he once played with a few Ethiopian friends. They entered shops as Ethiopian Israelis, speaking Hebrew with thick Ethiopian accents. They noted the shop assistants' attitudes: impatience, scowls, and so forth. Then, they pretended to be Canadian tourists, Moshe speaking in fluent English while the others remained silent. The shop assistants welcomed them warmly.

Some young people look at the nature of Israeli society to understand Israeli racism. Alemu points to the ideological importance of the Hebrew language in Israel: 'If you do not speak Hebrew in Israel, you know nothing.'

A number of Ethiopian Israelis explain the issue in terms of Israel's own struggles as a new European country.

> Admass: 'Israelis do not respect us. They think that we are here just because we were poor in Ethiopia. They mean us no harm, but they have their own problems, trying to be equal to the Europeans and they want nothing in their way. We, uneducated people, are not good for that.'

Others take an opposing, somewhat cynical, view: Ethiopians, they say, have a positive image compared to Russian immigrants precisely because Ethiopian ignorance poses no threat to Israelis; Russians, who arrive as trained engineers, doctors, and artists threaten Israeli jobs and seats in Parliament.

Moshe: 'Israelis do not like Russians because they are afraid that they will take their jobs. Ethiopians however they like because Ethiopians sweep the streets!'

The notion that Israelis fear Ethiopians' advancement was taken to extreme by an overwhelming number of Ethiopians, both young and old, to explain the relatively high death-rate of Ethiopian soldiers in the army (Ethiopian leaders stated that over twenty Ethiopians died in service, and not in combat, from 1992 to 1996; the official figure is 10).[10] The army authorities stated that the youngsters had committed suicide, but many Ethiopian Israelis maintained that the '*farenj* kill our soldiers when they think that the Ethiopians will go beyond them'.

On the morning of the 5th January 1996, Assefa Birhun, a former neighbour of mine, was found in his soldier's room, dead from a bullet wound in his stomach. He was a nineteen-year old boy, unanimously described as full of joy and life, a loving son, brother and friend. The army officials announced a death by suicide. Ethiopians refused to believe this: the army was lying, the boy was killed. They argued that given the precise location of the bullet wound, it would have been impossible for it to be self-inflicted. Local residents staged a demonstration on the streets of Afula to protest against the army's mistreatment of their youngsters.

The killing of the soldiers became an issue on everybody's lips and was a catalyst in sparking off the fury unleashed over the Blood Crisis.

The blood crisis

The depth of Beta Israel's sense of rejection is illustrated by the January 1996 Ethiopian mass protest against the Blood Bank's policy of discarding blood donated by Ethiopians.

The demonstration

On Thursday 25 January 1996, I met with my friend Aster to go shopping in town. However, the normally quiet restrained young woman was flushed and angry. 'Have you not heard?' she said, 'they have been throwing away our blood! They say that we have AIDS!

My brothers arrived here at the age of eight and ten – how could they have caught AIDS? They gave blood and it was thrown in the garbage! It is racism!'

Aster's anger was felt throughout the country, and, three days later, over 10,000 Ethiopian Israelis assembled in front of the government offices in Jerusalem. Ethiopians filled the numerous buses sponsored by the Ethiopian Umbrella Organisation, and when these were full, other buses were hired at the passengers' own expense. Six buses and two mini-buses left from Afula.

As we approached the House of Parliament around 11 am, we could see thousands of Ethiopians, many draped in their white shawls, and hear their slogans and cries. As soon as the bus stopped, the youths jumped out, and started to run towards the gathering holding up the banner they had prepared. They shouted at passers-by: 'Don't come near! I have AIDS!' One youth picked up a gardener's pick and walked off holding it high above his head. He replaced it twenty yards from the bewildered gardener.

The crowd was trying to force entry into the parliament compound. The police responded by showering water and tear gas. The cries of pain from burning faces and eyes were drowned by the chanting of slogans. In the distance, a group of priests, with their white shawls and colourful Ethiopian umbrellas, prayed under a tree.

Written slogans – in both Hebrew and English – included:

> 'Although our skin is black, our blood is as red as yours and we are as Jewish as you!'
> 'Did Apartheid leave South Africa for Israel?'
> 'Apartheid! The second Holocaust! Genocide in the Holy Land!'
> 'Our dreams are being stolen when racism comes to our homeland!'
> 'Our blood is also red, it is not black!'
> 'I am a proud Ethiopian but a disappointed Israeli!'
> 'We are brothers in blood.'
> 'My blood is good enough for the army, but it is worthless'.

The crowd quietened for a while and stood facing the Parliament, waiting for an address by Addissu Messelle, the Ethiopian leader of the day, and by the Minister for Absorption. Slogans were chanted in unison, calling amongst other things for the Health Minister's resignation. Addissu spoke in Amharic, his clenched fist forward, the crowd repeating his refrains and clapping. He said that he and a number of priests and representatives were to meet with the Prime Minister and that they would not exit without a satisfactory answer. Everyone waited patiently, at first.

Suddenly, boys in the front of the crowd began to throw stones at the riot police. Others soon followed. Youngsters took position on the hill and threw rocks from there. The police retaliated with tear gas and rubber bullets. Tear gas bombs flew in both directions, Ethiopians picking them up in time to hurl them back to the police. Many older Ethiopians and women ran off to safety behind the Ethiopian firing lines.

Eventually the crowd quietened down, but only after dozens of police and a few Ethiopians were injured and many cars vandalised.

Ethiopian youths walked about proudly with a victorious look in their eyes. They boasted their feats:

- 'My stone smashed a police van window!
- I hit a soldier on the forehead with my umbrella!
- This is like the *intafada*!'

I asked youngsters why they had been violent:
- 'Every time I read an article in the newspaper [about the throwing of the blood] it was as if I was hit in the head with a stone!
- They started, they sprayed us with gas! That could kill someone!
- Now people will listen to Ethiopians!
- Arabs got want they wanted by throwing stones, so can we!'

Discourse about the blood crisis

Why should the discarding of donated blood spark such fury? The official explanation was straightforward enough: given that Ethiopian immigrants had much higher rates of HIV infections than other Israelis.[11] Ethiopian immigrants were deemed a high risk group, and so in the interest of the safety of the national supply of blood, their donations were not used. An exception was made for Ethiopian donations from rare blood groups which were not discarded. The reason for *secretly* discarding the blood – that is accepting it and then throwing it out rather than not accepting it from the start – was to avoid stigmatising the Ethiopian population and cause embarrassment to Ethiopian soldiers, who would have had to stand aside as the other soldiers in their unit gave blood.

Most Ethiopians claimed that this policy implied that they were all infected, failing to understand (or choosing to ignore) the distinction between a group perceived to be high risk and a group fully infected with HIV. Indeed, dozens of times, I heard the retort 'just because a few Ethiopians might have dirty blood, this does not mean that all Ethiopians do!' As Yeshe put it: 'Because one person's blood is not clean, why is the blood of all the Ethiopians thrown away?' Ethiopian Israelis were devastated at the thought of being all cast together, and all tainted with the blasphemy of dirty blood.

> Samagn, an educated Ethiopian leader: 'It is the way that the policy was enacted that infuriates me as much as the policy itself. They lumped all Ethiopians together as if we were all the same and did not take the trouble to explain to us what was going on. Why did they not speak to us from the start instead of throwing out the blood in secret? My friend Avraham has been here twenty-seven years and his children were all born here, and they cannot give blood – that is absurd!'

Ethiopians were particularly upset that it was their blood which was discarded because 'blood is life', 'blood is the soul (*nifs*)'.[12] They compared the spilling of their blood to killing. Ethiopians repeated again and again, to each other, to me, on the radio, in the press:

> 'Throwing our blood away is like taking our life. It is like killing us!'

Several Ethiopians made extreme comparisons:

> 'Only an enemy can bring about a spilling of blood. We make no difference between those who spilt our blood and the Hamas [killing Jews in suicide bombs].'

> 'Throwing away our blood is no different to what the Germans did [in the holocaust]; it is like killing all the people.'

> We prefer our blood to be spilled in front of the government's office [i.e. to fight and maybe die in the process] than to be thrown in the garbage.

The blood revelations gave rise to a sense of betrayal.

> Old Mama Tsay: 'We always said that the *farenj* are our brothers and sisters, and our children serve together with theirs [in the army], but now they say that our children's blood is not good enough. We have no language, we do not know. But we are all Jews. So we trusted them like parents and we followed them. We

went with them when they took us to hospital. Even the clothes they give us, which have already been worn by them, we accepted even without washing them – we never would have accepted such clothes in Ethiopia! We trusted them. So now why have they done such a thing?'

As Lisa Anteby points out, the discourse about the Blood Affair varied according to age group.[13] Older Ethiopian Israelis interpreted the throwing away of blood as a rejection by Israeli society on account of their religion, while for younger ones, they were rejected because of the colour of their skin.

One of the demonstration's placards combined both these views: 'Although our skin is black, our blood is as red as yours and we are as Jewish as you!'

For older Ethiopians, the throwing away of Beta Israel blood was a slur on the purity of the group. Concepts of purity and impurity are central to Beta Israel ideology.[14] By suggesting that Ethiopians' blood was infected, Israelis were implying that their blood was impure. For the Beta Israel, impurity normally results from failing to observe Beta Israel marriage laws (e.g. not marrying kin) or Biblical purity laws (e.g. segregation of menstrual women), which are the cornerstones of Beta Israel Jewish identity. Thus, following their reasoning, discarding Ethiopian-donated blood means that the Beta Israel are thought of as having infected blood, that is impure blood, which implies that the Beta Israel are not proper Jews.

The following quote illustrates well this equation between religious purity, that is the observance of marriage rules and Biblical purity laws and clean blood, free of HIV infection. It also shows the vehemence of the rhetoric of religious rejection.

A priest explained his reasons for attending the demonstration: 'We are black, but our blood is clean. We do not marry relatives (*zamad*), we do not eat unclean animals [...], we do nothing that is forbidden by God, we are clean (*netsu*) people. But now they say: "You are black and your blood cannot be mixed with ours," and they threw out our blood and we became very angry. It is like the Germans when six million were killed! The only difference between us and the *farenj* is that they are White and they do not observe the Bible in the way we do and they marry their cousins and go naked – that is forbidden! They do this kind of thing and yet they throw out our blood. It is a matter of life and death – that is why we demonstrated!'

For the young and the educated elite, the scandal was more an issue of colour and racism than religious discrimination or purity, although the symbolic importance of blood was as strong for them as for their parents.

Taddesse expressed his feeling of stigmatisation: 'The blood thing is pure racism. They do not want Ethiopian blood in their bodies! It is terrible the way that they have stigmatised our community. I cannot walk down the street looking good now. I feel that everyone looks at me as if I have AIDS. I could never ask an Israeli girl out now. Israeli girls may just as well look at us like Arabs!'

Aster made explicit the link between refusal to mix blood and otherness. I asked her whether, were she in hospital and needed blood transfusion, she would accept blood from an Israeli Arab. She was horrified at the mere thought of Arab blood in her body. She asked me whether I really was a Jew to be able to pose such a question.

Like Aster and Taddesse, Ethiopian Israelis felt that throwing out Ethiopian blood implied that Israelis do not want to mix with Ethiopians: Israelis don't want to mix their blood (quite literally, as if it were non-Jewish Arab blood), nor mix socially and sexually. Ethiopian Israelis felt that their aspirations to integrate with other Israelis in their homeland were thwarted; with the discarding of their blood, they were metaphorically being thrown out.

For weeks and months after the Blood incident, Ethiopian Israeli young people expressed deep disappointment: they had felt part of the country and strove to serve it, but after the blood incident they felt separate, on the outside, 'as if I was not a real Israeli'. They questioned their position in Israeli society and emerged with grave doubts. I often heard throw-away comments like 'what job will I get? I am just an Ethiopian!' 'Hah! How can I expect a good position in the army? They will just see me and think that I have Aids!'

Osnat, a young mother was particularly virulent: 'I want to leave the country! I used to feel Israeli, but after this, what is it to be Israeli? If you live as a Jew in Israel and they do such things, what is there left to feel? They think that you are not a Jew, you are not Israeli It is because we are black. Did we not show them our Jewish culture? We observe Sabbath three or four times better than them! Before, I strictly maintained my Israeli identity. Now, I have nothing left to maintain.'

Conclusion

On the Amharic chat show radio programme a few days after the Blood Bank demonstration, a man quoted an Amharic saying: 'You invite him so that he does not feel left out, but then you do not serve him food.' Another added: 'They are building a wall between us and them that the strongest technology will not be able to destroy.'

The reaction of Ethiopian Jews to the policy of discarding their blood was vehement because it challenged their sense of belonging to Israel. For the young people, the policy was an overt demonstration of Israeli racism and unwillingness to accept Ethiopians into their society. For the older generation, the discarding of Beta Israel blood was a slur on the communal purity of the group.

Ethiopian Israelis accounted for the vehemence of the Blood Crisis demonstration by saying: 'We hold things in our tummy a long time, but when it gets too full, it bursts.' The demonstration was an outlet for the pent-up daily frustrations and rejections that Ethiopian Jewish immigrants had stored up since arrival: the silence of their non-Ethiopian neighbours, the rudeness of officials, the taunting at school, the lower positions in the army, the doubts on their religious status. Alongside the positive relations and the sense of belonging which Ethiopian Israelis do experience in Israel, they feel rejected by their host society; and on the 28th Jan 1996, their tummies burst.

7

On Becoming Deaf

Introduction

Abba Negusse, my adoptive father, is an old man, tall and strong, with bright eyes which appraise everyone and everything around him. He is usually quiet and dislikes people who go 'blah blah blah' all the time – 'you should speak only when you have something to say!' He is a cheerful man and his neighbours often congregate in his front garden to chat in the afternoon breeze. Abba Negusse loves to recount the days when he was a wealthy farmer and renowned weaver: 'I had land from here, right up to the bank', his arm stretches out towards the local Bank Hapoalim, some five hundred metres away. 'I had cows and sheep! And a mule! And I had a gun with so many bullets!' At other times, especially when a dispute is the topic of the day, he loves to speak of the elevated status he acquired in his village: 'For five years, I was a judge (*dagna*). People came to me with their problems. I listened and then I said: "This is good. This is bad. Do this. Do that."'

Abba Negusse became accustomed to my questions but when I asked him about practices specifically in Israel, he lost his fluency, and claimed ignorance: 'You must ask people who know, who have studied. Now, if we were in my country, I could tell you everything! Here what do I know? I have become *dinkoro* (ignorant, lit: deaf)! I used to know so many things; but now I have forgotten. You study on your computer and it contains lots of information; my stomach is full [of knowledge], but it no longer works. It has become crazy (*angol*). I have no more energy or strength, just sadness.'

The older generation of Ethiopian Jewish immigrants – above the age of about thirty five – describe themselves as becoming *dinkoro* in

Israel. The literal meaning of *dinkoro* is unambiguous: deaf/the inability to hear. However, Ethiopians love to speak in riddles and to use words with several layers of meanings;[1] the word '*dinkoro*' allows just such interplay.

Leslau, in his authoritative Amharic-English dictionary defines the verb *deneqwara*, from which the adjective *dinkoro* is derived: 'To be or become deaf; to be unable to think or perceive due to vexation; to be ignorant, to not understand or remember what one has been taught; to be stupid.' When Ethiopians complain of deafness, they refer, in the first instance, to their inability to 'hear' or understand the language around them, Hebrew. They are also describing their new found state of ignorance in their new environment.

> Alemitu illustrates these two meanings: 'In our country, you grind *teff* (a local grain) and you make *injera*, but in this country, you need a brain. Here, for those of us who have not studied, the problem is language. For the children, and for those who have studied, this country is good. As for us, we do not know the language and secondly we do not know where the bus station is, and we cannot find our way around the country to visit our relatives.'

The Ethiopians' choice of a body metaphor to describe their problems in Israel follows Ethiopian custom of attributing physical pain in a particular part of the body to describe emotional or mental ailments. For example, Ethiopians make frequent reference to the stomach – the seat of knowledge, pain, frustration, and desire.[2]

> Aster told me that she ate and ate when her father died, but she could not fill her tummy [for her tummy longed for her father].

> Aveva: 'Ethiopians have much patience but when it breaks ... The tummy is bigger than the world, but if it fills, it explodes.'

> Worku warns me to be less open: 'Keep feelings in your tummy!'

> A lament at a funeral: 'Are you feeling it? I can feel my stomach. There is no-one to listen to us and we did not say good bye.'

Just as a tummy ache denotes emotional troubles, 'deafness' is a metaphor for Ethiopian Jewish immigrants' difficulties in Israel.

An Ethiopia Jew today, Afula, Israel, 1996.

'We have no mouth'

Worku, a middle-age man: 'Our ears do hear, but we do not know the language ... so that is why we say that we are *dinkoro*.'

When Ethiopians say that they are *dinkoro*, they mean in the first instance that they are unable to communicate verbally, they cannot 'hear' the language around them, and they cannot express themselves in this language. Other expressions are also used to convey their inability to communicate: 'We have no mouth' or 'we have no language'.

Mama Tsay is a tall woman in her sixties. She was talking to me about what a good country Israel is for the Ethiopians. She broke her narrative with a sigh: 'But the problem for us is that their Hebrew and our Amharic do not meet. If only they could understand our Amharic!' She went on to explain the non-chalance I had noted in her elder brother Abba Brhan when he spoke about his new job. She blamed his difficulties at work by his 'deafness', by which she meant his inability to speak Hebrew.

Mama Tsay implies that her brother's problems at work, and Ethiopians' problems in general, are caused by a lack of Hebrew. On further questioning, she, and her brother, described the kind of problems which I had previously assumed were paramount such as cultural differences, lack of appropriate technical knowledge, the low status of the job and lack of control over the work. But the problem she chose to stress was language. Although the significance of these other problems cannot be under-estimated, the immediate level of experience concerns language and the inability to communicate in Hebrew. Moreover, Mama Tsay stated a tangible problem – language – because that was easier to verbalise than all the other difficulties her brother experienced. As Alelign, an educated Ethiopian Israeli, said to me: 'They do not think like you! They are not educated. They cannot give reasons and explanations, they just say something briefly.'

At the immediate level, as Mama Tsay explained with reference to her brother's work, 'becoming deaf' means suffering the daily humiliations and frustrations which result from not being able to understand and speak the language of the new society. The frustration of 'not having a mouth' is constant: when the TV in on, at the shops, with children's teachers, social security officers, and neighbours, and at work.

> I visited Dinke, a middle-aged woman, after I had seen her earlier in the day at the social security office, flustered, angry and quarrelling with several officials. She had gone to find out why her payments had stopped. 'It is so hard in this country. No, it is good, but when you have a problem, it is hard. At the *betuar leumi* (social security offices), if you cannot speak Hebrew, they just say *'besseder, besseder'* [OK, OK, Hebrew]. If you can speak they give you what you want. They think that if you cannot speak Hebrew, then you are deaf and stupid. Without a mouth, this country is hard!'

Ethiopian Israelis are also frustrated by their inability to communicate with non-Ethiopian neighbours beyond a standard 'hello' and 'how are you?' Ethiopians regret this greatly, especially faced with Israeli neighbours who express goodwill towards them, or conversely those to whom they want to return abusive language.

To fully appreciate Ethiopian Israelis' distress at their inability to communicate in Hebrew, I turn to a brief discussion of the importance of verbal communication in Amhara culture and Ethiopian immigrants' difficulties in acquiring Hebrew.

Language in Amhara culture

It is no coincidence that the metaphor Ethiopians use to express their difficulties is 'deafness', a metaphor which places verbal communication centre-stage. Ethiopians' particular concern with language became apparent from my first days of fieldwork.

When I was struggling hard with Amharic language, my hosts and neighbours often asked me to say words in English. As I had to reel off word after word in English, I quickly became irritated: why should they care how to say 'good morning' or 'horse' in English when they were trying to learn Hebrew and me Amharic? As my fluency in Amharic increased, they stopped asking for these words in English. I later understood that this was one of their discreet and charming ways of making me feel at home amongst them; they were encouraging me to express what they assumed I held dearly – my language – and were relating to the frustration of being unable to express oneself as 'an adult'. Indeed, my Amharic words often provoked peels of laughter because I spoke 'like a baby'.

I was often described as 'clever' (*gobaz*, '*ras alat*', lit. 'she has a head') not so much because of my years of education or ability to absorb Ethiopian cultural practices, but because I spoke many languages and was a keen learner of Amharic. For example, Mama Fantae said: 'You have a good brain, you grasped our language'. When introducing me to new-comers, my language proficiency was invariably singled-out to serve as introduction (and recommendation). To test my 'cleverness' and willingness to engage, I was continuously subject to verbal provocations. If I succeeded in responding 'cleverly', that is using a play on words, my companions clapped with delight.

Levine's seminal *Wax and Gold* has made Amharas famous for their 'clever' use of language.[1]

In a later work, Levine recalls the source of his 'love for ambiguity': 'In the late 1950s I spent three years among the Amhara of Ethiopia, where I encountered a culture whose devious imprecision was necessarily vexing to an American of my age and time, but a culture that finally attracted me deeply with its flair for artistically ambiguous utterance.'[4]

Wax and Gold discusses the ancient Amharic form of verse of that name (*semna work*). The verses contain two semantic layers. The apparent superficial meaning of the words is called wax and their hidden deeper significance is the gold.[5]

Levine provides the following example of an Amharic wax and gold verse:
Since Adam your lip did eat of that Tree
The Saviour my heart has been hung up for thee.
He explains: 'In this couplet the wax of Adam's sin and Christ's crucifixion on his behalf has been used as a form in which to pour a love message. A literal translation of the wax couplet is:
Because Adam ate of the apple from the Tree of Knowledge
The Saviour of the World has been crucified for thee.
To savour the gold of the couplet fully, one must know that the verb meaning 'was crucified', *tasaqala*, may also signify 'is anxious to be near'. So a literal translation of the gold would be:
Because of your [tempting] lips
My heart is anxious to be near thee.'[6]

Levine argues that, albeit less elaborate, everyday speech is permeated with this type of ambiguity and the enjoyment of verbal ambiguities plays a significant role in conversations and stories:

'When [an Amhara] talks, his words carry *double entendre* as a matter of course; when he listens, he is ever on the lookout for latent meanings and hidden motives. As an Ethiopian anthropologist once told me, wax and gold is far more than a poetic formula: it is the Amhara way of life'.[7] Thus, 'one is considered a master of spoken Amharic only when one's speech is leavened with ambiguous nuances as a matter of course. Even among other peoples in Ethiopia the Amhara have been noted for extremes of symbolism and subtlety in their everyday talk.'[8]

Levine's observations are easily born out by the Beta Israel. On my very first day of fieldwork I was entertained with an Ethiopian story where the punch-line centred on a play with words.

Abba Gebrahanu, the hero of many an Ethiopian tale, was visiting an acquaintance. He received a plate of food from his host. A mouse had just run off the plate and the host did not clean it before presenting food on it to his guest. When Abba Gebrahanu departed, he made a blessing, 'May this plate never be empty', which can also mean in Amharic, 'this plate has a mouse'.

'Good speech' is essential to make progress in life, and to manipulate authorities in particular. As Chaim Rosen, who has spent many years living and working with Ethiopians (Jews and non-Jews) notes, 'language becomes, for many Amharas, their primary means of both self-defence and also of offence. One must live a long time in the midst of Ethiopians, speaking with them in Amharic (or Tigrinya), in order to begin to appreciate how much calculation is invested in each phrase (...). That he who desires to do harm may always be polite, or that he who wishes to deliver an insult may include it in a finely-wrought compliment, is part of a general understanding of human nature.[9]

> Abba Alemu and Abba Negusse were chatting about the old days, and in particular, Abba Tarik's wealth and land-ownership, which was rare for Beta Israel. Abba Alemu commented by way of explanation: 'Abba Tarik was always mixing with the authorities (*balasiltanoch*) for he had the ability to speak well.'

> Katama's son was studying in a place for 'people who have no brain' (a school for low academic achievers). She lamented her inability to 'speak well' with the authorities, for had she this skill, she could have got him placed in a better institution.

'Good speech' is also required to conquer hearts.

> Abba Alemu told me the type of man I should marry: 'You have to choose someone who is educated like you, who knows much, who helps you, whose *speech is attractive* and who is handsome.'

> Abba Negusse: 'When I was young, I had a friend and she used to say to me: "Negusse, my body, you are leaving today, when are you going to come back like a ripe chickpea? – you will be finished on the way!" You see I used to live in the village, and her in the town, and thus she was afraid someone else would "pick" me on the way!'

Ethiopians love to create and sing verse couplets, called *getem*.

> At celebrations, after the disco equipment has been taken away, a few men start to sing, often accompanied by a *masenko* (a traditional two-stringed Ethiopian instrument) and drum. The *masenko* player sings favourite *getem* and creates verse relating to the moment. He also sings verses dictated to him by other members of the party. In the case of an engagement, these tell funny stories about the bride, since the musicians and guests are

her relatives, and include sexually explicit verse, to the amusement of all.

Sorrow and respect for the deceased are expressed with improvised *qetem*. At funerals relatives and specialists sing couplets – often incredibly moving – in memory of the deceased:

He is like a flute [meaning also bright young man], do not bury him, people will walk past and admire him [even while he is dead].

My flower, my brother, the time has come to cut your time short.

'Let it eat me, oh Abba Mucha, what kind of woodcutter is he, when I told him to cut the branch, he cut the root. He cut the tree at the root and made the birds cry!' [the tree cut at the root means that the father is dead and the birds crying are the children]

'My country Ethiopia ... Oh, my relatives ... the ox of mourning ... come be ready to plough, because the hero is dead.'

At the funeral of a young soldier:

'Ah, Tadesse Telahun, you have been harvested while still green!'

'Oh, my village! At my sister Meles's [the mother of the deceased] house, the in-laws came, the relatives were invited, they were received all together like the wedding of before!' [everyone should have gathered for the boy's wedding not his funeral]

'Oh, the poor mother! She carried him in her tummy for nine months, she carried him on her back for two years, she breast-fed him two years. What kind of son is he? He has returned to her tummy, tying up her intestines!'[10]

As well as its 'ambiguous' construction, Amharic is also striking in the elaborate and loving way with which it is used. Greetings are no simple matter, and contain a variety of different expressions for different times of day. Stories and daily events are reported in detail, with as much elaboration and humour as possible. The simplest of events, such as an interaction at the supermarket or the greeting with a relative, is reported to a third party (most often coffee partners) in minute detail, including all direct speech, and any clever use of language contained therein. Such narratives, lasting up to ten minutes, are rarely interrupted. Certain individuals gain reputations as good story tellers, and entertain others for hours.

Muluye always livened up a social gathering. During the long evenings of the wake after his cousin's death, he entertained the company with his stories. The following two stories, for instance, each lasted about ten minutes, as no detail was spared, and direct speech was quoted verbatim:

A man went to a prostitute and wanted 'it' five times, but she only accepted three times and so he did not want to pay her.

His cousin Makwanent was looking after the cows in the hills and waited for his lunch. Finally, very late his mother brought a plate of *injera* to him, but by then he was so hungry and angry that he threw the plate down. He then had to wait till evening to eat!

I have elaborated on the richness of Amharic language to show the centrality of the metaphor of 'deafness' and why 'having no mouth' is so acutely crippling for the Beta Israel: Self-professed masters of language are reduced to speaking 'like a baby' in Hebrew, if at all.

Learning and not learning Hebrew

Hebrew classes

Within weeks of arrival in Israel, all Ethiopian immigrants take up free intensive Hebrew classes, called *ulpan*.[11] These classes are aimed to equip all new immigrants to Israel with sufficient Hebrew to communicate verbally and to use the Hebrew alphabet, as well as to offer an introduction to Israeli culture and Jewish traditions. Ulpan classes were modified and extended for Ethiopians given that most of them were previously illiterate. Instead of the usual five months of classes, they received ten months to compensate for 'learning difficulties'.[12]

Young people and formerly educated adults learn Hebrew well, and quickly become orally fluent and able to write, often extremely well. People who immigrated in their twenties and thirties, who were uneducated or received minimal education in Ethiopia, usually acquire enough Hebrew for everyday conversational purposes and some are able to write and read basic Hebrew. Those who received no education in Ethiopia or/and elders tend to acquire very little spoken Hebrew and no written Hebrew, other than occasionally the ability to sign their name.[13] There is much individual variation. Men who worked often speak better Hebrew than their wives, while wives of unemployed men often succeed better than their husbands because of greater interaction with Hebrew-speaking children. In the latter case, embarrassment results because men expect to be intellectually more able than their wives.

> Fantanesh and Telahun are a middle-age couple. Fantanesh is an exceptionally bright woman who completed four years of schooling in Ethiopia. Telahun is the joker of the neighbourhood, but perhaps not the sharpest of men. Fantanesh, who can read and write Amharic better than him, has now learnt more spoken Hebrew than him, and is able to discern a few written words. Her increased competence in both languages is a source of embarrassment for her husband. Faced with a letter in Amharic, he pours over it studiously and she gently takes it from his hand and reads it quietly. She deals with the daily mail by fetching it herself from the mail-box and opening the letters before reaching her husband to minimise the fact that she is reading them. Similarly with spoken Hebrew. After their eldest son had skived off school one day, the head-teacher summoned the parents. One of them had to remain behind to take care of Fantanesh's old mother. Telahun, as the head of the household, asserted that he would go to the meeting. However, he knew, she knew and I knew that given his non-existent Hebrew, he would not be very effective there. At the last minute, the pretence was broken, and Fantanesh went. A little unkindly perhaps, I asked her why Telahun had changed his mind and she said, after a pause, 'he is unwell.'

On the whole, Ethiopians have not done well in ulpan classes and their level of spoken Hebrew is low and their written Hebrew practically non-existent. Lisa Anteby, who followed the ten months ulpan course with new immigrants, and wrote her MA thesis on the subject, concludes that 'at the end of the ten month teaching course, I realised the extent to which the teachings of the ulpan was not assimilated by the majority of the immigrants and the extent to which their competence in both written and spoken Hebrew remained poor'.[14] She supports her conclusion by making reference to a handful of other studies undertaken on the subject.[15]

Difficulties and motivations in learning Hebrew

Learning Hebrew at ulpan clearly poses a number of specific difficulties for Ethiopian immigrants. For many, the ulpan is the first experience of formal education and the first time that a second language is learned (though many Tigrinya-speaking Beta Israel from the Tigre region had already acquired Amharic as a second language). Also, a number of Hebrew words have no reference in Amharic and thus learning a new word is not only new vocabulary but also requires the assimilation of the usage and the social role of the named object, as well as new conceptual categories. Ethiopians face particular difficulties in learning to write and the ulpan methods presuppose prior literacy and the knowledge of graphic conventions such as page numbers in books. Furthermore, Ethiopians have to adapt to new cultural norms: Elders often have to learn from a young Israeli woman dressed in Jeans, women have to speak in front of men, and youngsters in front of elders, resulting in the 'blurring of the hierarchic frontiers'.[16]

Despite all these difficulties, Anteby concludes that Ethiopians could have achieved better. She notes that the central prerequisite for learning a new language are motivations and need. Given the high levels of absenteeism in the classes, she concludes that learning Hebrew is not a priority for Ethiopian adults during their first stages in the country.[17] I too witnessed a lack of motivation for the Hebrew continuation classes (classes for immigrants already in their sixth year in the country) laid on especially for Ethiopian immigrants in Afula. Classes were frequently missed for non-essential activities and few students completed their homework. Anteby argues that Ethiopian adults do not feel that they need Hebrew since their children can help to read, write and translate, and the notion of having an intermediary in daily negotiations is culturally acceptable in Ethiopian society.[18] It is easier to depend on youngsters than to learn Hebrew, and Amharic is sufficient for social relations within the group.[19] However, relying on children, hierarchically lower in status, is a source of distress for adults. Furthermore, whilst Amharic is not always sufficient for communication amongst Ethiopians, since young children and an increasing number of teenagers do not communicate adequately in Amharic. I return to this question in Chapter Twelve and suggest that the Beta Israel's lack of motivation at Hebrew classes is sometimes a manifestation of a subtle form of resistance.

'Deafness' as an inability to read

Ethiopian Israelis also feel *dinkoro* because of their inability to read Hebrew. However, this aspect of their 'ignorance' is less keenly felt than verbal difficulties because most Beta Israel have always been '*dinkoro*' in this way since most of them were illiterate in Ethiopia.[20]

Furthermore as Levine[21] points out, Amhara people have always had an ambiguous relationship to writing skills. 'The act of writing was considered to be inherently shameful: like any manual activity other than farming and fighting, writing was regarded as degrading work, the business of scribes whose status was thereby not much higher than that of potters and metal-smiths'[22] But this form of 'deafness' does become more acute in Israel since the written word plays a significant role in daily life. An Ethiopian feels *dinkoro* each time he is faced with a price label, the writing on packaged food, a bill, official letters, medical prescriptions, destination of buses and road signs. Each time, he must seek the help of a willing youngster and suffer loss of pride.

> An old woman dressed in her white Ethiopian dress prowled up the aisles of the supermarket, searching for something. Observing her, I soon noticed that she was not after a specific product, but a willing scamp to direct her to the goods she required. She finally collared a young boy who was charging out clutching an ice-cream. She only released him after he had filled her shopping basket and extracted the coins from her plastic purse to pay the bill.

Ethiopians manage to operate within the labyrinth of the written text through the help of children, helpful social workers and literate relatives. However, whenever a letter comes through the door they are reminded of their 'ignorance' – especially since many of them have yet to differentiate between important mail and junk mail. I recall many a poignant moment trying to reassure Abba Negusse and his wife that the latest printed circular for a new clothes catalogue was not the latest dreadful bill and could happily be chucked in the dustbin. Some aspects of daily life remain difficult, irrespective of the amount of help. Anteby notes in particular the inability to use a calendar and thus register and memorise dates for appointments.[23]

A pressing concern is the difficulty illiteracy causes for travel: which bus to catch, when to get off, and navigating through nameless streets.

Abba Negusse was looking forward for weeks to his sister's religious celebration in Ramle. On the day, he unexpectedly failed to find an escort. He nonetheless went to the local bus station in the hope of spotting an Ethiopian who happened to be going in that direction. He was unlucky and returned home.

When older Ethiopian Israelis go to a new place, they tend to find someone to accompany them for the first few times, then they venture alone, remembering, via a series of landmarks, when to get off the bus, and where to walk from the bus stop. Street names are not taken into account. When a change of bus is required, a literate Ethiopian is nabbed to point out the correct bus. Failing this, a friendly-looking Israeli is approached. Once the correct neighbourhood has been reached, there are usually Ethiopians around who can lead the way to the desired household.

Deaf about technology and bureaucracy

As well as language difficulties many Ethiopian Israelis feel 'ignorant' about technological knowledge. With a resigned tone of voice, a young man who earns his living in the hospital laundry says: 'It is a bad job, but what else could I do? I know nothing in this country!' This lack of knowledge is explained by Ethiopians' lack of education.

> Worku: 'The Russians learn quickly here and go [easily] into the hospitals and offices. They grew up at school while we were in the fields and making pots and cloth. If you had three boys, only one would go to school. There was not much education in Ethiopia, that is why we are *dinkoro*.'

A sense of 'being deaf' overcomes Ethiopians when they come into contact with Israeli bureaucracy. Anteby captures these difficulties in characteristic elegant prose:

'Un nouvel ordre temporel scande la vie du group. Cette temporalité, exprimée par un horaire fixe, un emploi du temps precis, une datation rigoureuse et un climat et des variations saisonnnieres inconnus, impose des decomptes, des segmentations, des regularités et des moyens de mesure etrangers aux immigrants. Perdus, desemparés, desorientés dans cet univers spatial geometrisé et ce monde temporel fragementé, ils n'ont tout d'abord plus aucun moyen de reperes ni aucun point de reference'.[24]

Daily life is full of confrontations with officials and frustrations with the bureaucratic systems they deal with.

Abba Negusse noticed that his pension was lower one month and he also needed to get a bus pass for pensioners, so he decided to go to 'the office'. He knew where to get off the bus and confidently strode up to the local social security office. He walked straight through the doors, but was called back by the door attendant. He returned, and ignoring the mass of people waiting to be given numbered tickets to mark their place in the queue, he said '*Cartis, cartis*' (ticket, ticket, Hebrew). The attendant got stroppy: 'For which office?' The people in the queue started to grumble and the attendant gestured for him to wait his turn. After a while, another attendant said, in Amharic, 'Old people?' 'Yes', he answered with a smile, appreciating the Israeli clerk's efforts. The smile was not returned and a ticket was handed to him.

On his way up, he looked around, lost. The proud man, in control of all and everything at home, was flustered and confused. His face lighted up when he spotted a young Ethiopian cleaner: 'Ah! She will translate for me.' He greeted the girl, who tried to decline his request on the grounds that she was paid to clean, not to translate. 'Please', he implored, 'I have no mouth here!' Finding it impossible to refuse an elder, she led him to the correct door and translated for him. His reduction in income was not a result, as he suspected, of an error or theft on the part of the bank, but due to the fluctuation of the dollar, on which social security payments are based. He implored the official for more money, lamenting that he did not have enough to pay the bills. The young Ethiopian woman was embarrassed – as if a clerk could alter a government set national pension figure – and she only translated some of his words.

In the next office, where his task was to obtain the bus pass, a similar *langage des sourds* took place. Abba Negusse was not content with the clerk's assurances that the pass would be sent to him by post and he strolled off, discontented.

He regained his composure and confidence on arrival at the open market which was teaming with Ethiopians: so many people to explain properly how to go about getting a bus pass. He saw his brother and nephew, the former equipped with a pass, and the latter was soon roped into returning to the office the following day to help him.

Ethiopians on unemployment benefits often fail to attend offices on the specified day, especially if that day clashes with a funeral, and they lament the harshness of the officials who then refuse to pay them their dues. In this way too, many a hospital appointment is missed, or the relevant signed papers from the GP are not brought, so that the process of referral has to begin afresh. Each time such a slip-up happens, the Israeli official in question, often a relative youngster, does not spare the Ethiopian's pride and berates him or her in, what is taken as, a most shocking and offensive manner. The demeanour and facial expressions of Ethiopians in public offices is generally withdrawn and 'closed'. They regain their smile and good humour over coffee on return home.

One morning, after coffee, I joined Abba Negusse and his nephew Worku to pay the house bill. We set off in fine spirits. We reached the *amidar* office (council housing) and when our turn came, we entered the appropriate room and the Israeli women, dressed in shorts and black tights, did not raise her head to greet us. She spoke in a rough tone of voice and snatched the papers from Abba Negusse's hands. Worku did the talking and an argument erupted. As we were exiting the room, Worku's sister entered and Worku took her card and papers to liaise on her behalf. As he handed over the papers, the woman at the desk, thinking that he was still dealing with Abba Negusse, pushed him violently aside. She realised her error, although did not apologise. Abba Negusse and Worku were shaken by the experience and did not regain their composure until safely back home, when over the second round of coffee, they were able to make fun of the rude Israeli woman.

Some younger Ethiopians feel that they are progressing in their knowledge of Israeli bureaucracy and technology. They refer, for example, to difficulties at work in the past: 'Before, everything was so difficult, but now I know'. Or they bemoan their previous refusal to take out a government mortgage to buy a house, blaming their former state of ignorance.

Tsega is a young mother of four who lives in a council house in Afula, the other end of the country to where her mother lives surrounded by several of Tsega's siblings. I asked her why she was not closer to her mother, whom she always spoke of with longing. 'We were offered the chance to buy a house at first, and we could have done so in Ofakim, near my mother's, but we did not want to go into debt, we were new [in the country] and did not know. The man at the absorption centre suggested a council house in Afula and we just said yes, we did not know.' Several other Afula residents had recently realised the missed opportunity at not having bought a house and blamed their 'lack of knowledge' as new immigrants.

On the whole however, these difficulties in operating within an Israeli system must not be over-stressed because, as Chapter Four demonstrated, Ethiopian adults have adapted remarkably rapidly to practical life in their new environment:[25] few are the difficulties which cannot be overcome with help from kin and neighbours.

'Deaf' about Israeli ways

Ethiopians say that they are 'deaf' with respect to Israeli social behaviour: loud speech, forthright young women, immodesty, and brashness. In actual fact, they are less ignorant on these matters than they make out, and they frequently adopt a superior attitude and assert that the foreign behaviour is plain wrong and that Ethiopian ways are correct. But this superior standpoint occurs 'after the event', back home over coffee, while during the interaction itself, alone amidst Israelis, Ethiopians can feel bewildered and 'stupid' (*dinkoro*).

The young accuse their parents of being '*dinkoro*' due to apparently irrational ways of thinking in modern Israel. For example, many Ethiopians turned down government grants of up to US$ 120,000 to buy houses. Younger Ethiopian Israelis explained that their reasons stemmed from ignorance: they feared entering into debt, unable to grasp the fact that 90 per cent of the money was a non-returnable grant, and they were afraid of a monthly mortgage for twenty-five years ('We will be dead by then!'), even though the sum to be paid was roughly equivalent to council house rent, their preferred alternative.[26] Youngsters complain that cherished Ethiopian cultural traits, such as expressing agreement to an interlocutor, particularly one of superior status, become 'ignorance' in Israel.

Mama Tsay's daughter Workie explains: 'My mother agrees to everything that she is told. If someone said 'I will kill you', she would still answer '*ishi*' (OK)!'

Fantanesh is also aware of this problem and apologises for failing to obtain a copy of her son's Bar Mitzvah's video for me: 'When I got to the shop, they only had the one tape, with no copies, even though Galia [her daughter] had asked them previously for more copies on the phone. I do not know Hebrew so I just said "*besseder* (OK, Hebrew)"'. In fact, Fantanesh's Hebrew is easily proficient enough to have pressed the shop assistant to make the promised copy. But she felt too intimidated of the brash Israeli video-man to argue, even though she was perturbed at the thought of breaking a promise to me.

On becoming a donkey

More frequently still than the statement 'we are deaf', Ethiopians make throw-away comments like, 'in this country, what do I know?'

Mama Tarikye: 'If you have no language, you are *dinkoro*, you are like a donkey!'

The effect of feeling ignorant about the ways of the country is that Ethiopians become 'ignorant' as people: they become 'donkeys'. Abba Negusse expressed this feeling in the chapter's opening quote with another bodily metaphor: 'My tummy no longer works, it has gone crazy!'

Alequa Birre put it this way: 'This is why we say that we are *dinkoro*: by not respecting our laws and not accepting our religion, they make us primitive [term in Amharic]. They keep us inside.'

Alequa Birre's words are extremely evocative: because of their 'deafness', Ethiopians have become 'primitive' in their homeland. They are forced out of the realm of public life, they are 'kept inside'. I shall examine the effects of this sense of enclosure in the next chapter: over and above rendering everyday life frustrating and inducing an overall sense of ignorance, 'becoming deaf' drastically reduces Ethiopians' control over their life, and over that of their children.

Conclusion

This chapter has focused on the difficulties of immigration which arise for the older generation in particular as a result of their inability to communicate in Hebrew and lack of experience of modern urban living. However, their difficulties of adaptation to Israeli society are not acute. On the one hand they succeed in overcoming them with the help of their children who act as intermediaries. On the other, they avoid them altogether by enjoying social life within the Ethiopian community and minimising their interaction with Israeli society. The essential problem of the older generation is not so much their 'deafness' in Israeli society per se, but rather the effect this has on the internal organisation of Beta Israel society, and the resulting sense of loss of control over their lives. The following chapter addresses these issues.

8

Losing Control

Mulu, aged thirty-five: 'People who were clever in Ethiopia cannot manage in this country. Today, the clever ones are the children.'

The previous chapter showed how many Ethiopian Israeli adults feel that they have 'become deaf' as a result of their lack of Hebrew and the unfamiliarity of their new environment. Most of the older generation can minimise the impact of such difficulties by avoiding Israeli society as much as possible and, when contact is necessary, by enlisting the help of their children to translate. The fundamental difficulty faced by Ethiopian Jewish immigrants, this chapter suggests, is not adaptation to the dominant society as such, but the disruption of the hierarchy amongst Ethiopian Israelis themselves. Ethiopian adults feel that they have lost control over production: over land, livelihood and work. Ethiopian men are the worst affected since women are able to maintain their domestic role quasi-intact.[1] Men's loss of status and the influence of the dominant society's cultural norms result in a reduction of their authority over the household, their wives and daughters, and in religious matters. Worse still, for both men and women, is the impression of being unable to discipline their children and instil social norms upon them. Loss of control is most evocatively expressed in Ethiopians' feeling that they are unable to cure their illnesses in Israel.

Two caveats are required at the outset. First, unlike the idiom of 'becoming deaf' which I heard from the Ethiopian Jews themselves, the expression 'loss of control' is my own. I trust that the ethnographic content of the chapter will demonstrate the aptness of the phrase, even though I never heard an Ethiopian Israeli use it. Second, just as I did not suggest that Ethiopian Israelis *are* becoming deaf, I am not suggesting that Ethiopians *are* losing control and the chapter concerns itself with Ethiopian *perceptions* of loss of control over their lives.

Losing control over production

Most older Ethiopians, above the age of about forty, do not work in Israel.[2] Ethiopian men resent this loss greatly: not only are they left at home 'just sitting doing nothing', but also they have lost control over the livelihood of their families.

Unemployment

Abba Negusse often spoke of the expanse of his land in Ethiopia, the resulting barrels full of grain, the huge size of his herds, his hunting prowess, his renown as a weaver, and the time in his youth when he was a soldier with the Italians. 'Here I just sit all day and go to the bank saying "give me money!" like a beggar... Work keeps you fit and bright (*gobaz*).' He lamented that he has grown old in Israel because he does 'nothing'. I once suggested that he might be feeling 'old' in Israel because he was older now, by six years, than he was when he was last in his village. He defended himself ardently, sprang up from his seat, and started to mime the tasks he would still be doing back home.

Remaining at home, in the way of one's wife, not only leads to listlessness, it is also a great source of shame. For Ethiopians place an extremely high value on hard work: an idle person is berated ('Get up, do something, stop being so lazy (*sanaf*)!'), a hard worker, whether at school, work or the army, is constantly praised, and the much sought-after quality *gobaz* is defined as youthful, strong, clever and energetic.

Unemployed men avoid idleness by constantly seeking activity. They go out for strolls, leaving the house with a great air of determination, with hat and scarf and stick, only to gather a few hundreds yards away, with other men under the shade of a tree to chat. A few succeed in finding temporary part-time work as watchmen, cleaners, gardeners; they call this 'old people's work'. The purpose of this part-time work, as the sister of one such worker pointed out, is to avoid just 'sitting and thinking/worrying (*masab*)'. Others become 'professional wanderers', visiting one relative after another in different parts of the country.[3]

Unemployment entails a loss of status for men in particular since providing for the family is considered to be the man's responsibility. Welfare payments deprive men of this important source of social prestige: it is the government which is now feeding their families. Women do not generally suffer from this loss of status since they have kept intact their former role of running the household and have not therefore lost their principal occupation.

Livelihood and the physical environment

Both men and women suffer from a loss of control over the *source* of their livelihood.

> Mama Gevianesh loved to rant about the difficulties 'in this country', especially after her forty-year-old daughter was 'killed' by Israeli doctors. Government money was a frequent source of complaint, even though she never omitted to thank God for it. She explained: 'In Ethiopia, you could always manage because everything – food, money, clothes – was in your own hands. In this country however, it is in the hands of another person. Suppose I go to the bank and they say that there is no money, then what can I find? If the government says 'no, it is finished!', where can we find since it is in other peoples' hands?' She tried to dispel my astonishment at the notion that Ethiopian agriculture and the vagaries of weather could be considered 'safer' than a government welfare payment, by proceeding to explain to me in detail the coping mechanisms she used when the crops failed – resorting to money-lenders, selling handicrafts and foraging for wild foods.

I doubt that Mama Gevianesh really believes that her daily income is less secure in Israel than it was in Ethiopia, since she so often speak about the bliss that is Israel because 'you never go to bed hungry'. Rather, she is expressing her anxiety, helplessness, and loss of pride at the fact that her welfare, and that of her children, is no longer under her control, or as she would say 'not in her hands'. Like a baby, to use a typical Ethiopian metaphor, she feeds from the breast of the government. Like many Ethiopian Israelis, she does not trust the welfare system and were welfare payments to cease, she would be helpless. Before, she could always manage to feed herself and her children whatever the circumstances, because she felt she knew intimately the source of her livelihood: the environment in which she lived.

Mama Gevianesh's complaint that she has lost control over her livelihood hinges directly on a sense of loss of knowledge about the workings of her new environment. In Ethiopia, she was safe because even when her regular source of sustenance failed her (i.e. her crops), she could still operate skilfully in her local environment to find alternative means of livelihood: she could make use of the natural products of the land because she knew where to look and she could resort to social and economic fall-backs. In Israel, she feels that this knowledge, and hence security, is lost.

The interesting point is that *in fact* if Mama Gevianesh was really in financial difficulty in Israel, she *would* know how to obtain a bank loan or to squeeze a hardship grant out of an affable social worker. She would be successful as she is a particularly shrewd woman or if her confidence failed her, she could easily obtain the help of one of her two literate children.

Yet, she feels economically impotent in Israel. Her feeling of inadequacy derives not from her inability to obtain what she wants – which is *not* diminished in Israel – but rather from her sense that she is no longer in control of the space around her, which for a former villager who knew every detail of her landscape, is bewildering and frightening. Gone are the fields she knew so well and the socio-economic context in which she was a successful operator. Around her are streets, cars, council estates, and markets in which a foreign language is spoken.

> Twenty-eight-year-old Fanta remembers Ethiopia in a free flow of words: 'I remember ... the country [i.e. the landscape], the place where we lived, the field, the way in and the way out [i.e. how to get about], the market, and the people.'

Fanta's words refer to the landscape and significantly her ability to move within and know that landscape, including its market. The implied contrast is clear: here she cannot find her way in the landscape and market.

The landscape of Israel is socialised by the network of kin which extends throughout the country, but the area between these islands of kin remains foreign and difficult of access in the minds of many Ethiopian Israelis. They were appalled by the spate of suicide bomb attacks which killed over fifty people in early 1996. They spoke about them incessantly: the attacks confirmed their worst fears about the dangers of living in this unknown urban maze.

> Turunesh: 'In Ethiopia, you could go anywhere, sleep in the field at any time. Here if you go into a bus, you die! I saw it on the TV, the parents of a baby killed! Ah, life in this country is hard!'

This landscape is of particular concern for parents of young children.

> Fanta: 'We worry so much about the children. There, they just looked after cattle; here, there are electric sockets and cars on the roads.'

Ethiopian Israelis not only feel that they have lost their ability to operate easily in the physical space around them, they also regret loss of control over the usufruct of the land. Until the 1974 revolution, Beta Israel generally did not own land but they rented it and had usufruct rights to common land.

> Worku: 'Here you go to the shop to buy soap – there you could just make your own, although the water there was so good that one did not usually need soap anyway! In this country, everything is from the government. There, I could dig and make a well for my cattle to drink. I cut wood as I wanted. Here my house belongs to the government. I pay rent. There I had a *gwaro* (back yard) of my own and I could build my own house.'

Ethiopian Israelis' attitude to their loss of access to land is perplexing. They complain that they have no more land, yet most households who do own a small back garden, let it run wild. Only a minority plant vegetables and trees in their gardens. These plots render the Ethiopian neighbourhood I lived in extremely colourful in the spring as chick peas, sweet-corn and onions ripened alongside the roses of the Russian immigrant neighbours.

> I asked Abba Negusse why he did not grow vegetables in his garden: 'Yes, I could plant a few onions and a bit of this and that ... did you see the *walka* (ploughed land) [in my village in Ethiopia]? It was so big. I had seven pieces of land and two sets of oxen ... Now I am old, I am no longer young like you!'

This answer is evasive. Abba Negusse says that he is old, but in other contexts, as in the opening quote to this chapter, he boasts his physical strength, and in any case he has plenty of grandsons and children in the neighbourhood to help with manual work. He switches the conversation from his unused small garden in Israel to the large amount of land he cultivated in Ethiopia. Expert agriculturist that he is, cultivating a few vegetables appears paltry. Similarly, offers to live on a *kibbutz* or *moshav* (farming village) were turned down by all but a few Ethiopian families. Ethiopian Jews may be disdainful about agricultural work because of its associations. It reminds them of the village life they left behind to join a modern country, where they consider agricultural work should be done with machines and by low status Arab workers,[4] not by Ethiopian Jews. Given their aspirations to integrate and modernise discussed in Chapter Four,[5] they avoid agricultural work, even in their own back garden.

Another aspect of the Israeli physical environment which troubles Ethiopian immigrants is the weather. The pleasant Ethiopian climate which is never too hot or too cold is contrasted with Israel's bitterly cold winters and burning hot summers. Ethiopian weather is portrayed as reliable and predicable, and droughts, for example, were never mentioned.

> Samagn: 'In Ethiopia, all year, you wear the same clothes. Here in the summer you are too hot and in the winter too cold!'

As the latter part of the chapter elaborates, the extremes of temperature make the Beta Israel sick.

Work

While unemployed Ethiopians suffer from lack of work, many employed Ethiopians hardly appear more contented.

> The disgruntled Mulu (about 32 years old): 'In our country we worked just one season. Here you work both summer and winter; there is no holiday. You work so much but the money they give is not enough. There we worked as we wanted: we were not ordered by others. If you were tired or unwell you could take the day off work and you could attend your relatives' weddings and funerals as you wanted. Here if you say: 'I do not feel well' or 'my uncle died, I want to go to the funeral', the boss will fire you. With the boss, there are always quarrels ... also, when a White starts work, he becomes manager within a week. We remain at the bottom.' Mulu also routinely complained of the nature of his work: the unpleasant smells and deafening noise of the factory.

The majority of Ethiopian Israelis under the age of forty and a few elders go to work. Except for a small educated elite, Ethiopians worked as unskilled or semi-skilled labourers.[6] Mulu's narrative introduces the problems that many Ethiopian adults face at work:

low salary, drudgery, lack of permission for days off, difficulties with the employer, the position at the bottom of the work hierarchy, and the foul nature of the work.

The highest Ethiopian prerogative is to attend kin's funerals, a relatively frequent occurrence. But Israeli work schedules do not allow for such frequent days off work. Ethiopian workers often complain about the intensity of working hours, and remember fondly their former working lives when they 'only worked one season', for the rest of the year was the 'wedding season', spent attending celebrations and visiting relatives.[7]

Ethiopian Israelis are aware of their place at the bottom of the social hierarchy in the work environment. They frequently complain that their work companions are Arabs because they hate being identified with a minority which they think of as despised by dominant society.

The nature of work is also disliked: 'It is smelly' and can be 'deafening to the ears'.

> Alemwork, a hospital cleaner: 'It is so awful! I hate the smell! I cannot eat there. I eat in the morning, and then I fast all day until I reach home.'

Not eating at work is a significant rejection of the work-place since, for Beta Israel, the sharing of food is symbolically important and a means of creating social bonds and common identity.

Fortunately, not all workers dislike their work as much as Alemwork and Mulu. Women in particular sometimes compare wage labour in Israel favourably to their previous work-load.

> Fantae is a cheerful woman in her mid-thirties. In her first job in Israel, de-skinning grapefruits in a tinning factory, she worked shifts, one week starting at five a.m., and the next at four p.m., returning home past midnight. She also had her house to run, with four young children to look after. Her husband rarely helped her. She succeeded in obtaining a job with more sociable hours in a seedling warehouse. She never complained, on the contrary: 'It is better than in Ethiopia. There you had to fetch the wood and water, carrying it for a long way on your back, and work bending down in the fields. Here, work is just sitting all day, doing this and that with your hands!'

Having a job is positively valued, and Ethiopian men hate to be out of work. Yet men rarely mention their jobs: work is often taboo.

Work held such little prominence in daily discourse that towards the end of fieldwork, I realised that I had little information about it: following my informants, I had unwittingly ignored it.[8]

> Abba Falag, Abba Negusse's brother is a pensioner who has taken on a part-time job as a lavatory cleaner. He loved to speak about his former work in Ethiopia, stressing his dominion over his land, animals and labourers, and his knowledge: he knew when to plant and how to stop animals eating the seedlings, and he often checked the fields. He used his sound judgement and was an excellent farmer. And he was his own boss. Here, 'they take you by the hand and say, "Do this and do that!"' His hand is taken, like a child. He would not elaborate on the nature of his work or work relations, and closed the conversation by commenting on the TV programme: 'Look, the rider has fallen off his horse!'

Work in Israel where Ethiopian men are 'deaf' and treated like children: contradicts their image of themselves as knowledgeable masters, proud farmers and craftsmen. As a result, while work in Ethiopia was depicted as part of a harmonious daily cycle, in Israel, it is cast aside. Men must work to earn a living, but their job is not considered part of meaningful daily life and is excluded from their self-image. Men return from work, and then begin their day in earnest with a coffee session and a visit to a neighbour. Work is outside the moral society of Ethiopian Jewish neighbours and kin.

Losing control over the social order

Men's loss of control over production has reduced their authority over their wives. Worse still, for both men and women, the influence of new norms and behavioural patterns has resulted in a loss of control over the social order and the socialisation of children.

Men's loss of control over women

> A man joked with me: 'Can you cook *injera*? Can you obey orders? Yes? Then you can marry an Ethiopian. Mind you, in Ethiopia, his wife obeyed him, but now ... only sometimes!'

Women's relative standing in the household has increased in Israel. A number of factors account for this increase. Women's greater financial independence thanks to employment and social security benefits has shifted power relations between husbands and wives. Men complain that their wives say: 'I have money! I do not need you anymore!' In Ethiopia, Beta Israel households were largely self-sufficient. The relatively small amount of money which entered the household of a married couple came from the man's sale of his agricultural produce and crafts work (e.g. weaving and blacksmithing) and his wife's sale of her crafts (e.g. pottery and embroidery). From my informants' accounts, the man's monetary contribution was usually considerably higher than his wife's. In Israel, for couples on social security, or when the wife brings home equal or more wages than her husband, the situation is altered. Social security is paid to a couple together, and women feel that they have equal rights over this 'government money'. Moreover, women regard child benefit as 'their' money, so they have an addition personal source of income. And in the case of divorce or separation, women know that the council house and child benefit will remain with them since they will keep the children. Their husbands, in this respect, are at their mercy.

> During a marital dispute, Tsay exclaimed triumphantly: 'He [her husband] has to be nice to me! He knows that if we separate, I will get to keep the house because of the children!'

> Fantanesh told me that before emigrating to Israel, her husband had wanted to divorce her in order to marry a woman who owned at least five heads of cattle. But before finding a suitable person, they emigrated. Now that she receives so much government money for the four children, he no longer wants to leave her. I noticed that in their household, Fantanesh held the money-bag, and her husband came to her for petty cash. As she said on another occasion: 'Many people quarrel over money. Often the woman wins and she holds the money. Then her husband has to come to her to beg for money when he wants to visit his relatives. She gives him fifty shekels. "Give me more!" he pleads, "No, that is enough!" she says.'

Women's position in the household is also enhanced by their access to external influence and power. Men complain that they can no longer hit women, because the latter will 'just call the police'.

> A priest, possibly bemoaning the reduction of his mediatory function in disputes, complained that women now go to the social

worker the moment that there is a problem in the house rather than trying to make things work out with the help of elders. He concluded that 'in this country' women, like children, were being spoilt.

Ethiopian men feel that state institutions such as the social services and the police take the women's side, and the latter are therefore prepared to make full use of them.

The status of Ethiopian Jewish women is also influenced by the cultural climate of their new country. Ethiopian Israelis say that, in Israel, women are treated 'as equals' (lit: 'men and women are the same '*and naw*'). Women quickly begin to develop new expectations about gender relations, even if actual changes in behaviour are slower to develop.[9]

> Abba Brhan hit his wife lightly on the bum with his cane when she did not rise fast enough to fetch him some water. Before rising to obey the command, she muttered, 'What is the matter with you? Why do you hit me?' I doubt she would have made such a comment in Ethiopia.

> A young woman complained that her husband was not treating her as he should 'in this country'. 'Here', she explained, 'men should do half the work in the house; he does nothing!' One day, when I jokingly criticised the cup of coffee he made me, she said: 'Why do you complain? He has not once made me a cup of coffee in eleven years of marriage!' When it suited him, he too made use of female emancipation: when his wife complained about the lack of money in the house, he said 'You too could work!'

If the hold men have over their wives is loosening, that over their grown-up unmarried daughters still living at home is weaker still – a loss of control shared by their wives.

> Tauvesh, a twenty-two year old unmarried girl, sometimes slept with her boyfriend, staying over at a friend's for the night. She knew that her father knew, despite his silence. 'What can he do about it?' she said, with an air of satisfaction.

> An old woman asked her eldest stepdaughter to come and visit: 'You are the only child I have. Yesterday I asked Gennat [her only daughter, who lives at home] to make *injera* and she would not. Her mother is ill and she does not make *injera* and *wot* (stew)!'

Children

The turmoil in gender relations is slight compared to the loss of authority over children and the resulting inability to socialise them according to either Ethiopian or Israeli norms. One of the key-stones of Ethiopian culture is the idea of respect towards elders, particularly from children towards their parents. In Northern Ethiopia, in the presence of adults, children should be seen and not heard. Their unruly behaviour in Israel is therefore a cause of grave distress to their parents.

> I went with a neighbour to his parents for the monthly family *kuvie* (credit society). For the whole week-end, the two bedroom flat was bulging, with six adult siblings, their spouses, and an assortment of their children. The good humour, chatter and laughter was marred only by Gennat's two boys. Moshe and Avraham were three and five years old and totally undisciplined. In front of everyone, they hit, kicked, and spat at their mother. She vainly repeated 'No! No!' and sometimes pinched them hard. The father did not intervene, and, trying to make peace, embraced the boys who came to him for comfort, screaming after a hard pinch. They were just as disobedient towards him, failing for instance to close a cupboard at his request or to put down a large bottle of Coca-Cola which was about to spill. Both parents were embarrassed. The rest of the company tried to ignore the bad behaviour, except for when the children's attention-seeking screams made conversation impossible. The uncles and aunts stared at them, not knowing what to do. At one point one of the boys kicked and hit his grandmother. She raised a slipper to the child. She was visibly disgusted. The children's misbehaviour was all the more conspicuous given the self-consciously 'Ethiopian' atmosphere which pervaded this large family gathering, where Ethiopian etiquette was particularly pronounced.

Socialisation of children

Small children enjoy a period of total freedom till the age of about three; they can do what they want and are never reprimanded.

> Etan is eight years old. He is on his way out to join his friends when his mother tells him to play with his younger brother, a

toddler. Etan reluctantly agrees. His brother starts to misbehave and Etan raises his voice. His mother intercedes: 'Let him be! He does not know. He is just a baby!'

Babies and toddlers rarely leave their mother's side. Many Ethiopian women carry their babies in home-made slings on their back, although a growing number of mothers, and young ones in particular, prefer to use push-chairs. In Ethiopia, babies were breast-fed until the age of two or three – in Israel, they are generally weaned within a year. Babies and toddlers are the focus of everybody's affection – until the birth of the next child who takes on the privileged role.

Abba Telahun spent his days reading and copying religious texts in bright coloured felt-tips. He gave little attention to his grandchildren. Whenever his baby grandson was in the room however, his face lit up and he kissed, cuddled, and played with the baby, whom he nick-named Shimbra (chick-pea). When Abba Telahun left the room, he kissed only the infant, walking straight past Shimbra's four-year-old sister.

Small children's naughty behaviour is excused and laughed at.

Alemwork explains: 'Children do not know until the age of eight or so, only then do they learn the difference between good and evil.'

In Ethiopia, disciplining started around the age of four/five.[10] Parents and other closely related adults take on the role of teaching a child about 'good and evil' and to 'show respect'. Children learn by watching and from verbal discourse and physical beatings. Eventually, if the apprenticeship is successful, by the age of about eight years old, the child acquires 'a heart' – that is the capacity to act morally. As well as learning from elders, children acquire parents' characteristics by heredity. Hot debates rage about which of the two parents a baby most looks like. Ethiopian youngsters are said to be 'strong' and particularly adept at the army because they are the off-spring of strong soldiers who 'could fight for eight days without water'. Conversely, a lazy teenager is cast off as the child of 'that bad man'.

An old learned man explained to me that he did not go to school, but learned from his elders (*abatachin*) and the learning stayed in his head, in the same way, he added that his words stay in my tape.

Aviva tells me that her younger sister knows more than her [about Ethiopian customs] because the latter did not go to school and therefore was at home all day hearing elders speak and watching them.

Ethiopian values continue to be taught in Israel. A little girl pleads with her great-uncle to help her get her stick back from her brother. He ignored her at first and then took the boy's side, saying somewhat sternly: 'He is a boy and you are a girl!'

In Ethiopia, from the age of about five, girls were expected to help with household tasks and boys to mind the herds. Both sexes were ordered to fetch things for adults and older siblings, and act as general dogs'-bodies. In Israel, children are rarely asked to do anything; and when they are, they tend to refuse.

Aviva's fourteen-year-old son finally joined her in Israel after his (Christian) father's death, six years after the rest of the family. When he first arrived, he ordered his younger half-siblings about: 'Fetch me Coca-Cola!' 'Move that chair!' 'Stop making so much noise!' The children were too bemused to refuse him at first, but the tensions soon grew and he learned fast that in Israel, children were not as they had been in Ethiopia.

Naughty children

Ethiopian children who arrived in Israel from about the age of five onwards are generally charming and well-behaved. However, children born in Israel or who arrived as infants are frequently uncontrollable and naughty – the socialisation process described above has failed. They neither respect basic Ethiopian customs, such as getting up from their chair for an adult or offering their cheeks to be kissed by older relatives, nor do they obey their parents. These children can generally understand basic Amharic although they are unable (or unwilling) to speak it. My field-notes are filled with examples of children's behaviour similar to that of Gennat's children and their parents' bemused reactions.

Worku was relaxing one Sabbath morning under the tree in our front garden, chatting to his uncles who were visiting from another town. His seven-year-old came to ask for Coca-Cola. Worku was embarrassed at the rudeness of his daughter in front of his relatives, asking for a drink away from her own home, which by Ethiopian standards is akin to begging. He told her sharply that there was none and suggested she drink water. She began to make her way into the house, and he reprimanded her, telling her go fetch water at his sister's house opposite. She whined, saying that she wanted water here, and continued, slowly, to push the door open. He raised his voice and said: 'Go!' She whined further until he picked up a pebble and raised his hand as if to throw it at her. She laughed uneasily and finally scampered off in the direction of her aunt's house. The conversation resumed, without a mention of the incident, which was keenly observed, and noted, by all present.

A small child throws pebbles into the living room through the open French windows. His father tells him to stop and the boy continues. After an embarrassed silence, the adults in the room all laugh.

The helplessness on a parent's face is visible when his/her child refuses to turn down the TV when guests are trying to talk over coffee, and the child turns up the TV again even after the parent has turned it down.

Parents do not know how to react to such behaviour. Despite the obvious distress it causes, it is rarely talked about. Anteby stresses the resonance of Ethiopians' silences:[11] no silence is more eloquent than that provoked by the naughtiness of children.

When children are well-behaved, the pleasure and relief which suffuses a parent's face is as palpable as the distress which adorns their faces at other times.

Worku looks on fondly as his three-year-old eats *injera* (most little children refuse to eat Ethiopian food).

Melissu's ten-year-old entered a room full of relatives, and despite obvious apprehension, went round each in turn saying whose son he was and offering his cheeks to be kissed. Melissu's proud and contented smile was a joy to behold.

The loss of the children is epitomised by young children's refusal to partake in the two most central Ethiopian activities:

eating *injera* and speaking Amharic. Young children are fed chocolate desserts, chocolate drinks, white bread and chocolate spread, pasta with tomato sauce, eggs, *bamba* (a savoury snack) and the occasional schnitzel (fried turkey). They say in a resigned tone of voice: 'The children refuse to eat *injera*, this is the food that they want.' New immigrants are apparently unaware of the low nutritional value of this diet.[12] Parents speak Hebrew to their children as far as their Hebrew language ability permits them. They explain that children refuse to speak in Amharic and that speaking Hebrew with their children is a good way for themselves to learn the language.

Parents' analysis of children's naughtiness

Ethiopian Israelis have a number of explanations for the naughtiness of their children. They say that children are learning the ways of this country, emulating the behaviour of 'spoilt' white children. In other words, children are no longer learning from their parents but from negative external influences.

> A former primary school teacher regrets his life in Ethiopia, conceding though that at least Israel is good for the children because they can study so much. After a little reflection, he said: 'But in some respects it is less good here for the children. In Ethiopia, those who went to school studied so hard. Here they do not. They copy things from Israeli children: they wear their hair long, they smoke ...' He spoke with a tone of inevitability in his voice. Because of negative external influences which he felt were beyond his control, this former school-teacher had lost his power to make his own children study well.

> Qes Yalew's wife: 'If you speak to them, they do not hear. They see *farenj* films on TV, they go to *'flimia'* [Ethiopian elders' pronunciation of *'pneumia'*, boarding school, Hebrew] and that is what teaches them, not anything else! If Qes Yalew gets angry, they do not hear!'

Alternatively, parents explain naughtiness by saying that the children are bored. They say that, in Ethiopia, children could play outside but in urban Israel they must stay indoors because of the cars. Children are not allowed out unless they are supervised, and yet most of them have few play things in the house. In addition, in

Ethiopia, children lived with their extended families close-by, which provided them with both entertainment and authority (all older relatives can exert their authority over their relatives' children). In Israel, children are brought in up nuclear family households, often with only their mother – approximately 30 per cent of Ethiopian Jewish households are one-parent families.[13] Moreover, in Israel, children accept the authority of their relatives even less than that of their parents.

> Enat, is a spirited twelve year old girl. One day, she refused to obey her uncle Fanta's order to take his two little children home, as she did not want to leave the social gathering she was much enjoying. He struck her. She screamed, ran off and did not speak to him for six months afterwards. Enat's parents and relatives told her that, as her uncle, she has to obey him and that her punishment was rightful. In private however, I heard them discuss the issue in less dogmatic terms, wondering whether 'in this country', Fanta had a right to hit his niece ...

Occasionally, environmental factors are given as a cause for unruly behaviour.

> Aviva, a young mother of two uncontrollable children: 'The children's behaviour has changed. I do not know why. Maybe because of the water or the country [i.e. the environment, the weather].'

The most common explanation which Ethiopian parents give for their children's misbehaviour, however, is that the Israeli authorities do not allow them to punish the children physically.

> A young woman: 'In Ethiopia, the kids were so well behaved: you hit a child once and because he was afraid, he would not do it again. Here a mother says 'Do so and so!' but the child can just say 'No!' and what can the mother do? If she hits the child, he can tell his teacher who will tell the police and she will be put in prison. I know of several people who were put in prison.'

Parents can no longer adopt an Ethiopian style of child raising since it is so much at odds with the norms in Israel, where childhood is idealised and corporal punishment outlawed, yet they have failed to develop an alternative way. As this father of four explained: 'In

Ethiopia, parents had a way to bring up children. Here they are not allowed to follow that way. They have not yet found a method to bring up their children in accordance with Israeli customs.' The result is erratic behaviour on the part of parents which does little to improve children's behaviour towards their parents.

Melash accepts a lot of 'un-Ethiopian' style behaviour from his nine-year-old daughter. She often fails to obey a command and he gently coaxes her into obedience. Sometimes, however, the smallest incident makes him explode. One day she fetched some cups of tea from the kitchen for a few people, including her father, who were assembled around the living room coffee table. She placed the cups all together in the middle of the table and returned to the TV programme which she had reluctantly left. He asked crossly: 'Where is my tea?' 'There!' she said, pointing to the cups. He raised his voice louder: 'Bring it here, closer!' The girl, not knowing whether he was really angry or just joking, giggled nervously. She played safe, and proceeded to push one of the cups nearer to her father.

Little Avi was exceptionally well-behaved and pleasant, and by contrast illustrates some of the factors which account for children's naughtiness.

I knew Avi from the age of three to five. His mother was a teenager when she gave birth to him, and he was largely brought up by his grandmother and mother's step-father, who was a neighbourhood elder. His mother lived at home and looked after him after work. Avi's step-grandfather took the child everywhere with him, and the child sat quietly on his lap or played with other children. Even in Ulpan language classes he remained well behaved and quiet compared to other children who frequently disrupted classes. Avi understood Amharic although he responded in Hebrew. On a return visit to Israel, when Avi was eight years old, he came to greet me, and his grandfather told him to bend to kiss my knees. Avi obeyed – the only child born and brought up in Israel that I saw perform willingly this Ethiopian custom.

Avi was brought up by his extended family, enjoyed lots of activity since his grandparents took him with them wherever they went, and both his mother and grandparents were relatively well adjusted in Israel, and happy within the household. Most children, however, are brought up by parents who are often confused about many aspects of life in Israel, including child rearing – and the children suffer.

Cattle-children

Police intervention does occur and there have been cases of Ethiopians jailed for physical violence, although more usually as a result of wife-battering than child-beating. But the importance given to external interference – seen as *the cause* of the children's unruliness – reveals the depth of the feeling about loss of control over children. Ethiopian parents feel that the basic matter of disciplining a child is taken out of their hands. This represents an overt manifestation of their loss of authority over their children, and their inability to socialise them.

> Aster, a twenty-six-year-old single mother of two, complains that her children no longer 'listen' to her, they say 'It is not your business.' She continues: 'Children do not have a heart anymore. If my son [a ten-year-old] is watching TV and I call him, he does not hear me, his heart is there in the TV, not with me.'

Aster is saying that she has lost her child ('his heart'); his concern, interest and allegiance, are now to the TV. She therefore feels excluded from her children and their new world. In the words of an elder:

> Our children have become like cattle in the field, not respecting their fathers or their religion. The children are not taught properly here. We lost our rights to raise them and to punish them when they do wrong because of the intervention of the police. The children, whom we raised [supported financially], got out of our words and this makes us very upset.

Religious and domestic affairs

Ethiopian Jewish adults bemoan their loss of authority in religious and domestic affairs. While this section deals primarily with older Ethiopian Israelis, the younger generation, including the (largely secular) political elite, is also vociferous about Beta Israel priests' loss of authority. They espouse the cause of Beta Israel priests for they see it as a battle for recognition as an ethnic group of equal standing to other groups of immigrants in Israel, who tend to have their own ethnic Rabbis and synagogues.

On the day of the blood demonstration in January 1996, the lack of Ethiopian synagogues and the low status of Beta Israel priests were part of the main issues of discontent which the Ethiopian delegation presented to the Prime Minister.

> Alequa Ayelign: 'We were very religious people and we are here as if we know nothing. They see us as *dinkoro* (deaf, ignorant), but our heart is full of thoughts! The Yemenites, the Russians, everybody's rights are being respected. They have their synagogues. But we have no synagogue, the prayer cannot be given, the *mergam* (menstrual women) cannot be separated, our people live just by crying when it comes to religion.'

These words are powerful and express the thoughts and words I heard so often: Ethiopian Jewish religion is devalued in the eyes of other Israelis and Beta Israel priests have lost their religious authority and can no longer perform weddings or divorces. Given that religion is all-encompassing for Beta Israel, they feel that their knowledge and wisdom, and hence themselves as persons, are devalued in their new society. This sense of devaluation, their recently acquired 'deafness' makes them sad, and taints their new-found material wealth.

> Abba Fatag: 'Us elders (*shmagleotch*), we are happy to have food and clothes in this country but our religion is being lost. All that we eat therefore, we cannot enjoy.'

Worse still than devaluation in the eyes of other Israelis, elders suffer from the loss of their own youngsters' morality: young Ethiopian girls dress in short skirts, menstruating women continue their daily life unabated, young people have sexual partners before marriage, and a growing minority are failing to observe even the most basic of Jewish practice, such as observance of the Sabbath.

In a short speech following a Bar Mitzvah blessing, the priest bemoaned the fact that although God had brought the Beta Israel to Jerusalem, the young were no longer observing the Sabbath, and he called on everyone to respect traditions.

Parents fear that their children will grow up with norms and values at odds with their own.

> Melissu, a young woman, is despondent about her five-year-old's future morality: she would like her daughter to keep her virginity until marriage, but she fears that she hopes in vain:

'What difference will my wishes make? She will go with whoever!'

Alequa Ayelign, a respected medicine man, whose children are older than Melissu's, acutely feels loss of control over his ability to instil his norms and values in his teenagers. He laments that 'they stay away from us', in the army and at boarding school. He complains that his children are with 'them' and that his children eat impure '*farenj* meat'. Children, he maintains, should have 'a right' to do as their parents showed them. He concludes: 'When there will be democracy, we can marry our children in good time [i.e. young], we can help the children to build a home and we will be like anyone in the country.' He uses a language of rights, but no-one has denied his children their 'rights' to follow their father's injunctions – the children themselves have chosen to integrate Israeli norms and food into their daily lives. Rather than directly voicing his sense of loss of control over his children, Alequa Ayelign is thus constructing an alternative discourse, less damning to him personally: it is Israeli democracy, rather than his own authority, which is not strong enough to enable Ethiopian Jews to maintain their traditions in Israel. He attempts to cling onto a vestige of control by blaming the state for his own loss of authority and by portraying an idealised future in which this control will be regained. Alequa Ayelign's eldest son, a thirty-seven year old priest, also adopts a language of rights. He would like the liturgical language Ge'ez to be upheld and learned. 'But,' he laments, 'how can we encourage our children to learn when we have no rights?' Like his father, he is deflecting his loss of control over the younger generation onto a political problem with the country – a more bearable – because remediable – problem.

Elders have also lost much of their former social function as guardians of peace.[14] Recall Abba Negusse who loved to speak of the prestigious status he acquired in the village: 'For five years, I was a judge. People came to me with their problems. I listened and then I said: "This is good. This is bad. Do this. Do that."'[15] Priests and elders do still mediate in times of strife, but this function is rapidly being taken over, or supplemented by, social workers. The latter have become an integral part of daily life – the first port of call for complaints about housing, money or marriage. Elders resent them because not only do they operate with totally different attitudes, norms and in a foreign language, but they have also usurped their own role as mediators in domestic affairs.

Ethiopian adults' loss of authority is illustrated by their discourse on divorce rates. Though the divorce rate in Ethiopia was extremely high,[16] they claim that the Beta Israel hardly ever divorced in Ethiopia, while in Israel many Ethiopian couples are divorcing because of the lack of the elders' beneficial interventions. Moreover, the disruptive effects of divorces are said to be much graver in Israel, sometimes with fatal consequences.

> A middle-aged woman, twice-divorced: 'In Ethiopia, it was so easy to divorce. If you had problems, the elders would come and if after they had tried to resolve the problem, it still remained, you would agree to separate. The belongings would be divided and you would return to your mother's home. There, you would make some *talla* (alcoholic beverage) and ask your relatives to come and build you a house. It was so easy. Here though you have to get the social worker and then there is no house to go to and it takes so long. Some people cannot wait and so they kill themselves.'

While elders suffer from their drop in status, the worst hit are men in the thirty to forty age group, whom I call the 'in-between generation'. Older men have the status of 'elders' and do not need to even try to integrate into Israeli society since they do not have to work thanks to their state pension nor do they have young children to bring up as young Israelis. Younger men received training on arrival in Israel and find it easier to learn Hebrew and find a place for themselves in the new society. The middle-aged men, however, are too young to be 'elders' but too old to successfully integrate. They cannot find decent jobs, if any, and they cannot learn Hebrew well, and yet they have young families to bring up and need to earn the respect of their children.

> Yinework, a thirty-year-old father of four explains: 'This country is good for elders – they can just sit and chat merrily – and for the children, because of education. But for those who came between the ages of twenty and sixty it is hard – we do not understand [how to operate successfully in] this country.'

As mentioned above, women in the 'in-between generation' do not suffer from this loss of status in the same way as their husbands. As in Ethiopia, their primary domain is the household, and their control there is undiminished.

Loss of control over well-being

Illness in Israel

Ethiopians tend to assert that they are sick in Israel while they were healthy in Ethiopia.[17] Worse still, they claim that when they were ill in Ethiopia, they could soon be cured, whilst in Israel, they remain sick. Illness and healing is one of the prime concerns of Ethiopian immigrants and one of the most frequent and contentious subjects of daily conversation. This is because, I suggest, many illnesses and the inability to cure them results from the loss of control suffered by Ethiopian Jewish immigrants in their new country.

The following two accounts illustrate clearly the imputed causes and nature of illness, the effect illness has on daily life, and the difficulties – and lengths sought – to cure illness.

> Yalew has a chronic head-ache. He is a tall, well-built man in his late forties, with a house full of children. For the first year that I knew him, though he often took sick leave, he held down a job as a hospital cleaner. But his headaches worsened, and he eventually quit his job. He sat at home all day, wearing a white turban around his head, looking morose. He believed that his headaches were caused by a female insect which had entered his head through his ear and had then reproduced inside his head, so that a swarm of insects were continuously buzzing away there and eating away at his flesh. Israeli doctors and Ethiopian medicine men in Israel failed to cure him and his only solution was to seek a cure in Ethiopia.

> With money saved from his credit society and financial contributions from relatives, Yalew set off. The medicine man that he saw near his former village removed the insects by applying certain herbal potions to his ear. Abebe returned to Israel with his illness cured. He took the jar which contained the six dead insects removed from his head to the doubting *farenj* doctor to prove to him the cause of his ailments.

> Within a few months however the pain returned. Some relatives concluded that he had failed to see the right person in Ethiopia, others thought that the new pain was caused by the wound left after the exit of the insects, where they had eaten away at Yalew's flesh.

Aster is an attractive young woman, single mother of two uncontrollable children. She was possessed by the same spirit that possessed her grandmother shortly after the birth of her first son, twelve years ago in Ethiopia. (This information was confirmed to me by the Amhara witchdoctor of Aster's village in Ethiopia who originally diagnosed the spirit possession.) There, Aster's spirit was under control: she could provide him with what he wanted – a red chicken, coffee, herbs – and so he did not make her ill. In this country however, she is ill; her left leg hurts her permanently, and she gets fatigue and headaches. *Farenj* doctors are of no help – they found nothing wrong. Sometimes, they give her a cream to rub into her leg, but it has little effect. She explained the problem: 'My *kole* (spirit) comes here. But what we do for spirits here is superficial. In Ethiopia, he is happy with what is done for him, so he leaves me and goes. You have to prepare coffee in a special way with incense and you prepare popcorn. In this country, when we use incense the neighbours are angered and ask why we use such things. Also, where in this town do I find a red chicken to slaughter? We cannot do things properly here. Therefore people are sick.' Here, even the Ethiopian doctors cannot cure her, because they do not have the right herbal medicines. So she too started to save up for a ticket to Ethiopia.

Both these accounts start from the idealised notion that in Ethiopia, though illness did occur, it was much less frequent than in Israel and it could always be cured. Both these individuals were finding Israel particularly hard to cope with: Aster, a traditional young woman, missed Ethiopian village life and her former Christian husband who was unable (or unwilling) to join her; Yalew, who was just beginning to acquire age-status in Ethiopia, found himself yet again at the bottom of the social hierarchy, a member of the 'in-between generation', too young to qualify as an elder and too old to acquire decent Hebrew and adapt successfully to life in Israel. Blaming Israel for their inability to cure their illness is a means of expressing their dissatisfaction and their sense of loss of control.

The causes of illness

The most frequent medical complaints of Ethiopians are heart pain, stomach pain, headache, colds, flu, asthma, and skin rashes. A small number of Beta Israel also suffer from various mental illnesses, for which there is a range of indigenous names and expressions (for example *moign*, lit: 'crazy, *menfas chinqat*, the name used by a herbal doctor for one of his patient's mental illness). Most illness is said to result from external agency – environmental, psychological, or supernatural factors, or a combination of these.[18]

Environmental factors are the most frequently attributed causes of illness. Ethiopians complain that the vagaries of the weather in Israel make them sick. It is either too hot or too cold and the strong wind, especially in the coastal towns, is particularly dangerous to health. Israeli water which, according to Beta Israel wisdom, has 'medicine' added to it and comes from a stagnant lake (i.e. the Sea of Galilee) rather than a flowing river as in Ethiopia, is blamed for both mental and physical illness. One young woman attributed her little children's unruliness to drinking water, while for another, water was the cause of the mental illness her grown-up sister developed in Israel.

Physical illness is often directly connected with problems at work or with emotional pain and difficulties.[19]

One young man attributed his stomach pains to his current worries (*assab*, lit: thoughts): unrequited love from a girl that he was wooing and some nasty quarrelling with his elder brother over money.

Alemwork said that she is ill (itchy body and headache) 'because' (*mikinyatum*) she is having problems with her husband.

Illness is also caused by the agency of malevolent spirits.

A teenage boy went mad – he looked distracted, he did not talk properly, 'he jumped off buses before they had stopped'. His desperate parents took him to see the greatest medicine man in the country who diagnosed that the boy had become possessed by a spirit.

Some people, called *balakole* (lit: owner of a spirit), are possessed by a specific spirit, who makes its host ill when his requests are not met[20] – as Aster illustrated in the above account. Not all Beta Israel believe in spirits though. Aster's sister and brother, for example, attributed her fainting at a mourning ceremony, not to her spirit, as the rest of the family did, but to her fear of large crowds.

People who are not possessed by a specific spirit fear sporadic attacks by roaming spirits – and they guard against them in a number of ways; they fill extra cups of coffee for the spirits, throw a little popcorn served at coffee over their shoulder, and light incense at set times.

I sometimes asked Mama Alefash why she threw a little popcorn over her shoulder before passing the dish around. She always laughed a little, with a touch of embarrassment and answered 'it is for the *kole* (spirits), so that they do not come and disturb us!'

A young university student home for the holidays invited me in for a drink late afternoon one day. At sundown, he lit some incense in the front room. He explained: 'It is for the *kole* (spirit). I do it for my mother because she is out today – I do not believe in this myself!'

Curing and failing to cure illness

Worku (twenty-six years old) was ill. He suffered from bad stomach pains and vomiting. He went to the *farenj* doctor but the latter, he told me, just gave him the kind of pills that they give people who are sick on the bus. Worku wanted to visit a private doctor in Ashdod, a *farenj*, who gives injections. What he really needs though to be fully cured is a trip to Ethiopia, to the holy waters (*tevel*).

The main problem with illness in Israel is that it cannot be easily cured. Ethiopians are dissatisfied with the treatments offered by Israeli doctors.[21] They complain that doctors only give pills, without giving enough injections, since these are what really cure. Beta Israel claim that pills are not very effective, especially if you just swallow them as the doctor says because they just go straight through your body and come out the other side. Older Ethiopians chew away at their pills in an attempt to increase their effectiveness. Moreover they feel that, irrespective of acute language problems, Israeli doctors do not relate to them properly, fail to listen, and treat them with disrespect and impatience.[22] While continuing to use Israeli medical services, Ethiopians increasingly turn to Ethiopian traditional medical practitioners.[23] As Alequa Ayelign, a reputed Ethiopian medicine man explained, people come to him when the *farenj* doctor cannot cure them.

Most treatment involves either extracting the harmful agent or substance which has caused the illness – remember Yalew's attempts at removing the harmful bugs from this head – or finding a way to put an end to its influence on the sick person, e.g. Asters' efforts to appease her spirit.[24] Beta Israel practitioners use one or more of three types of treatment: 'physical', herbal, and spirit possession.

Physical treatments have been much reduced in Israel: the former widespread practice of bleeding, for example, is now extremely rare. Still common are massages to sore areas of the body and uvulectomy for babies, whereby a specialist removes the uvula with a sharp instrument to prevent suffocation and other baby illnesses.[25]

> A young woman was distraught when her baby boy continued crying for the third day running. The medicines of the *farenj* doctor were apparently ineffectual. She asked her mother who in the area knew how to remove uvulas. Her mother, pleased at the suggestion, named a practitioner. The young woman was a little horrified at the thought of this man cutting into the throat of her child, but decided that unless the child's illness stopped within a few days, she would go for the operation. After all, she reasoned, she had had the operation as a baby, as had all her siblings. Fortunately, her baby's cries ceased before the appointed day.

Herbalists use divination techniques[26] and their treatment typically includes herbal medications, amulets[27] and instructions such as 'This month is not favourable for you, do not travel far from your house.' But Ethiopian Israelis complain that the medicine men cannot cure them in Israel. Both patients and doctors blame the lack of appropriate herbs and healing waters. To try to remedy the situation, patients, doctors and traders travel to Ethiopia to bring back appropriate curative herbs, and holy water from special springs.

Spirit mediums operate with the help of a spirit. The spirit gives him/her strength and power by revealing the cause of the illness and the way to deal with it: the Medium's spirit can converse and influence proper behaviour in the spirits which are troubling the patient.[28]

> After having accompanied Mama Alefash to several trips to the *farenj* doctor, she finally suggested a visit to the local Ethiopian medicine man Alequa Atnafu. We were ushered through the

living room into his consulting room. He sat cross-legged on a low bed, a blanket around his legs, a woolly hat on his head, and two long necklaces of beads around his neck. His eyes were sharp and lively. The walls were draped in colourful cloth and the display cabinet full of dozens of bottle of *arak* (a strong liquor) and dozens of unopened sets of coffee cups, given to him by grateful patients. On the floor a small tray was filled with coffee cups, covered with a small colourful cloth. The smell of incense pervaded the room. Popcorn littered the floor. We sat opposite the medicine man and Mama Alefash described the aches and pains in her shoulder and head. Alequa Atnafu took out a scroll, a long piece of paper with neatly written Amharic writing in blue, with a passage in red. He filled in two blanks, one with Mama Alefash's name and one with her mother's name. He made some calculations on some rough paper (an old bank statement). His speech alternated between ordinary Amharic and '*kole*' (spirit) talk, which sounded to me like gibberish with Arabic sounds and intonations. He gave her the scroll, which she later sewed into a small leather pouch which she wore around her neck. He suggested that she go to the hot water baths in Ashdod. He also gave her some twigs which she was to smoke under her body for three nights. He instructed her to return to him in three days for an appraisal. She placed a twenty shekel note on the coffee table.

Alequa Atnafu then turned to me and asked me my name and my mother's name and made appropriate calculations. He asked why I had come. I tried to explain that I was not ill but had accompanied Mana Alefash for my studies, to learn about his medicine. But perhaps I did not make myself clear: he proceeded to give me a powder which I was to apply with cream on my face to help me with my studies (lit: 'for your studies to enter you').

It must be said that Ethiopian Jews are not always keen to publicise their beliefs in spirits and visits to traditional medicine men since such beliefs and practices are antithetical to their proclamation of a strict adherence to the Bible.

A typical interchange between myself and an Ethiopian Israeli:
– 'I never go to those medicine men! It is against the Bible!
– So, where did you get that amulet from?
– Oh, well, I did go once ...'

Despite Ethiopian Israelis' frequent visits to both Israeli and Ethiopian medical practitioners, they continuously assert that they cannot be cured in this country: 'Here it just does not work'. Israeli doctors do not understand their illnesses and the powers of Ethiopian medicine men are lessened in Israel. To be fully cured, Ethiopian Israelis have to visit Ethiopia. Beta Israel have probably always voiced scepticism about the powers of their medicine men, but their current loss of faith is acute. Nudelman[29] states that health problems are exacerbated by a new lifestyle, changes in social role (namely the inactivity of elders) and the difficulties of dealing with life in urban Israeli society.[30] In Israel, Ethiopian Jews cannot remove the root cause of their illness – the new socio-environmental conditions in which they live and consequent loss of control over their social order; and so they remain sick.

Suicide

The ultimate loss of control over well-being is suicide. In 1985, Ethiopian immigrants suffered a six times higher suicide rate than the average population in Israel.[31] While there are no up-to-date figures, both Ethiopians and Israelis say that Ethiopian suicide levels are extremely high, and according to Ethiopians, much higher than in Ethiopia. It is hard to ascertain causes since Ethiopians often explain a particular suicide with reference to whatever happens to be the political issue at the time, whether family reunification, failure to gain university admission, inadequate housing or mistreatment in the army. Documented cases were found to relate to domestic problems and, increasingly, to positive tests for HIV.[32]

> My neighbours explained the unfortunate circumstances which led to the suicide of young Waga, a young mother of three infants committed suicide. Waga's sister-in-law told me that Waga had separated from her husband and was given a flat for a year. At the end of the year, the social security officials asked her to pay NIS 1,800 rent. But Waga had no money. They said that she should return to her original home and that they would get her husband to leave and give him alternative accommodation. But she said that she would not go back until he was out. So she went to her mother's home. After about one month there, she was found hanging from a tree, far from the house.

Fantanesh, my middle-aged neighbour: 'Waga must have thought and thought and found that there was no other solution ... There was no suicide in Ethiopia.'

Gennat, a young educated woman, understood well Waga's motivations. Waga did not know what to do, helpless and powerless in front of her difficulties. She could not cope with the bureaucracy nor having to take decisions and deal with all the Israelis. I said: 'But if only she had waited a while she would have got her house!' Gennat explained that Ethiopians have different ways of dealing with things: 'You wait and wait and accept and accept and then you explode.'

Kanubesh said that the cause of the woman's suicide was God's anger about the Beta Israel's current lack of respect for purity laws. She concluded: 'If you put me down once', says God, 'I will put you down seven times'. This means 'If you do not obey my words, I will cause damage in many ways'. So people commit suicide, die in war and die of illness because God is angered.'

What struck me in these accounts was that none of my informants expressed shock at the fact that a young woman with three small children should take her life. On the contrary, they spoke with sympathy and blamed 'them' (that is social security officials) for not giving her a house, and implicitly accused them of her death. Whatever Waga's motives, her neighbours spoke of her suicide as the natural outcome of her sense of powerlessness in the face of Israeli social services. For them, her suicide was a manifestation of the disruption, and sense of loss of control, over the social order in Israel.

Kaplan & Rosen suggest on the contrary that suicide is a means of regaining control: 'Unable to live in an honourable fashion in a country whose rules and customs remain unfamiliar, the Ethiopian seeks to exert at least a measure of control by dying with honour.'[33] Their conclusion is interesting, but it needs corroborating data – while my informants spoke of death in battle in honourable terms, they never did so about suicide. Indeed so dishonourable is suicide that it is difficult to convince priests to make the appropriate funerary blessings at the funeral.

Conclusion

This chapter has explored the consequences of 'becoming deaf' in Israel. It has portrayed the sense of loss of control over most aspects of life: livelihood, the domestic sphere and health. In the new cultural and social context, the accumulated knowledge of generations, of which medicine men are the proud bearers, is now becoming redundant.

> Such a healer, Alequa Ayelign, sums up the issue in these words: 'The traditions and knowledge that we brought with us from there, we cannot make use of here. They closed it for us, by saying that we had to study again here in this language. This is why we say that we are *dinkoro*. By not respecting our laws and not accepting our religion, they make us primitive. They keep us inside [i.e. out of public life].'

The healing powers of respected Ethiopian healers have diminished in this strange land; their former well-known landscape, in which every tree yielded fruit, wood, shade or medicine, has been replaced by an urban maze navigable only by buses which can explode at any moment.

PART TWO

Overcoming Difficulties

A young Israeli friend visited me and my Ethiopian family and neighbours. Within a few hours, he exclaimed in amazement: 'Everyone is so cheerful! From what I had read and heard about Ethiopians, I imagined that they would be miserable!'

Despite the positive aspects of their new country which were explored in Chapters Four and Five the Beta Israel have found Israel disappointing. Long-held Beta Israel practices are changing fast: daughters return home in mini-skirts, menstruating women cook the evening meal, and Ethiopian "cattle-children" are fast disappearing into an unknown immoral haze; the older generation feel that they are losing control over their lives and that of their children. The younger generation (sixteen to thirty years old approximately) suffer from a somewhat different set of problems. While they do not bemoan the relaxing of moral standards and their elders' loss of control, they too are stung by Israelis' rejection of the Beta Israel practice of Judaism. For them, the religious controversy is another manifestation of Israeli racism towards them. Ethiopian immigrants, they claim, are being discriminated against on all fronts, whether it be in the religious domain, at work, in school, or in government offices. Reminiscent of their status in Ethiopia, Ethiopian Jewish immigrants to Israel feel that they are once again cast in an inferior position by the dominant society – as Blacks, "improper Jews", and uneducated "primitive" people.

The Beta Israel could have chosen to deal with negative preconceptions and threats to their sense of belonging by abandoning their native traditions and integrating as rapidly as possible. Instead, they have formed a proud self-confident *edah* (ethnic group, Hebrew), almost obsessively asserting the superiority of their traditions compared to those of other Israelis. Beta Israel's strong affirmation of their traditions vis-à-vis a dominant majority is not new for them. The Beta Israel defined themselves in opposition to their former Amhara neighbours on the basis of their distinctive traditions, such as female purity laws, eating only Beta Israel slaughtered-meat, and religious custom. The former practice of *attenkuqn* (don't touch me), whereby Beta Israel had to ritually purify themselves after contact with non-Beta Israel, expressed their commitment to a separate identity within a multi-ethnic society.[a]

In Israel, the situation is more complex. On the one hand, the Beta Israel do want to merge with other Israelis; on the other, integration comes at a price: to join the bottom of the socio-economic hierarchy and to concede religious inferiority. Chapters four and five illustrated their efforts at integration. The following three chapters build on Chapter Three – the creation and maintenance of strong communal ties among kin and neighbours – to show the variety of ways in which Ethiopia Jews proudly maintain their identity as Ethiopian Jews in Israel. They develop strong ethnic bonds and they uphold Ethiopian cultural customs and Beta Israel religious practices.

The Beta Israel have found additional strategies to overcome the difficulties of immigrating to the dreamed-of homeland: they ideologically subvert Israeli disparaging attitudes to cast themselves as morally superior and they come to terms with their imperfect homeland by casting their visions into the future (Chapters Twelve and Thirteen).

9

Being Together as Ethiopians

An Ethiopian Israeli boy boards a bus in Tel Aviv. He realises that he has not enough money to pay the fare. Unperturbed, he walks to the back of the bus and he asks, in Hebrew, if someone can give him the eleven shekels he needs. The four Ethiopian passengers dig into their pockets, and the fastest hands over the required sum. The boy then takes a seat, near the Ethiopians, but not next to any of them, which suggests that he did not know any of them personally; he had approached them, as opposed to any other passenger, because they were fellow Ethiopians.

This incident is one of the many instances and situations when Ethiopian Israelis savour a feeling of communality in Israel. While Ethiopian Israelis often feel united in Israel, in daily life, they are often more aware of their specific group allegiances – their relatives, their neighbours, or their Ethiopian region of origin – and thus of the factors *separating* them from one another. The coming together as Ethiopians *per se* takes place in specific times and contexts – during celebrations and mourning in particular and when they feel under threat.

Internal divisions amongst Ethiopian Israelis

From the outside, Ethiopian Israelis appear as one group, and indeed as this chapter demonstrates, they frequently feel a sense of unity. However, within the group, there are many divisions and sub-divisions. In daily life, their allegiances rest with particular sections of the community. Kin and neighbours are the primary groups. All Ethiopians outside of the kin group are 'other'. Similarly, Ethiopian Israelis can experience a sense of 'other' towards Ethiopians in other neighbourhoods and use slightly derogatory tones towards their kinsmen in less prestigious neighbourhoods. Clearly, Ethiopian Jews have the same group allegiances as other members of society. These can arise, for example, from differences in education and employment, both former and current. An Ethiopian Jew who was the village school-teacher will certainly feel quite removed and different from an illiterate immigrant. The Ethiopian who works in the government office can feel world apart from the factory worker.

Internal politics is another source of difference and conflict. Following the advice of a number of educated Ethiopians, I avoided questions of Ethiopian Jewish political organisation in Israel in order to protect my neutrality as much as possible. Communal political issues are hotly debated and constitute an important part of daily life, especially for men. In 1992, there were fifty registered Ethiopian organisations, each with specific demands and many antagonistic towards one another.[1]

> In Afula, there were elections in 1994 for a 'committee' to run communal affairs and represent Ethiopian immigrants to the local council, but within a few months, further elections were held for a rival committee. The dissenters' animosity towards the Committee Chairman Moshe was extreme: 'Ah, I will not go to that celebration! Those are Moshe's people!' 'That Committee is nothing! They are all Moshe's relatives!'

> A prominent Afula resident who publicly condemns Addissu Messelle, the organiser of the Blood Demonstration, did not attend the demonstration, and forbade his wife to. He told me: 'Why should I go? Addissu just organised the meeting for his own political advancement, so that he can become a Member of Parliament!' Addissu Messelle did in fact subsequently become an MP, thanks in large part to the publicity generated by the demonstration.

Further internal divisions amongst Ethiopian Israelis arise from years of residence in Israel, region of origin in Ethiopia, and slave descent.

Years of residence

> Fantaoun, who arrived with Operation Moses, is trying to place Melash Tarakagn, a man spoken of in conversation. The first question he asks is: 'Is he new here [i.e. did he come with Operation Solomon]?'

There is a definite awareness of period of arrival – in the above example, the first marker to identify Melash Tarakagn is his period of arrival – and people who arrived in the same cohort have a sense of allegiance towards each other, and consequent separateness towards Ethiopians who arrived at different times.

Ethiopian Jewish immigrants who arrived with Operation Moses or around that time (early to mid-eighties), feel a bond with other immigrants of that period and express, amongst themselves, criticism of the newcomers, whom they call 'the Solomon people' (*yeSolomon sawotch*), after the Operation Solomon airlift. Ethiopians who arrived in Israel in the early eighties were airlifted to Israel after they had walked from their villages to the Sudan and spent months, and sometimes years, in refugee camps. They consider themselves pioneers who, under unimaginable hardships, paved the way to immigration. They pride themselves in having had a stronger ideology of 'return to Jerusalem' than later immigrants who came only once the path was clear and 'easy'. The latter were transported to Addis Abeba, where they were supported by Jewish Agencies before being flown to Israel. In addition, the early immigrants claim, settling in Israel was easier for later immigrants because the earlier ones were there to instruct the newcomers and the Israeli government had formulated better policies towards Ethiopian immigrants (such as offering them grants of up to 90 per cent of the price of a house and providing better translation services).

Eighties immigrants who arrived as teenagers to Israel, often alone with their families left behind in Ethiopia, complain that the new immigrant youngsters lack drive and desire for success. This is because, they reason, these youngsters have seen that the earlier immigrants' efforts at integration have born no fruit (i.e. that they have low career prospects and suffer from discrimination) and so they are less keen to make efforts. In addition, veteran youths claim that while they arrived in Israel straight from the village and refugee camp, innocent, humble and reserved, the 'Solomon youngsters' were adversely influenced by their prolonged stay in Addis Abeba where they acquired a taste for low life, and became *'duruye'* (vagabond). They say that the latter smoke cigarettes, are not timid, wear immodest dress, and that many of them have become drop-outs from school and roam the street of Tel Aviv around the central bus station.

Efrat came to Israel age sixteen in 1984 with her uncle and his family. Her younger sister Ronit came with their parents in 1991, with Operation Solomon. Ronit wears mini-skirts and lots of make-up and she regularly goes dancing in Ethiopian night-clubs. Efrat adores her younger sister, but she lamented one day to me about her sister's immodest dress and behaviour and said: 'The new people, the Solomon people, they are *duruye* (vagabonds). Look at their earrings (worn by the boys) and the short skirts. They go to the social security offices and do not leave until they get want they want. We were quiet.'

Muluye, who arrived prior to Operation Moses as a boy, states: 'The newcomers are *duruye*. You see them with their dreadlocks at the bus station. They smoke hashish. We came wanting to succeed, they do not.'

Ethiopian region of origin

Other than a few exceptions, the Beta Israel came to Israel from either Gondar or Tigre, two neighbouring regions of Northern Ethiopia. The two groups of Beta Israel spoke different native languages (Amharic and Tigrinya),[2] and social relations and marriages between the two groups were rare. As with the regions' respective Christian populations, they maintained long-standing hostility towards one another.[3] Recent evidence for this hostility came in the 1950s when Jewish agencies injected cash into Beta Israel communities and leaders accused one another of favouring communities from their own region.[4] While Beta Israel from Tigre were on the whole the first to immigrate to Israel and constituted the majority of immigrants from Ethiopia in the early eighties, Beta Israel from Gondar now outnumber those from Tigre by a factor of about ten to one. In Israel, the segregation between the two groups is apparent. Ethiopian Israelis from Tigre often live in close proximity to one another and certain neighbourhoods are known by Beta Israel from Gondar as 'Tigre' neighbourhoods. There is little social mixing and intermarriage between the two groups, and the older generation does not eat meat from animals slaughtered by members of the other group.

Abba Negusse's nephew married a woman from Tigre. Even though they live not far away and this nephew visited our house regularly, his wife never once came, in contrast to the spouse of his other nephews and nieces who visit regularly. The nephew occasionally brought his daughters to the house, but they were often taunted: 'You little Tigre, you!'

When a group of immodestly dressed young girls walked past the house, Aveva would mutter in disapproval: 'Tigre!'

I had a Tigre friend in Beersheva. After a year of waiting for his promised visit, I asked him to tell me truthfully why he would not come. 'Your [adoptive] family will not like me', he finally admitted.

Beta Israel from the two regions have developed elaborate stereotypes about each other.[5] Those from Tigre accuse Beta Israel from Gondar of never speaking openly or honestly and for holding grievances 'in their tummy' for ever. Beta Israel from Gondar claim to be more educated than their Tigre counterparts (a claim unsurprisingly denied by the Tigre Beta Israel). The Beta Israel from Gondar also express anger against Tigre Beta Israel because the first immigrants from Tigre, in the late 1970s and early 1980s accepted to undergo the Rabbinate's demands for symbolic conversion (Hebrew: *giyur*). They consider that his conversion lowered the image of the Beta Israel as a whole because it implied that they were not proper Jews to start with.[6]

Slaves and non-slaves

Early on in fieldwork, I joked to a young couple at a wedding celebration, that my adoptive mother ordered me around so much that I had become a white *barya* (slave). The pair giggled as if I had just mentioned a lurid sexual detail, and told me 'You must never make such jokes! It is forbidden to speak about slaves! People will not like you!' A few minutes later, however, the young man could not resist pointing out a group of dancers, and whispered in my ear: 'They are [slaves]!' Later, his wife took me aside and explained to me that I should never ever mention the subject of Beta Israel slaves, or I would be rejected from Ethiopian society.

The strongest line of division is that between 'slaves' (*barya*) and non-slaves (*chewa*).[7] Until recent decades, wealthier Beta Israel families, like their Christian counterparts, owned 'slaves', and the *barya* of today are the latter's descendants.[8] The *barya* adopted the same religious and purity practices as their masters.[9] *Barya* used to be bought and sold in the market 'like cattle' and according to non-*barya* have 'frizzy hair, white teeth, a flat nose, and are very very black'. After Ethiopia's revolution in 1974, the practice of slavery was officially abolished and former slaves were given land during the land reform campaigns.

The subject of slavery is taboo and it was difficult to get a person of slave descent to speak on the subject, but towards the end of my fieldwork I succeeded.

> Efrat, I found out one day, had not celebrated her marriage in the customary fashion with a large family wedding. I finally learned that her husband's family had rejected her and opposed the marriage. I immediately guessed why. One evening, when we were both visiting her mother's house, she spoke on the subject, bemoaning Ethiopians' backwardness in attaching such importance to 'it' (she never mentioned the word *barya*). She told me her brother Daniel had had to leave a girl-friend because of 'it'. 'With us, it comes from our grandfather's mother's grandmother – so many generations ago!' As we were talking, her mother entered the room, frowned on hearing the topic of conversation and, after failing to make us change the topic of conversation, ordered her daughter to attend the baby.

Efrat, it seemed to me, had comes to terms with her *barya* status, especially since her loved-one had not rejected her on account of it. However her brother Daniel held a chip on his shoulder and the rejection by his former girlfriend has been hard to bear. I knew the girl in question. She told me that her present fiancée was not as good as Daniel, neither in looks nor intelligence (Daniel was a university student and her fiancée a garage mechanic). But her parents would have forbidden her to marry a *barya*. I sensed that irrespective of her parents' wishes, she herself did not want to bare such stigma: in particular, she did not want to give birth to *barya* children.

Given the apparently wide-spread former practice of masters sleeping with slave girls, many kin groups are 'mixed', with one or more legitimate lines and one or more slave lines. This is because the Beta Israel father often brought up his *barya* offspring together with his legitimate offspring. In several cases that I knew, the head of the family had had at least two legitimate non-*barya* wives and at least one *barya* concubine. This resulted in several branches of the family – two from non-*barya* women and one from a *barya* woman. The *barya* and non-*barya* branches of the family treat each other as kin. However, the difference is known to all, including small children, and I sensed that members of the slave line can be particularly sensitive to slights made to them by the legitimate lines.

Intermarriage remains rare between *barya* and non-*barya*. In Israel, a new opportunity has arisen for *barya* to increase their social standing: to marry a *farenj*, who as the Beta Israel love to say, are unaware of the difference. They love the fact that the *farenj*, who think of themselves as so superior, are actually marrying descendants of slaves.

While intermarriage is rare, *barya* mix socially in the neighbourhood with the non-*barya*. However, jokes and comments were frequently made on the subject, which suggests a lingering unease and constant awareness of otherness.

> A young woman: 'I am inviting my co-godmother for coffee, my *barya* co-godmother!'

> Shalom tries to convince me to miss a neighbourhood party to celebrate the birth of a child and go instead to a wedding with him: 'What do you want to go to a *barya*'s party for?' His wife interrupts him: 'Do not speak like that! They [*barya*] are people too! The *farenj* in this country say that we are black!'

Shalom wife's comments reveal the irony of the *barya* issue: while Ethiopian Jewish immigrants complain incessantly about racism directed at them, they perpetrate their own form of colour consciousness within the group. In fact, irrespective of *barya* status, skin-colour is one of the most important physical traits.

> Returning from a wedding, neighbours invariably ask: 'Is the bride beautiful?' to which the answer is, 'Yes! She is light (*kay*, lit: red)!' or, 'No! She is black (*tekur*)!'

> Ofir told me that his parents named him 'Worku', which means 'the golden one', because they were so happy to have a light-skinned baby.

> An angry mother to one of her darker-skinned children: 'Run off you black thing!' Another describing her daughters: 'Tsahay is beautiful but Lemlem is black.'

'Being together' as Ethiopians

All immigrants, despite their aspirations for integration, maintain communal organisations such as self-help groups, political lobbies and associations of friendship networks.[10] Ethiopian Israelis are no exception; they ignore their differences in order to 'be together' (*abran*) to celebrate, mourn and pray. They are the most united when they feel their dignity is under threat.

Mourning and Celebrations

The huge celebrations and mourning rituals which punctuate daily life epitomise the 'being together' of Ethiopian Jews in Israel. Guests and mourners – between five hundred and one thousand for weddings and often considerably more for funerals – cut across all the above mentioned divisions: *barya*, non-*barya*, new immigrants and veterans, people from different localities and different kin lines, traditional elders, educated elite, trendy youths, children, students, and people from Tigre and from Gondar. All together, with hardly any non-Ethiopians, they celebrate and mourn.

Celebrations

The main celebration for weddings, and increasingly Bar Mitzvot, are held in large hired halls (*oulam*). The format of the evening is always the same.[11] The event is compered by an Israeli DJ who plays Western disco, Israeli folk tunes and, with the help of an Ethiopian youngster, Ethiopian pop music (Amharic and Tigrinya). After greeting the hosts who stand in line at the entrance of the hall, guests sit at tables laden with drink and food (little dishes of oriental-style starters). Israeli waiters serve a four-course meal. In the middle of the meal, the wedding ceremony, conducted by an Israeli rabbi, takes place according to Jewish custom under a *chuppa*. As soon as the customary glass is broken, the close relatives of the couple leap forward and dance and clap, lifting the bride and groom high up on their shoulder and dance around the room. Sometimes, the timid couple are forced to kiss in mid-air to the delight of the company. While many guests start to leave around midnight, but young people and close relatives continue to dance and chat until five a.m.

The Israeli setting reinforces the 'Ethiopianess' of the proceedings, evident in the dancing, music, greetings, the presence of a large number of kin, and the near absence of non-Ethiopians. At the same time, *oulam* celebrations allow Ethiopian Jewish immigrants to become proud Israelis: while they are often in a position of subordination and dependency vis-à-vis other Israelis, on this occasion, they pay a lot of money and are masters of the occasion.

Lamenting the dead

Ethiopian Jews have maintained almost intact their mourning rituals during and after funerals in Israel, even if the burial itself is no longer in their hands. In common with other Jews, Beta Israel mourning rituals are elaborate. After the funeral, a week's wake is observed by close relatives of the deceased in the latter's home. Days and nights are spent sitting, chatting and wailing in ritualistic manner when visitors arrive. Special ritual commemoration ceremonies and 'crying' sessions (*lksaw*) take place on the third, seventh, and thirtieth day after the funeral. That on the seventh day is the most elaborate, with a large feast of meat and *injera* served to hundreds of mourners throughout the day. On each anniversary of the death, a commemorative gathering is held, either with a feast or just with *dabbo* (holy bread).[12]

> On the morning of the funeral, bus loads of Ethiopians and groups of Ethiopians on foot converge outside the house of mourning, usually in the concrete area under the apartment block. Soon, up to two thousand people are gathered. As a group of mourners approaches, people emit a low humming sound, specific to funerals, and some emit wails and loud cries sporadically. Men cross their hands on their heads. Women also do this or hold up the tip of their *gabi* (white cotton shawl) over their mouth. Faces are constricted with pain, and those that are not shedding tears, screw up their eyes to make out that they are. The group advances in very slow steps and waits for an appropriate time to make its entry.
>
> The scene at this point could be a stage-set. At the centre of the space, a throng of people, clad in their white *gabi*, lament and wail. They are arranged in concentric circles around chief mourners. The latter are engaged in the most extraordinary

movements, a veritable funeral dance. They sway to and fro, hopping from one foot to another, going around in a small circle at the centre of the mass of people. They make abrupt bodily gestures, extending their arms forward, bringing them back, raising them, bending low to the ground and making circular movements with their hands. Feet bob up and down and bodies sway from side to side. Facial expressions are trance-like, eyes gazing in space: chief mourners are possessed by grief. In a corner, sitting in a circle under their traditional Ethiopian umbrellas, the priests sing their funeral prayers. Around the fringes of the space, groups of relatives sit in silence or chat quietly.

When a new group of mourners arrive, the chief mourners extricate themselves from the centre of the lamenting mass. Facing the incoming group, the chief mourners continue their wails and gestures with renewed vigour. Across an area of empty space, the new arrivals, humming and crying, watch the chief mourners perform their funeral dance before they advance rapidly to greet them. Each newcomer clasps the shoulder of each chief mourner and the gesture is reciprocated.

All the while, the mass of mourners lament: two at a time, mourners take turns to compose verses about the deceased, singing them out aloud, verse by verse, accompanied by the cries and wails of the rest of the group. Two framed photos of the deceased circulate, and a mourner wishing to lament takes hold of one of them. The lamentations, as illustrated in Chapter Seven, recall positive and salient aspects of the deceased's life, highlight specific memories, invoke previously deceased relatives, and describe the pain and longing felt at the death of a loved-one.

Coming together under threat

Ethiopian Jewish immigrants are the most united when they feel 'threatened': when an individual Ethiopian is affronted, all Ethiopians are affected.

After the death of Tafra Bahata by police gunfire, Moshe Bahata, 38, the chairman of the Umbrella Organisation for Ethiopian Immigrants, was quoted in *Ha'aretz* daily newspaper (13/7/97): 'Tafra's family lost a dear son. But the pain is that of the entire Ethiopian community.'

The unity of Ethiopians was manifest in dazzling strength during the blood crisis in January 1996. Days after finding out that the blood which Ethiopians had donated to the Blood Bank was systematically and secretly thrown out for fear of HIV infection, Ethiopians staged a mass demonstration. Disregarding internal divisions, over 10,000 Ethiopian Jews gathered in front of the houses of Parliament in Jerusalem.[13] The pride Ethiopians derived from staging the mass demonstration suffused them for weeks.

> Lemlem: 'The violence at the demonstration was good! Even wrecking all those cars. Why did the *farenj* leave their cars there anyway? They knew there would be a demonstration that day, but they thought of Ethiopians are like this [she made a gesture of smallness, bringing her thumb and index finger close together]. Now they know: Ethiopians are not small!'

More than a decade earlier, Ethiopian Israelis had staged another large demonstration. In 1985, after just a few years in the country, young political activists and Beta Israel priests organised a month-long sit-in to protest the Rabbinate's demands for Beta Israel symbolic conversion on arrival in Israel. Their demands were partially met.[14]

While Ethiopian immigrants object to many aspects of their treatment by Israeli authorities, for instance in housing and education, the issues which provoke such strong reactions are those which directly threaten their sense of belonging. For the Beta Israel, the demand for religious conversion implied that they were not considered 'real Jews', and thus questioned the very basis of their legitimacy in Israel, the country of Jews. The blood incident suggested that they were rejected for lack of pure 'Jewish' blood and that Israelis did not want to mix their own blood with Ethiopian blood.

They respond by developing a discourse of 'us' versus 'them', and strengthen their communal ties amongst themselves. Already in the early eighties, Abbink[15] noted that: 'With this semi-conscious 'we' ethos, expressed in mutual interdependence and communal solidarity, the [Beta Israel] compensate for what they find missing in their relations with the other Israelis ...' As the following chapters show, they reaffirm their religious and cultural traditions to transform themselves from low status individuals to the purest and most culturally refined of all Jews.

Conclusion: a community of Ethiopians

Ethiopian Israelis' strong communal life, and its vital role in ensuring their well-being, is typical of immigrant groups throughout the world.[16]

> Markowitz describes the community that Soviet Jews have created in New York and concludes 'in coming together [at Russian evenings and eating at Russian restaurants] to express [their] commonalties, Soviet Jewish immigrants are able to integrate the reality of their American lives with the values and self-image they have developed in a different context, giving shape and substance to their emerging community'.[17]

This chapter has examined one of the strategies adopted to counter threats to Beta Israel sense of belonging: the strengthening of communal ties between Ethiopians. While suffering from a lack of respect from Israelis – recall the teenage shop assistant growling at an elder for taking too long to find the correct change for the payment – they can enjoy, within their own community, the old systems of hierarchy and respect.

Ethiopian Israelis' sense of 'togetherness' – their 'community' – is constituted as much by 'repositories of meaning'[18] as concrete social institutions. For, while Ethiopians ostentatiously come together in glory and pomp for celebrations and funerals, and in numerous ethnic political organisations, the sense of 'being together' is experienced with great delicacy in the minutiae of everyday interactions.

> A young Ethiopian Haifa University student meets for the first time an Ethiopian Jerusalem University student and tells her in a quiet respectful tone of voice about his Ethiopian class-mates, detailing the latter's genealogies, so that the Jerusalem student soon 'knows' them, and the two youngsters' sense of 'being together' as Ethiopian Jews in Israel is enforced.

10

Proud Ethiopians

Introduction

Mama Tsahay was upset with the way in which a group of Ethiopian Israeli teenagers described Ethiopia after returning from an organised trip there. She berated: 'They spoke only of poverty and about the large trees which grow over their ancestors' grave. Ethiopia is not like that! Maybe there is poverty in Ethiopia now, but there was none while we were there. The children [who made those disparaging comments] were brought up here in wealth and so they saw only poverty there. They know nothing of the richness of Ethiopia: the rain which comes on time, the flowers, the seeds ... just the smell of the leaves is enough to move your heart.'

In Israel, the Beta Israel reaffirm their cultural heritage with ardour: they not only uphold many Ethiopian cultural practices, but they also engage in a discourse which marks their Ethiopian customs as *better* and 'tougher' (*kebed*) than the traditions of other Israelis.

Given Israeli society's radically different set of cultural norms and the abruptness of the change in environment, the Beta Israel are extremely conscious of social and cultural traditions and of their transformations;[1] traditions are constantly discussed, quarrelled about and laughed over.

Fanta, an eighteen-year-old boy, was helping me to understand the plethora of names of a few close relatives. He laughed a lot as he recounted the half-dozen names by which each was known. His laughter was not embarrassment at a strange custom. He laughed rather at the 'quaintness' of the custom, as if, though still adhering to it, he could now see it from a foreigner's eyes, and found it touching.

Alemu entered Worku's house carrying his baby girl. Worku, noting his male friend taking on a female role, laughed and said: 'So you have become *farenj* now!'

The Beta Israel assert that their customs are 'tough' (*kebed*), especially in contrasts to the lax standards of their host society.

My friend Fantanesh: 'For Ethiopians, the funeral is very important. It is not so for the *farenj*. One day I went into the shop and David (the shop-owner) was looking bad, so I asked him: "Are you OK?" He said: "My mother died and the funeral is today." But he was selling! For us if a mother dies, "Oh! Oh!"' She mimicked the body gestures of lamenting, hopping and bending to the ground with her hands above her hand. 'We would never work on such a day! [It is highly unlikely that an Israeli would work on the day of his mother's funeral. Fantanesh was probably embellishing her story to strengthen her point.]'

Abba Birre described the prohibition of eating meat which has not been slaughtered by a Beta Israel. He commented: 'We would go for a week only eating chick peas – we would never eat meat with the Amhara. Our traditions are tough!'

Avi, a 22-year-old, told me that he had already spent NIS 5000 (approx. £1000) of his savings for the *ametat* ritual to mark the anniversary of his mother's death. He commented: 'Our customs are hard, and I want to do it right!'

A young woman laments the difficulty of finding a suitable marriage partner given the strictness of Beta Israel marriage rules: 'Ah, our traditions are so tough!'

To introduce the following account of Ethiopian customs and beliefs, I present the basic tenets of Beta Israel identity as I discovered them, learning to live in an Ethiopian household: learning to 'become Ethiopian'.

When I drank Ethiopian coffee, I was told 'You are Ethiopian' or 'You will become black just like an Ethiopian!' When I visited a new household and was not offered *injera* (Ethiopian sour pancake), my companions quickly interjected 'Give her food – she is like us, she eats *injera*!' When I behaved as a good daughter – cleaning the house, running errands, serving drinks to guests – and as a good neighbour – visiting the sick, the bereaved, and women who had given birth, and joining a credit society – I was told 'You are really one of us, you are just like an Ethiopian'. My poor attempts at Ethiopian dancing, eliciting many a laugh, were always praised and appreciated, as was my Amharic language. When I was able to use Amharic in a 'clever' way, playing on words, I evoked such delight that I was kissed and wished the birth of a son. My identity as a Jew was always stressed to new-comers to the household, and right up till my departure it was jokingly questioned because of my vegetarianism: not eating Beta Israel meat suggested to them that I may be Christian or Muslim [since in Ethiopia, people only eat meat from animals slaughtered by a co-religionist].

When, on the other hand, I asked a question of someone while he was eating, failed to fulfil a promise, spoke too openly about myself and others, or lost my temper, I was reprimanded and asked if I had not yet learned how to be Ethiopian. I was also constantly questioned and criticised for my failure to get married and bear children.

When, for fun, my adoptive father Abba Negusse and I wanted to make out that I really was Ethiopian, we would say that my British grandmother went to Gondar at 'the time of the Italians' and had an affair with Abba Negusse; I was therefore his illegitimate granddaughter. The whiteness of my skin was accounted for by intermarriage and the lack of sun in England.

From these personal anecdotes, the principal elements of Beta Israel identity can be drawn: proper social intercourse, observing a number of traditional practices, maintaining a 'Jewish' identity. But to be *really* Ethiopian, Ethiopian parentage, at least on one side, is required, hence the joke about my grandmother's travels in Ethiopia.

Speaking of honey: the land of Ethiopia

Ethiopians love to reminisce about their former country, adopting a soft sing-song tone of voice, interrupting their words with doleful nostalgic clicking sounds, sighs and a chorus of 'Ah, Ethiopia! Ah, our country!'

Proud Ethiopians

The Beta Israel are proud Ethiopians. They distance themselves from black Africans – to the point where they do not even think of

Ethiopia as part of Africa. Educated Ethiopian Israelis stress that their country was the only African country never to be fully colonised.

> A ten year-old Ethiopian Israeli boy asked me: 'Is Ethiopia far from Africa?' After I explained that Ethiopia is *in* Africa, his mother exclaimed: 'Ah! So *that* is why the *farenj* say that we come from Africa!'

> Looking at my photos of Ethiopian tribes-people, Ethiopian Israelis were quick to point out that these people were *not* Ethiopian.

Ethiopia is remembered both for its beautiful landscapes and its way of life.

> When my suitability to marry an Ethiopian was discussed, I was warned that I would need to bake *injera*, make *talla* (home-made barley brew) and milk the cows. These activities were positively and affectionately depicted, even if humorously.

> Fantanesh: 'Ethiopia – it is honey! The water in Ethiopia tasted delicious and sweet – even when it was full of mud!'

> Mesganow returned from Ethiopia in an ebullient mood. It was all so wonderful: 'Here there are just houses and concrete, but there, there is so much to see: grass, cows, donkey, sheep. It is so beautiful! And the air is so good.'

> Worku: 'The market there ... so much food, so much choice, you could never be short of anything!'

As Lisa Anteby[2] points out, Ethiopian Israelis love to indulge their reminiscences of Ethiopia by watching video-tapes of the homeland. For the most part, musical video-tapes – *azmari* singing against an Ethiopian backdrop and professional dancers performing in traditional costume – are watched. Alternatively, an Ethiopian drama is enjoyed. As videos are watched, appreciative sounds are made and the children urged to appreciate the beauty of the country's traditions.

Idealising the past

The past is depicted in an idealised version. Ethiopian Jewish immigrants paint a picture of the perfect life in Ethiopia, which they themselves increasingly believe in. They are in effect recreating their history. The elements which they stress are precisely those which they have lost in Israel.

> Aster, a young woman who was often ready to criticise 'backward' Ethiopian practices, sometimes became doleful as she remembered life in the village she left at sixteen: 'Oh Ethiopia! It was so fertile! ... Everyone was together there! Men came from the fields, me from school ... all together, we drank coffee. It was so good!' She spoke with long sighs and clasped her hands. 'We left all that for this. Just problems here!'

They claim to have been a strictly pious and ritually clean people, who were wealthy[3] and who were respected, if a little feared, by their neighbours. Wedding celebrations consisted of no less than seven days of uninterrupted feasting and dancing. Work was hard, but it was under their own control, and nothing stopped anyone taking time off when they felt like it. The air, climate, food and water was so healthy that one rarely got ill; when such a rare misfortune did occur, a cure was instantly found.

Occasionally, negative aspects of Ethiopia are mentioned: the country's material poverty (especially its paucity of factories and poor infrastructure), political instability, and the lack of education. Women in particular recall the difficulties of everyday life: carrying water and wood long distances, grinding grain on a stone mortar, washing clothes in the river, sowing seeds ... 'Here [in Israel]', women exclaim, 'you can find everything in the house and do everything by machine!' Ethiopian Israelis who have returned on visits to Ethiopia were visibly shocked by the poverty they saw. To the impoverished villagers that they used to be, the towns and roads of Ethiopia appeared impressive and wealthy. But to Israeli urban citizens, these same roads and towns now appear dilapidated and poverty-stricken. However, they still succeed in maintaining the image of an ideal past by explaining the current poverty in Ethiopia as a recent occurrence which began *after* they left. People often made comments such as 'the roads are so bad now, there are so many beggars on the streets – it was not like that when we were there!'

> Witness Alequa Ayelign: 'Now Ethiopia does not look up, her neck is bent. During the previous government, there was no drought, no famine, plenty of milk and butter and plenty of grain. There was lots of *talla* and *injera*, wherever one went. There were

not the problems that exist now ... everyone married according to the customs. There were no prostitutes, and unless a woman was married, she was not suspected of having sexual relations.'

Another tactic to dispel any image that the Beta Israel were poor in Ethiopia is to claim that Ethiopian poverty is predominantly found in towns, rather than in the villages where they used to live. For example, if a youngster comments on beggars he saw on the streets of Ethiopia in a TV documentary, he is soon assured that poverty is only an urban phenomenon: in the villages the grain is plentiful.

The Beta Israel: the decorated edge of the shawl

Ethiopia is presented in glowing terms: so too is the position of Beta Israel relative to their neighbours. The literature portrays Beta Israel as a low status group, a despised caste, subordinate to their Christian neighbours[4] but the Beta Israel prefer to remember, and present, a different image. Unless I probed, no-one mentioned that until the last twenty years, Beta Israel were not able to own land, and that they had to supplement their agricultural produce with craft work and blacksmithing, which are despised in the region. They choose instead to remember themselves as proud farmers and expert artisans, respected and much needed by their Amhara neighbours.[5]

> Mama Tsahay, after her outburst about the teenagers' false accounts of Ethiopia, proceeded to present a detailed picture of the Beta Israel as the elite group of the village, highly religious, economically vibrant, and so much liked and needed by their Christian neighbours that the latter begged them not to leave for Israel, and even suggested intermarriage as an incentive for them to stay.

> At coffee, an elder recounted that in Addis Abeba, a Christian Amhara had told him how difficult life would be for the Christian villagers, now that the Beta Israel had gone, since the latter were 'the decorated edge of the shawl' (*t'beb*) [i.e. the most precious and distinctive part of the traditional Ethiopian cotton shawl, *netala*]. The company repeated several times in delight 'the decorated fringe of the shawl!' '*Tbeb*' also means wisdom. It is used in the saying 'To fear the Lord is the beginning of all wisdom (*Igziabiheren mefrat yetbeb hullu mejemeria naw*).'[6]

Young Avi's father was killed by local Christians shortly before his family migrated to Israel. The Christians, Avi said, were angered by his father's decision to leave for Israel because he was the best blacksmith in the area and they needed him.

Ethiopian Israelis also refer at times to negative treatment received at the hands of their Christian neighbours. In particular, they recall being called names, such as 'kayla' and to be accused of possessing 'the evil eye' (buda) and inflicting supernatural harm to their Christian neighbours.[7] Harsh times with neighbours are recalled when Ethiopian Israelis want to identify with other Jews to emphasise their common experience of anti-Semitism. When they stress this side of their past, they are endorsing the prevalent rhetoric in Israel that the Israelis 'saved' and 'rescued' the Ethiopian Jews from persecution.

Ethiopian cultural traditions

The Beta Israel are extremely proud of the social norms and customs that they have inherited as Ethiopians.

Respect

The most frequent complaint about Israelis is their lack of respect for elders and their bad manners, manifest in loud voices, physical abruptness, and lack of formalised terms of address. Respect (kber) is fundamental to social intercourse: visiting others, speech, dress, greetings, and even the choice of marriage partners, are predicated on this notion. An attitude of respect is required in relations with persons senior in status. A junior should always defer to his seniors in matters of judgement, serve them, greet them as superiors, listen attentively when they speak, avoid contradicting them, and eat after them. The very name used to address an older person must show respect: it cannot be the same as the name used by that person's elders. Thus each person has at least two first names, one used by older persons, and the other by younger – in fact individuals tend to have at least four names, for a new relationship requires a new name, thus, for example, a young bride is given a new name by her in-laws.[8] The choice of marriage partner is influenced by many factors, but respect is said to be the key. If a potential marriage is found to contravene the marriage rules, it will be renounced 'out of respect' to the parents and relatives. Conversely, when two people marry without paying heed to the marriage rules, they are said to have shown 'no respect' and are universally disregarded as a consequence.

Foreign commentators can be critical of Ethiopian 'respect': 'Politeness is (like truth and love and much besides) a commodity to be traded with in Amhara society, and the courtesy that has charmed so many may not always be spontaneous and come from the heart. In many cases it is a mere pose and pretence.'[9] But what for Molvaer is '*mere* pose and pretence' is essential for an Ethiopian: the form of social interaction is as important as content.

Strength

Ethiopians pride themselves on their 'strong' (*kebed*) and steadfast nature. They can withstand deprivation and physical hardship:

> Alequa Ayelign: 'We are able to fight for up to eight days without water.'

Ethiopian Israelis contrast Ethiopian strength with Israeli weakness. A classic example of the latter provides the subject of a favourite Ethiopian anecdote:

> During *astasreyo* (the Day of Atonement, on which it is necessary to fast for one day) you hear ambulances all day coming to fetch the *farenj* who have fainted!

> Referring to the Israeli habit of taking an afternoon siesta, I was once told: 'You are like Ethiopians – you do not need to sleep in the middle of the day.'

Reserve and suspicion

Ethiopians do not 'speak the content of their stomach', hiding the truth to keep knowledge away from unwelcome ears. An Ethiopian does not automatically say where he has been, and sometimes gives a false answer when asked, just to avoid a nosy question even when he has nothing to hide. Lying, or saying, 'I do not know' when you do know, is acceptable social behaviour. A clever person (*gobaz*) discloses just what is strictly necessary. Molvaer is critical of Ethiopian reserve. He states that the Amhara want to keep life secret 'to an almost ridiculous extent'. He notes that they tell 'blatant lies' about quite harmless things, such as where they were the previous evening ('and nothing sinister was involved').[10]

I was often reprimanded by my Ethiopian hosts for being 'like a baby and saying everything'. 'Keep things in your tummy!' I was frequently told. Even a verbal expression of affection in public is uncomely behaviour for an adult.

Ethiopians rarely express extremes of emotion such as anger, passion and joy.

> In two years of fieldwork, I only witnessed the expression of anger three times – and not once from older Ethiopians. I found that the constant need to be cheerful and repress feelings of anger or depression was one of the most warring aspects of Ethiopian Israeli neighbourhood life. Once, an adoptive cousin purposefully upset me in front of the family and I stormed out of the room, slamming the door. Later, when peace was made, he told me gently that if I wanted to be 'like an Ethiopian', I should not behave like that. I had to concede that I had never witnessed an Ethiopian expressing his feelings so openly and publicly.

Given this high level of reserve, suspicion is viewed as a necessary and valued quality.[11] A clever person is one who doubts whatever is said to him, even by his own brother, and who can quickly evaluate the verity of a statement. 'To trust a man, you have to bury him first', goes the Amharic saying. Ethiopians often assume that a person is guilty of deceit until proven innocent.

> I asked Shlomo: 'Why are you always so quiet?' He replied: 'People are bad so I stay quiet!' I doubted the sincerity of the answer, but the point is that Shlomo implies a notion of inherent human 'badness', which he, being 'clever', does not want to be fooled by, and so he keeps his thoughts to himself.

> An Ethiopian proverb goes: '*Farenj*, like children, believe everything they are told.'[12]

The idea that people, especially the Israelis, are out to 'get you' is common. When an Ethiopian dies in hospital, for example, his relatives often explain the death as the result of 'killing' by the doctors, rather than their inability to save life. Ashkenazi[13] argues that Ethiopians operate with a concept of 'malevolent coincidence' – that personal ills are caused by an external agency, a spirit or a human, so that accusations of specific or vague nebulous intent by specific individuals or institutions accompany almost any adverse incident. He details a number of cases in which Ethiopian immigrants blamed welfare workers (whether Ethiopian or Israeli) for being 'the cause' of a rise in rent, or the accident of a child.

Gossip

As much as the qualities of reserve and suspicion are valued, gossip is criticised. This critique is all the more vehement given the fact that gossip is in fact rife in Ethiopian neighbourhoods.

> I accompanied a young girl to a secret appointment in hospital. She was terrified when we encountered an Ethiopian member of the hospital staff. I tried to reassure her: 'Don't worry, she won't tell anybody.' To which the response was: 'She is Ethiopian!'

> Abba Negusse spoke in a quiet tone of voice about a neighbour who had claimed to be in financial difficulty: 'Ha! She has plenty of money in the bank: NIS 8,000!' His nephew put his hands to his ears and said in a harsh tone of voice: 'Ah! do not speak about people like that!'

> A young friend of mine, newly wed, would rarely go out of her house for fear of what her neighbours would think and say about her 'wandering'.

Food: *injera* and meat

Abba Negusse describes the bewilderment of his first days in Israel: '... I did not know what anything was ... then the neighbours gave us *injera* and then we bought a *mugogo* (a large frying pan to make *injera*) and we made *injera* and thus we lived happily until today.'

At the end of my stay in Abba Negusse's home, I offered to leave him the furniture I had acquired: 'What good will these be to us, now that you will not be here to say 'How are you?' and to eat *injera* with?'

A funeral lament about a deceased former neighbour: 'Oh! My neighbour! We who ate together and drank together, how we cry when the other dies!'

Muluye told me that Worknesh complained that her husband 'eats' elsewhere all the time, which meant, Muluye added, that he has another woman.

These examples illustrate the symbolic importance of food, and *injera* in particular: in the first example, it is the symbol of a 'normal' life – only when *injera* was prepared and eaten in the home, could life in Israel begin in earnest; in the others, it symbolises pleasant co-habitation and sociability. Together with eating *injera*, the coffee ceremony is one of Ethiopians' most cherished customs and a basic requirement for proper sociability.[14]

Injera, a flat, sour, porous pancake, is the staple diet of Northern Ethiopia and remains that of Ethiopian Jewish immigrants in Israel. In Ethiopia, high-quality *injera* was made from *teff* (*eragrostis vulgare*) flour, which is cultivated in Northern Ethiopia. In Israel wheat flour is substituted, and the Beta Israel complain about the resulting decrease in nutritional value and taste. Over the last few years however, thanks to Israeli traders (both Ethiopian and non-Ethiopian) *teff* has become available, albeit at much higher cost than wheat flour, and most women prepare their batter with a least 10% *teff*. *Injera* with a higher portion of *teff* is served daily in affluent households, as well as to convalescents and to people possessed by spirits who demand *teff injera*.

An *injera* pancake is served with a stew called *wot*. *Wot* is made from vegetables, potatoes, pulses, meat or fish and is generally served in a small pile in the centre of an *injera* pancake. The dish is eaten by tearing a small piece of *injera* from the edge with the right hand and making a bite-sized parcel with a little *wot*. Meat *wot* is the preferred accompaniment to *injera*, and is a prerequisite for ceremonial occasions, such as receiving relatives from a distant town and celebrations. Meat *wot* for home use and vegetarian dishes are prepared by women in the kitchen, but meat *wot* for celebrations is prepared out of doors by men in large pots over make-shift fires.[15]

Conclusion

This chapter has explored a number of key markers of Ethiopian Israeli identity: the memories, customs and practices that the Beta Israel brought with them from Ethiopia. Ethiopian Jews are proud Ethiopians, they are also proud Jews. The next chapter turns to the purest and most authentic of all Jews.

11

The Purest of Jews

Introduction

Alequa Birre loved to speak about Ethiopian religious superiority over the *farenj*: 'There is no connection between the *datiim* (religious Jewish men, Hebrew) religion and ours. We take out the animal's *shulida* (biblically impure sciatic nerve); the *farenj*, however, do not slaughter meat properly; we therefore cannot eat their meat, but they can eat ours because we slaughter according to the Bible. All this [he details several purity laws] was the law given to us by Moses. When a baby girl was born the mother stayed in a hut alone for eighty days. Here women who have given birth stay at home! We follow it [the Bible]! They call this country 'Israel', but it is just a name, we are the true Israel! [He is making a pun on the name of the country 'Israel' and the name that Ethiopian Jews give themselves, which is also 'Israel', short for Beta Israel].'

Just as many Ethiopian Jews speak of the cultural traditions they brought with them from Ethiopia as "better" and "tougher" than Israeli practices, so too do they claim religious superiority compared to other Jews: they are the purest and most authentic Jews. Witnessing the predominantly secular character of Israel, where, with the exception of the religious minority, Israelis drive cars on the Sabbath, dress immodestly and generally fail to observe religious precepts, Ethiopian Jews assert that their religious practice is more intense and fervent, and lament the negative impact of immigration on their youngsters, who increasingly adopt lax standards of observance. They pride themselves on the nature of their religious belief and practice because it rests solely on the Orit,[1] unadulterated by later Rabbinical texts; while all other Jews dropped or substantially modified biblical purity laws and marriage rules, the Beta Israel proudly uphold the faith of their ancestors.[2]

Religious practice

Ethiopians also reaffirm their togetherness when they come together in religious observance. In Israel, different *edot* (lit.: community, Hebrew – a term used to denote Jews from the same country of origin) maintain their own regional variations, worship in their own synagogues and celebrate ab number of particular ethnic annual holidays.[3] Even though there is much internal variation in Judaism, Beta Israel practice and belief is markedly different from other Jewish groups. Unlike all other Diaspora Jewish communities, in Ethiopia, the Beta Israel did not pray in Hebrew and were unacquainted with post-Biblical Rabbinical writings and teachings. They did not therefore celebrate significant Jewish holidays such as Bar Mitzvot, *Hanukkah*, the *seder* night and *Purim*.[4]

Religious belief: the Bible

Abba Wuvie loved to write out verses from the Bible. He sat bent over the coffee table, writing in large letters with coloured pens into a large notebook. He never went to school but learned to read and write from priests. He often read the Bible to himself, his voice just audible above the sound of the TV.

Beta Israel religion is based on a strong belief in the Bible. The Bible is regarded as being the word of God handed to Moses, and its authenticity is never questioned. Religious practices and moral standpoints are legitimised by reference to the Bible. Thus Beta Israel purity laws, marriage rules, and codes of conduct are adopted because that is what is laid down in the Bible. Whenever I inquired about the difference between an Ethiopian and *farenj* practice, the former was always justified on Biblical grounds.

Qes Mulugeta defended the Ethiopian practice of prostration in the prayer house: 'The *farenj* do not prostate because they think that it is like Islam.' He then recounted the Biblical story of Daniel who continued to prostrate despite the king's orders and was thrown in the lion's den, but God protected him.

Ethiopians believe in the Bible *only*. Other Jews are criticised for their adherence to 'books written not by God but by men like you and me', that is Jewish texts such as rabbinical commentaries and the Talmud. The Beta Israel consider themselves to be the last 'true Jews' who follow strictly the scriptures of the Bible and unashamedly know nothing of subsequent Rabbinical writings. Many Ethiopian Jews, and elders in particular, have a detailed knowledge of aspects of the Bible, particularly eventful stories and genealogies, which they love to recount.

Ethiopians believe in a supreme Being, who exists 'out there' and watches over people in life and judges the deceased.[5] God is present in, and to a large extent determines, daily life. Daily speech is full of references to God such as 'what do I know? It is God who knows!', 'by the will of God!', 'thank God'. God is also evoked in all daily greetings: 'Hello' in Amharic means literally 'may He grant you health' (*tehna yistellin*).

> Alequa Birre, referring to election outcomes, said: 'It is God who votes.' His wife, always more moderate, corrected him: 'God provides the rain and we plant.'

Daily practice: prayers and Sabbath (qidame)

Religion is part of everyday life for Ethiopians: elders pray several times a day, religious blessings are uttered whenever coffee is served, the Sabbath is strictly observed by all adults and the majority of young people, regular fast days are observed, and God is invoked in daily speech, his wrath feared in daily behaviour. In addition to daily practice, in common with other Jews, the calendar is punctuated with religious holidays.[6]

The Prayer House

The Ethiopian house of prayer in Afula Tse'era is housed in the *moadon* (Hebrew).[7] The Beta Israel refer to it by a variety of names: *tsolet bet* (house of prayers), *mesgid* (Muslim prayer house), *bet knesset* (synagogue, Hebrew). The room is sparse: a small table is used for offerings of food and drink, a few dozen chairs are arranged in rows, Hebrew prayers books are displayed on a small shelf, and glasses are stored in a cupboard. Sabbath prayers take place at sundown on Friday, and early in the morning and at sundown on

Saturdays. Prayers are also held in the prayer-house on religious holidays and for mourning rituals.[8]

When people enter the prayer house, they prostrate, often with their hands and knees on the ground, taking their foreheads down towards the ground, ideally touching it. This gesture is repeated several times, ideally ten. The men sit in rows of chairs in the front of the room. The women occupy seats lining the wall, to the side of and behind the men.

Until the last month of my stay, the neighbourhood lacks a resident priest. As a result, prayers are spontaneous and individuals often recite their own prayers separately from one another. A learned man, who had undergone a few years of training as a *qes* (priest) in his youth chants prayers in Ge'ez, the Ethiopian liturgical language. Others follow him or read slowly from the Bible in Amharic. Young men rarely attend, but when they do, they tend to read from a Hebrew prayer book. Most men stand or sit in silence. Altogether a strange uncoordinated sound is produced. Old women sit or stand, their arms a little forward, with their open palms fluttering up and down gently. Younger women sit in silence or chat quietly. At specific points during the service, individuals prostrate themselves several times, or make body movements to that effect.

When priests visit for the Sabbath and when a priest, after much persistent requests, finally takes up residence in the neighbourhood, prayers become more formal. The priest(s) chant the service loudly in Ge'ez. The congregation remains silent most of the time, but participates by prostrating and saying 'amen' and occasionally a few verses at the appropriate moments. The atmosphere is generally pensive and solemn, albeit relaxed.

After about two hours, in the absence of a priest, a consensus emerges about when to bring the prayers to a close, and the most senior man present makes a closing blessing in Amharic. Then, with smiles on their faces, everyone stands and greets each other in both Amharic and Hebrew, saying '*shabbat shalom*' (peace on the Sabbath).

When the Saturday morning service is over, around eight am, the congregation chats merrily, drinking beer and eating home-made Sabbath bread which women donate. Whoever provided the crates of beer for the occasion goes forward and states the purpose of his offering: in memory of a deceased relative, the birth of a grandchild, the celebration of a Bar Mitzvah. Small blessings are made and, where appropriate condolences or felicitations, are offered. At this time, formal announcements (e.g. forthcoming meetings and organised trips) and discussions (e.g. strategies to get a resident priest) are sometimes held. Eventually, congregants go home in pairs and small groups to make blessings over the Sabbath bread at home and eat breakfast.

Judging from second-hand accounts and my visits to other neighbourhoods, the above description of Afula Tse'era's prayer house is typical of informal Ethiopian prayer houses throughout the country. In 1995, there were about three more formal Ethiopian synagogues, all of which are housed in purpose-built buildings. These follow normative Jewish practice more closely and combine standard Hebrew prayers and Ge'ez prayers.

Daily prayers and blessings

Older Ethiopians pray at regular intervals throughout the day, at dawn, dusk, and prior to consuming coffee, alcohol and food.

> Just visible in the first light of dawn, Abeba, a middle-aged woman, was standing by the window, draped in her white *gabi*, fluttering her outstretched palms. She was muttering a prayer in a supplicant sing-song tone. After a little persuasion, on another occasion, she let me tape her evening prayer: 'He who gave us a peaceful day, may he also give us a peaceful night. Our creator, our maker, Blessed be you. May you make us healthy. People who go out to work, may they return in peace and health. People who travel to other places, may they return peacefully. [This prayer was said in early March 1995, just after the spate of Hamas suicide bomb attacks on Jerusalem buses.] Do not bring us anything bad, only good.'

Alequa Birre blessed *Shavuot* (Harvest Festival, Hebrew), over *dabbo* (home-made bread) and coffee: 'Today it is *mayrar* (Harvest Festival). May you be healthy. May God send the bad away from us and bring the good closer. May God make this a place of wisdom and long life. May he make this a country of peace. May God give us more and bless us more. May God return us to the old days of our forefathers. May God widen the narrow road, return the lost way. May He bring a time when all can live according to the beliefs of their fathers. May God prevent us from eating more than we need and from becoming intoxicated. May God bless this country for our children, even after we have passed away. May God not take away the wealth that we now have … May [Archangel] Michael bless this day and give us food … It is said that anybody who has done good things will live longer … May God accept our offering.' Alequa Birre then recited a standard prayer in Ge'ez: 'Blessed be He the God of Israel, the God of Everything….'.

Sabbath: a Saturday affair

Abba Samagn: 'The main thing for us is *qidame, sanbat* (Saturday, Sabbath). God created the world and rested on the seventh day and said to Avraham, Yizhac, Yaacov and their children: 'I created the world, heaven and the earth and the animals, and on the seventh day I rested and so this is a sign between you and me.' This is an order from God, this is our sign.'

On the Sabbath, called '*qidame*' (lit: Saturday), the vast majority of Ethiopian Jews obey the Biblical prohibition on work, which means a ban on most daily activities such as cooking, driving, watching TV, writing, and so on.

Saturday morning at Fantanesh's. Once Fantanesh's husband Wuvie had returned from the prayer house, and most of the children, and visiting cousins had risen, everyone assembled around the coffee table. Wuvie cut the home-baked Sabbath bread, reciting standard prayers in Amharic, and we each received a small piece in our cupped hands.[9] The daughters started to prepare breakfast by crumbling the bread into a large bowl, adding home-made milk curd, salad and hot chilly sauce. Fantanesh stirred it all around, and served us in bowls. One of the daughters offered tea and instant coffee, made with hot water from the Sabbath hot plate.[10]

Saturday is a day to receive guests, visit neighbours and kin, and sleep. On warm days, the streets fill with small groups of Ethiopians, often dressed in their traditional Ethiopian clothes, making their neighbourhood tours. Chairs are brought out to the front garden for neighbours to sit, chat and laugh together. Youngsters climb over the school fence to play football on the school grounds. Towards the end of the afternoon, the older men congregate in the shade by the supermarket before making their way to the prayer house for closing prayers. When they come home, their wives have already got the TV on and the coffee ready. The next-door neighbours are invited and the Sabbath is ended over much needed coffee, often accompanied by popcorn which is a favourite coffee *kurs* (accompaniment for the coffee ceremony).

The Sabbath is spoken of with pleasure and anticipation during the rest of the week, a day to spend relaxing with kin and neighbours, a day to obey God and demonstrate religious fervour. The Sabbath is also a day in which all the hassles and difficulties of everyday life in Israel can be forgotten. On Saturday, the Beta Israel are not working in factories like Arabs: they are proud Jews and good Jews, like other observant Israelis.

A fundamental precept of Judaism is that the Sabbath, and all its prohibitions, starts an hour before sunset on Friday. In Beta Israel theory, Sabbath also starts just before sundown on Friday. However, in practice, the vast majority of households I got to know, did not obey Sabbath prohibitions until Friday evening well after sunset. In a household which is extremely strict on Saturday (in which for instance the elders do not drink hot drinks from the hot plate as this in their view goes against the spirit of Sabbath), on Friday evening, no Sabbath prayers are recited at home, no Sabbath candles are lit, the TV is on, food is prepared for the morrow, and the hot plate is switched on just before bed-time by the teenagers. I once even saw an Ethiopian priest drive to the prayer house on a Friday evening, a good half hour after the official start of the Sabbath. Some households made an effort to observe Sabbath prohibitions on Friday evening, but the timing was lax and Sabbath started when everyone had finished getting ready and the last cup of coffee had been drank, often at least two hours after sunset.

To my knowledge, no other ethnographer has noted Beta Israel laxity on Friday evenings. Soroff, in her study of Ethiopian Jewish religious practice asserts that the Sabbath began on Friday evening, in common with other Jews.[11] Her study was conducted amongst 1981 immigrants, and it is possible that these have had more time, and a greater desire, to adjust to the country's norms. Shelemay, who conducted research among Beta Israel priests in the early

1970s in Ethiopia, noted that Beta Israel continued to eat well after sun down on the eve of Yom Kippur, in effect starting the fast on Yom Kippur morning.[12] Another researcher, Schoenberger,[13] mentions that after the fire burnt out on Friday evening, the Beta Israel lit kerosene lamps. This confirms my observations that religious holidays – such as the Sabbath and Yom Kippur – in practice begin in earnest for most Beta Israel on the morning of the holy day, rather than at sundown the evening, which is the case for other Jews.

A number of young religious Ethiopian Jews, who studied in religious boarding schools, did follow standard Israeli practice and ceased all activities by the official start of Sabbath, one hour before sunset on Friday. For the older generation who wanted to follow Israeli-style practice, confusion often arose.

> An elderly woman in her sixties lit the Sabbath candles according to Jewish custom, covering her eyes. She recited a blessing in Amharic and asked her seventeen-year old nephew, the oldest male present, to cut the *dabbo*, but he refused. The two were negotiating cultures: she wanted to attempt Israeli style and therefore asked him, as a man, to cut the Sabbath bread; he, however, was respecting his aunt according to Ethiopian custom, whereby her seniority made her the rightful person to cut the bread.

Annual Holidays

I once asked old Abba Wuvie about Beta Israel religious traditions. He answered quoting God in direct speech: 'The main thing for us is *qidame, sanbat* (Sabbath) ... Second, 'I took you out of Egypt, away from Pharaoh, and you shall respect that wherever you live and eat *kitta* (unleavened bread) for seven days'. That is the *kitta ba'al* (Passover, lit: unleavened bread holiday). Third 'from the time that I took you out of Egypt, in the month of Nissan, seven months after is *brhan sereqa* (Ethiopian New Year, lit: the light appeared), it is a happy holiday and you will celebrate. We came out of the dark into the light, respect this.' Fourth, after ten days, there will be *astasreyo* (the Day of Atonement), a day on which we ask for forgiveness. It is like dropping the load we carry, we drop the sins we committed. From night till night, fast and praise God and make your body weak. Fifth, five days later it is *baal meselet, das ba'al* (the holiday of the tabernacles). Make a *das* (a temporary hut) in front of your house from leaves and be happy for eight days.'

From Abba Wuvie, we learn that the Beta Israel celebrated all the biblical holidays, but not the post-biblical holidays such as Hanukkah or Purim.[14] Older Beta Israel still mark certain traditional non-Jewish Ethiopian holidays, such as Ethiopian New Year and lunar holidays.

> On the morning of the twelfth of September, on the Ethiopian New Year, Abba Negusse was up by six am and came into my room to fetch his best white Ethiopian clothes from the cupboard. He told me to get up to drink coffee. I battled with the live chicken in the bathroom before joining the cheerful coffee session, with freshly prepared popcorn. I downed my glass of straight *araki* (an aniseed liquor, similar to Ouzo), which is served in the morning of special days. To my relief, Abba Negusse then slaughtered the chicken which his wife proceeded to prepare. I left with him to greet neighbours for the New Year.

Beta Israel's interpretation and practice of Jewish holidays remains at times quite different to that of their Israeli counterparts. For example, the Day of Atonement, traditionally the most sombre day in the Jewish calendar, was the most cheerful day in Afula Tse'era, and brought together in song and dance neighbours of all ages, with greater merriment than the most up-beat wedding. Shelemay[15] observed an *astasreyo* service in Ambover, near Gondar, in 1973 and, similarly, commented: 'For a Western Jew accustomed to sober observance on the day of repentance, the Beta Israel *astasreyo* was an extraordinary contrast.'

> The Day of Atonement, Wednesday 4th October 1995, Afula Tse'era. In the prayer house, in the morning, the atmosphere and prayers were similar to a normal prayer day, except that the attendance was quadrupled. In the afternoon, the mood changed totally. The entrance to the prayer-house was full of people, young and old and kids chatting joyfully. The number of teenagers was surprising given that they usually stay well clear of the prayer house. Inside, men, women, youngsters and children all together formed a large circle which moved slowly around. They sang a short refrain and danced rhythmically, a sort of hopping-cum-jumping, arms inter-linked. The singing was

interspersed with bouts of hissing and ululation. Everybody was smiling and laughing as they danced (unlike dancing at a wedding where facial expressions are often stone-rigid). In pairs, worshippers enter the circle and dance facing one another – old Abba Wuvie, the keepers of the Prayer House keys, enters the circle with his five-year-old grand-daughter, spinning round and round with huge smiles of their faces.

At about 4.30 p.m., people went home to fetch beer and home-made bread to break the fast. There was some argument as to what time this should be: some said five p.m., some six. In fact the fast was broken in the prayer house when everyone had reassembled with their offerings, at around 5.30 p.m. as the sun was setting.

Educated Ethiopians, who knew of the sombre style of the day in non-Ethiopian synagogues, accounted for the dancing and jumping as a method of fulfilling the alleged biblical commandment of exhausting oneself. The Day of Atonement was explained to me as a day when you forgive people with whom you have quarrelled. Most older Beta Israel spoke of a 'happy holiday'.

An old woman: 'On the seventh month, it is *astasreyo* (day of atonement). It is a holiday of joy (*yedessita ba'al*).'

A young woman: '*Astasreyo* was so wonderful in Ethiopia! My younger brothers, you would not believe it, fasted from the age of six and seven. All day was spent in the prayer house. The *zelen* (special chants for the day) were so beautiful as we danced like this, like that!'

Beta Israel purity practices

Purity laws

My neighbour Fantanesh and I made a deal: in exchange for English lessons for her children, she would give me lessons in Amharic language and Ethiopian customs. She selected the topic for our first lesson: purity practices. She told me vividly about the sojourn in the menstrual hut surrounded by a ring of stones, seven days during periods, forty days after the birth of a boy and eighty days after the birth of a girl. I asked whether the confinement was not lonely: 'It was nice. You were never alone – always two or three women, or otherwise a child would stay with you. My mother brought me food.'

Purity laws in Ethiopia

Beta Israel purity laws closely follow the biblical injunctions of Leviticus. In Ethiopia, women were segregated in a specially built 'hut of the curse' (*mergem gojo*) for seven days during their menstrual periods and for forty days after the birth of a boy and eighty after the birth of a girl.[16] Men who touched a corpse were unclean for seven days and those who had a wet dream were unclean for one day, and they had to remain outside their homes during this period. For both men and women, the end of the unclean period was marked by ritual immersion in the river, a thorough wash of clothes, and in some cases a purification ritual led by a priest.[17]

Contact with an impure person also caused impurity.[18] This led to a number of stringent rules, which, in former times, socially segregated the Beta Israel from their Christian and Muslim neighbours. The practice of *attenkugn* ('don't touch me!') precluded Beta Israel from touching non-Beta Israel. According to my informants, this practice ceased in the course of the twentieth century, although its symbolic value in terms of boundary maintenance remained important.[19] Indirect contact was also avoided, resulting in a prohibition on eating non-Beta Israel food. While these rules relaxed in modern times, the ban on eating meat from animals not slaughtered by a Beta Israel, remained in force.

Mama Tarikye: '... at weddings in Ethiopia the Christians were invited but they had their own tent set apart from ours and we did not touch them. We gave them a vat of *talla* (home-made alcoholic beverage) and a sheep for them to slaughter and prepare for their own consumption. We told them to take home whatever left-overs they had ... If my grandfather touched an Amhara, before entering the house, he would immerse himself into the river with all his clothes on. The reason for all these things is not that we hated the Amhara but because Amhara women do not stay out of the house during their menstrual periods. For us this is strictly forbidden. That is why we did not touch them.' Mama Tarikye subsequently explained that ritual prohibitions on contact with Amhara were slackened after the 'time of the Italians' (1935–1941).

Menstruation

In Israel, Ethiopian Jews continue to consider menstruating women 'unclean' (*erkus*). The latter do not have the option of secluding themselves away from home given the lack of available housing, but they do sleep separately from their husbands during this period – usually in one of the children's rooms. Menstruant women carry on with their daily household chores as normal, including cooking, although they don't prepare the holy bread for Sabbath nor host coffee ceremonies. They tend to avoid large scale celebrations, and if they do go, they remain at the peripheries so as not to pollute the communal space. Physical contact with priests and elders and entry into the prayer house is strictly forbidden.

> It took time and persuasion on the part of my adoptive father and closest neighbours for me to be allowed to enter the local prayer house, given that a few older men were concerned that I may defile the whole assembly by entering the premise 'unclean'.

Some priests avoid touching all women, in case one of them happens to be menstruating – but this behaviour is frowned upon by many Ethiopian Israelis as being too extreme and unsociable in Israel.

> A respected priest lives in a difficult situation, his wife Mama Tauvesh explained to me one day, because his three pubescent daughters live at home. The girls do not say when they have their periods so as not to embarrass him, but when they do, they avoid him, and refrain from cooking. To be on the safe side Mama Tauvesh always cooks the Sabbath bread and as far as possible she cooks the priest's *injera* herself, even if one of her daughter's has prepared the accompanying stew.

Post-partum women

According to Beta Israel tradition women must enter a period of seclusion after giving birth, forty days for a boy and eighty for a girl. In Israel, women try to mark the seclusion period as best they can.

They cannot go to a separate dwelling, since there are none available, and in any case they cannot abstain from their household duties for such long periods of time. They compromise. For three weeks, they shut themselves up in one of the children's bedrooms, going out only to the bathroom and to attend their post-natal appointments at the clinic. A close relative comes to look after the house, the family, and the continuous stream of guests who come to congratulate the mother. Close neighbours help too: one takes the other children to school, another brings cooked dishes, another encourages the husband to come and eat with them. After three weeks or so, the women begin to resume household duties, but they sleep separately from their husband for the full duration of the prescribed period.

> Balaynesh is ready to return home from hospital three days after the birth of Tarikye. Balaynesh's husband puts on his fine cloths and picks her up in a taxi to bring her home. She enters, and mindful of the pollution that she is causing in the house so soon after birth with no prior purification ceremony, she moves rapidly across the living room to the end bedroom, eyes to the ground. For three weeks, she barely ventures out of the room. Her sister-in-law came daily for a couple of hours to attend to household chores. Women from the whole neighbourhood and kin from other areas visited her constantly, always bringing plates of food and drink. All close neighbours and kin visited at least once to congratulate her and slip a twenty shekel note in the baby's cot.

Ethiopian Israelis differ in the amount of physical contact they have with post-partum women. In most cases, household members and close kin and neighbours enter the 'polluted' (*erkus*) woman's room to sit and chat with her. Some people kiss and touch her and the baby, while others enter without touching. Stricter men and women remain at the doorway of the room or avoid entering the house altogether. Such differing interpretations of 'proper behaviour' often result in confusion and embarrassment.

> A group of women are sitting and merrily chatting in the post-partum woman's room on the day of the baby boy's circumcision. Abba Abebe, a respected elder, keeper of the prayer house keys, comes to the entrance of the room. He pauses and then makes a step inwards. The women turn towards him in astonishment. He breaks the embarrassed silence in a good-

humored tone of voice: 'So, do you not get up when an old man enters the room?! Ah, this country!' He laughed and the women quickly rose, laughing shyly in their turn.

The women had been so stunned by his entry into the polluted room that they had failed to observe basic social custom – standing up when an elder enters the room. He deflected his embarrassment at the situation by laughing and by pointing to the women's breaking of the rules rather than to his own position, previously abhorrent and unthinkable, of being in close proximity to a polluted woman.

The period of seclusion is concluded with a purification ceremony and celebration called *cristenna*.[20]

> My God-daughter Tarikye was eighty days old. Close neighbours and kin were assembled in the living room. A large loaf of *dabbo* was on the table and alcoholic and soft drinks flowed. Abba Taddesse, the most senior elder present, conducted the purification ceremony. He complained that Tarikye's father had failed to obtain a bottle of blessed water from a priest, but he made do with a bottle of tap water. He told Tarikye's mother to sit outside with the baby, and there he stood facing East and blessed the water, blowing on the open bottle three or four times. He then sprinkled water on the mother and instructed her to smear the baby's lips with it. Next, he sprinkled water all around the house and on the guests. The host joked as he sprinkled the marital bedroom. 'Yes, here is the most important place!' Abba Taddesse returned to the living room and made a blessing over the bread, entreating God to make the baby girl a dutiful daughter and lead a fulfilled life as a married woman. The bread was consumed, and the merriment resumed. As guests departed, they each made a short blessing. The mother relished a plate of *injera* after her day of fasting.

The sprinkling of water, the blessing, and the mother's fast are the main ritual requirements of *cristenna*, but the celebration can vary from a small scale offering of beer and bread to a full-scale social event, at which hundreds of guests consume meat and drink, dance all night and make substantial financial contributions. In recent years, the lavish style celebration is increasingly becoming the norm. In Ethiopia, on the other hand, my informants told me, the celebration was more restrained, while the ritual was more elaborate and was conducted by a priest. In former times, the sacrifice of an animal was made, although, in recent years, this had largely been replaced by holy bread *dabbo*.

> I attended a traditional style *cristenna* ritual at the prayer house of the holiest Beta Israel of all, the *melukusse* (monk). He berated the young mother for failing to shave her head, checked whether she had fasted all day, and made her prostrate ten times while he chanted a blessing, then he sprinkled her and the baby with water that he had previously blessed. He gave the woman's father-in-law a bottle of this blessed water to purify the house.

Meat

The Beta Israel follow biblical injunctions with respect to meat. They eat cows, goats, sheep, chicken[21] and do not eat 'impure' meat such as pork and other animals proscribed in Leviticus. In addition, in Ethiopia, they only eat meat from animals slaughtered by Beta Israel, never consuming the meat of their Christian and Muslim neighbours.[22]

> When I asked people to explain the differences between Beta Israel and Amhara, they often started with 'we did not eat Amhara meat'.

Most Ethiopian Israelis above the age of thirty or so refuse to eat *farenj* meat – that is kosher Israeli meat, on sale in supermarkets and butchers and served in public places such as wedding halls. Instead, they go to great lengths to secure their own meat. A group of men go to a local kibbutz or Israeli Arab village. After much haggling, they purchase a live animal and slaughter it according to custom. The slaughter, based on my own observations, proceeds as follows. The slaughterer, a respected Beta Israel male, preferably a priest, sprinkles the knife and the animal with water and a blessing is recited. The head of the animal is turned to face East. The knife is sharpened and the throat slit in one go so that the animal dies instantly. The beast is skinned and the meat cut up into small bits. It is then washed thoroughly and salted so that all the 'impure' blood comes out. The sciatic nerve, which is considered impure, is removed. Transport is arranged – often with the Arabs from whom the animal was purchased – and the meat is taken home.

When the meat is for a celebration, the host organises a male work party to cut up and cook the meat in large vats on a make-shift fire out of doors. When the meat is for daily consumption, it is divided between the number of people who have contributed to its purchase, and each household cooks its share separately at home.

Ethiopians explain their refusal to eat *farenj* meat in the following ways:

– 'If you ask me why we do not eat *farenj* meat, it is because they do not slaughter it properly. The Rabbi himself does not kill the animal. Whites have a professional slaughterer who was trained, it is just his way of earning a living. They do not take out the *irm* (impure parts) such as the *shulida* (sciatic nerve), so we do not want to eat it.'

– 'My tummy cannot receive *farenj* meat. It smells like rubbish. It is like *baden* [an animal that died naturally without being killed, which is forbidden to eat].'

– 'If you want to eat meat, you must go to see the cattle with your own eyes, and if you like it you take it to be killed. Then you are impatient to eat the meat! What is this that they bring wrapped up, how can we know what it is? How can you trust what it says on the packet? It might even be forbidden meat [e.g. pork]!'

Refusal to eat *farenj* meat on account of its impurity compared to 'pure' Ethiopian meat (*yeEtiopiawi sega*) is a strong marker of Ethiopian Jewish pride. Given the primacy of sharing meat as a symbol of commensality and togetherness – as exemplified in the centrality of meat-eating for celebrations, mourning rituals and honouring guests – the refusal to eat *farenj* meat is all the more striking.

Marriage rules

Marriage rules are one of the first factors Ethiopian Jews mention to set Beta Israel apart from – and above – other Jews,[23] and the infringement of these rules is a great source of concern to elders and youngsters alike.

The rules

It is forbidden to marry within one's kin group or the kin group of one's ex-partner. This means that not only is marriage to blood relatives up to seven generations forbidden, but it is also forbidden to marry a blood relative up to seven generations of one's ex-partner.[24] There are no prohibitions on marrying in-laws such as the brother of one's sister's husband – the prohibition is on relatives of an ex-partner. Given the large size of the kin group and the small overall number of Beta Israel, the rule effectively excludes a large segment of the population, and finding a suitable marriage partner is a tough ordeal.

> Kanu was a young single mother of two, eager to remarry. She rarely met young men socially since it was improper for her to do so. But by word of mouth, it was known that she was single and a few men telephoned her. Over the course of a few months, she liked the sound of two of them, but one turned out to be a distant kin and the other a relation of her first husband.

> A young neighbour of mine, another single mother of two, explained her problem in finding a husband: 'It is hard to find a clean person. There must be no illness in the family, that is no *zar* spirits, no *barya* (slave descent), good behaviour and most importantly, no kin relation. One man came for me recently but his ex-wife is a relative of mine to five degrees. As for the next one, you won't believe it! Listen: My father has a half-brother, called Fantaun, from his mother's side. Fantaun has a half-brother, Melash, from his father's side. Now my suitor's ex-wife was my uncle Fantaun's niece, Melash's daughter. She is no relation of mine but she is my uncle's niece, and I too am his niece, so, for the sake of my uncle, we could not get married.'

Breaking marriage rules

Despite the strong rhetoric of marriage rules, marriage to kin does in fact occur frequently, both formerly in Ethiopia and now in Israel – albeit rarely between kin separated by less than four generations. People are reluctant to speak of such illicit marriages within their own kin group because these are a source of great shame. Even worse than breaking the kin group is marrying the ex-partner of a relative: '*Kewarsa zemdenna mefras yishalal*' ('breaking the kin bond is better than a brother/sister-in-law [uniting]').

Breaking the marriage rules is said to lead to ostracism from the kin group and the community as a whole.

One woman recounted an extreme case which took place in Ethiopia a few years earlier: the bridegroom had boiling water poured over him, and the couple fled to Asmara and were never heard of again, presumed to have emigrated to the USA.

Half-way through field-work, I noticed that within the kin groups I knew well, I had failed to meet several key individuals, particularly from the younger generation. Invariably, after wading through smoke-screens, the story was the same: the 'disappeared' had recently married a kin and therefore no longer attended celebrations and remained outside the visiting circles. Generally speaking, as years went by, such exclusion tended to slacken and the offending couples were eventually reintegrated into the circle of kin.

When a couple marry against Beta Israel rules, it is said that their offspring will be handicapped. Ethiopians can be particularly vociferous as they depict the likely malformations in the babies of such unions. Often, when we saw a handicapped child on TV, somebody would say 'that is the child of a kin marriage'. The Ethiopians loved to quote the statistics that Arab Israelis have more handicapped children than Jewish Israelis: they attribute this difference to the former's practice of marrying first cousins. When I referred to children of kin couples who appeared fully healthy, I was told 'just wait till these children's children and grandchildren are born!'

The worst effect of unions against the prescribed rules is that the kin group is said to break (*zemdenna farswal*). This has two far-reaching consequences: social relations are disrupted; and former relatives can now get married.

> Yinework, an educated man in his early forties, explains: 'When the kin bond breaks, kinship still exists in the flesh (*besega*), but the families have become in-laws (*gebi*). This means that from now on, people within the former kin group can get married because they are no longer kin. Second, they cannot continue their social relations as relatives. Before the marriage, they felt connected as relatives, but after, they become like strangers (*ba'ad*).' Yinework proceeded to give me a real life example within his own family. He drew a detailed family tree, starting five generations back at his grandfather's grandfather's siblings. He wrote in full the branches which led down to the two faulty individuals, showing how they are related to within five generations. Apparently, the mother of the bride had agreed to

the wedding because she claimed that the kin bond had already been broken in a previous generation. However when the father of the groom arrived in Israel (he was still in Ethiopia at the time of the wedding), he was very angry and has not spoken to his son since. The wedding was not celebrated in a wedding hall according to custom, but in private with just the couple, an Israeli rabbi and witnesses.

In a similar vein, Abba Negusse told me about a recent encounter with an ex-kin [the uncle of his niece's illicit husband]. 'He came to greet me, calling me "my uncle" and I said "what uncle? Is the kin relation not broken between us" He answered: "Ah! What can we do? The children did that!"' I asked Abba Negusse whether he would treat this man's children as his relatives: 'No, the kin relation is broken now.'

For the Beta Israel, the rationale behind the rules is straightforward:[25] 'The Bible says so'. In *Leviticus* an injunction forbids sexual relations with a first degree relative or in-law. As to the Beta Israel extension to seven generations, most people said that it is 'Ethiopian custom' (Amhara Christians observe the same marriage rules), while one priest pointed out the special religious significance of the number seven: God had created the world in seven days, and Passover has seven days. Marrying out of the kin group is explained by the Beta Israel in functional terms, as a means of increasing contacts and in-laws 'so that you could have people to stay with when you travel in distant villages'. The prohibition on marrying the ex-partner of a relative (or the relative of an ex-partner) was accounted for in terms of border maintenance. A common saying goes: 'Taking your sister-in-law is like crossing the border [between two neighbours' land]' (*'dember yeferesa warsa yewarsa and naw'*).

Ultimately, the importance attached to marriage rules is an extension and reinforcement of the ideology of 'being together' as kin. The sibling relationship is sacrosanct in Beta Israel kinship ideology[26] and incest between siblings is abhorrent. But kin are said to be 'like brothers and sisters'. So, given that a relative is considered to be a brother/sister, it is therefore deemed abhorrent to have sexual relations with him. This conclusion is supported by the fact that the marriage prohibition extents itself, albeit less rigidly, to any two people who are 'like brother and sister'. These include co-godparents and their children; *misie* (the person who accompanies the groom and bride during the marriage ceremony) and their children; and non-kin who grew up together, as close next door-neighbours or in the same household.

> Fantanesh explains: 'If two unrelated families, who are neighbours and are very close in their daily lives, so close that the children eat in each other's houses, then these children would not marry. They live close together, with much love, like brother and sister.'

The force of the ideology of 'being together' as kin also explains the dramatic consequences incurred when two relatives do marry. A union between two relatives is tantamount to increasing the social distance between the two individuals because it suggests that they are *not* like brother/sister. By extension it increases the distance between all the kin of the couple. But, given that it is impossible in Beta Israel ideology to have *distant* kin – relatives are 'like siblings' – it follows that if two relatives do marry, the kin bond must break. In other words, it is preferable to have no kin bond at all than a weak kin bond. The same logic applies to the ban on relatives of ex-partners – given that it is forbidden (in the Bible) to covet your wife's sister, the rule extends to all her relatives.

The infringement of Beta Israel marriage rules had a definite, and necessary, outcome. In its ideal formulation, Beta Israel marriage rules were not practicable in Ethiopia since there would not have been enough legitimate marriage partners given the potentially huge size of kin groups. The group of kin of any one individual, in theory at least, is enormous. Taking a conservative estimate of three surviving offspring, an individual would have 3^7 (three to the power seven), that is 2,187 relatives just within his/her generation on one parent's side. Given that the total population has not greater than a few dozen thousand individuals in modern times, the number of potential marriage partners would be exceedingly small. It is, ironically, defaulting couples which keep the whole system going. An illicit marriage not only provides the two individuals in question with marriage partners, but henceforth, all members of their kin groups are permitted to marry since the kin bond has been broken. In this way, each defaulting couple reduces dramatically the size of their respective kin groups and opens the way for countless further acceptable marriages, which without the union of the defaulting couple, would have been illicit. The proper functioning of the Beta Israel marriage system thus rests upon its infringement.

12

Subverting Negative Ascriptions

The previous chapters showed the ways in which the Beta Israel affirm their ethnic identity as Ethiopian Jews. This chapter turns first to another of their strategies to subvert negative ascriptions: speech. Next, it concludes this discussion on ethnic identity by showing how Ethiopian Jewish immigrants choose consciously the pace and nature of cultural change. These choices, I suggest, are made in accord with the exigencies of daily life and the balance sought between integration and maintenance of cultural identity.

The power of speech

Socialising difficulties

During a coffee session, Qes Ayelign recalls a story in which he had the last word over an Amhara: 'I was walking along a path near Ambover when an Amhara woman carrying a child approached from the opposite direction. Before our paths crossed, she covered her child's face. I said to her: "What are you afraid of?" The woman answered: "*Buda*! [evil eye]". I responded [to her fear of the child-eating *buda*-hyena]: "Why should I want to eat your dirty child?"' The coffee drinkers laughed heartily, delighted at Qes Ayelign's success at turning the tables round by making out that the Amhara child was not clean enough for him to consume!

Just as the Beta Israel sought to subvert Amhara derogatory discourse about them, they do the same with Israeli discourse. They use humour to socialise their difficulties and outwit the *farenj*, if only over a coffee session. After their experiences as deaf, ignorant, people, 'outside' (*bewuch*) – in town, at work, at the welfare office –

Beta Israel come home to a space in which they are *not* deaf. Their 'tough traditions' allow them to feel pride in the face of disparagement. Behaving like Ethiopians – e.g. quiet speech and respectful gestures and terms of address – also reinforces ties of kinship and neighbourhood. It allows social relations between Ethiopians to be framed and marked out as separate from those with the outside world of the *farenj*. In the sanctuary of the home, with characteristic humour and levity, Ethiopian Israelis recount recent humiliations and transform them into hilarity.[1]

> Over coffee, a young woman related: 'Abba Kabadu wanted to buy a light bulb. But he did not know what it was called in Hebrew and so he started to point up with his walking stick to the light in the shop. The shopkeeper thought that he was mad! I came in and explained what Abba Kabadu wanted, and then we could come home.' The coffee drinkers, including Abba Kabadu, all laughed.

> Etan: 'When my cousin was in the army, he worked as a mechanic for army vehicles. One day, two Israeli soldiers got stuck in a truck on the road and my cousin was sent out to help. When he arrived, they laughed at him: "What does a *kushi* (Hebrew: black, term of abuse) know about motor problems?!" My cousin immediately saw that they had simply run out of petrol. He told one of the soldiers to go to a petrol station down the road, without giving him a lift in his car. Then, when the soldier returned with the petrol, he told him to pour it into the tank and announced triumphantly: "Now you are ready to go!"'

The language of purity

In Ethiopia, Beta Israel purity laws not only maintained a separation from Christian and Muslim neighbours, it allowed Beta Israel to think of themselves as *superior* to the dominant society: rather than neighbours refusing to touch them on account of supernatural fears associated with despised crafts, it was the Beta Israel who refused contact with the Amhara. In Israel, the older generation resist attacks on their Judaism by once again developing a strong rhetoric of communal purity: not only are Beta Israel real Jews, they are the *best* Jews. The older generation only eat Beta Israel slaughtered meat because Israeli meat is 'impure'. While they have been unable to fully maintain in practice their female purity practices and marriage rules, they compensate by developing a powerful rhetorical discourse of purity.[2] When they speak about themselves, they describe their former purity laws and marriage rules in the present tense, as if these were still in practice today, as if there was no 'blood in the house',[3] and as if children were not marrying their relatives. Often, when I tried to raise a question about the form of ritual practice specifically in the present, such as *current* wedding or purity practices, my stress on the present was ignored and I was given a description which was situated in the past, i.e. how the practice used to be carried out in Ethiopia. In sum, even though Beta Israel are no longer 'pure' in practice, their strong discourse of purity allows them to maintain their self-image as the purest of all Jews, and thus subvert Israeli judgements on the inferior status of their religion.[4]

For the older generation, the discourse of purity achieves a further purpose. They are suffering from loss of authority with respect to the younger generation whom they see adopting *farenj* practices; the Beta Israel social order is in disarray. Talking *as if* nothing had changed helps them to negate this loss of control and overcome feelings of helplessness.

Usurping a religious ritual: a Bar Mitzvah celebration

While many Beta Israel have made little effort to adopt normative Jewish practices, they wholeheartedly celebrate Bar Mitzvah – the Jewish initiation rite which marks the thirteen-year-old boy's entry into adulthood, a practice unknown to them in Ethiopia.[5] A parallel initiation for girls, called 'Bat Mitzvah', is also now widely practiced. I was often told, 'We did not do Bar Mitzvah. At that age, we married our children!' Ethiopian Israelis have adopted the Bar Mitzvah ritual, only to usurp and use it – at least in speech – to replace a defunct, yet highly important practice, the parents' celebration of their teenage children's weddings.

The religious part of Bar Mitzvah is usually conducted at school; the family is barely involved and often fail to attend. New immigrants remain distinctly uncomfortable during Israeli-style ritual, such as during male circumcision, Bar Mitzvah, and prayers at the grave on day three, and absenteeism is therefore high. However, Ethiopian Israelis who have been in the country longer and whose sons do not attend boarding school, often arrange the religious aspect themselves.

Parents, siblings and close relatives of the Bar Mitzvah boy filled the Afula Tse'era Sephardi synagogue. They sat quietly, a little nervous, more observers than participants to the proceedings. After the service, the boy's parents laid on customary (Israeli) festive food on a large table in the synagogue hallway for all worshippers to share: soft drinks, kosher wine, sweets, biscuits, fruit. Then, the Ethiopians, together with a few non-Ethiopian neighbours, departed back to the hosts' home. A non-Ethiopian Israeli took the boy on his shoulders, as is customary, but he had to be asked to slow down as he walked too fast for the Ethiopians. Some younger Ethiopians tried to initiate the singing of appropriate Hebrew songs; older Ethiopians were willing to join in, and clapped their hands, but a feeling of unease overtook the group. Then some uncles began to sing celebratory Ethiopian songs, prancing about and clapping their hands, the women ululated and the mood lifted. At home, in the back garden, guests sat at long tables which were set with plates of food and drink. A blessing was made in Hebrew by a young man over the Israeli *chola* bread, and the Ethiopian *dabbo* was blessed in Amharic by an elder. Relatives ate large quantities of *injera* with meat stew and chatted all day. As soon as the Sabbath was over, they sang and danced to traditional Ethiopian tunes played on *masenko* (Ethiopian stringed instrument) and drums until the early hours of the morning.

The celebration of a Bar Mitzvah is a new ritual for the Beta Israel, yet there is a sense of continuity; it replaces the former practice of the parents' celebration of their child's wedding. This slippage is so clear-cut that many older Ethiopians speak of the Bar Mitzvah as a wedding (*surg*), and refer to the Bar Mitzvah boy as the bridegroom (*mushera*).

Abba Telahun: 'Bar Mitzvah is like a wedding. We pay for it, slaughter a cow and invite everybody. Later when the children get married, it is their affair. Bar Mitzvah, it means that we are marrying them.' Abba Telahun urged his son to look after himself during the week preceding his Bar Mitzvah celebration: 'Do not go into the sun [so as not to darken], you are the *mushera* (bridegroom)!'

Like the Ethiopian wedding, which often took place around the same age, the Bar Mitzvah marks the transition from childhood to adulthood. Parents explained to me that in Israel since their children organise their own weddings themselves, the Bar Mitzvah takes its place and becomes 'like a wedding'; it is their last chance to hold a big party for their child. The celebration felt very much like the parents' day, rather than the child's: people referred to 'Telahun's Bar Mitzvah', where Telahun was the father of the child, and during the celebration itself, parents always received more attention than their child. The Bar Mitzvah celebrations allow parents, for the last time, to take control over an important event in their child's life, to reassert their importance as parents now that so much of their child's life is beyond their understanding, let alone control. The ritual part of the Bar Mitzvah – the lighting of the candles and the prayers in the synagogue – is unfamiliar to them, and they let Israelis take control over these parts. It is the celebration which is important – an opportunity to reaffirm bonds with neighbours and kin, to display their ability to hold a large celebration, to recoup debts owed from their own donations at earlier celebrations, and to regain a sense of control over the lives of their children.

Racism as rhetoric

Another means of subverting a low image is to tackle it head-on. Ethiopians, especially the younger generation, frequently state with vehemence that Israelis are racist towards them and reject them. I was struck by the ardour and uniformity of such statements during the months following the January 1996 blood demonstration. Individuals who were relatively soft-spoken about Israeli attitudes suddenly adopted a militant rhetoric and it became 'fashionable', especially amongst the young, to deplore Israeli racism. In this mode of discourse, all problems faced by Ethiopians were the result of racism perpetrated by teachers, social workers, politicians, neighbours, officers in the army and health workers, sometimes with fatal consequences – soldiers and patients were said to die as a result of racist mistreatment.

A similar process of subversion is the propagation of 'alternative discourse' which contradicts official Israeli views.[6] For example, even educated Ethiopians, who read a daily newspaper, claimed in the media and in private that the policy of discarding Ethiopian blood signified that Israelis thought that AIDS was widespread amongst Ethiopian Israelis. Similarly, they misquoted medical findings to lower the true figures of Ethiopian HIV infection.

At one point during the crisis, many Ethiopians throughout the country were saying that only two Ethiopians were HIV infected. 'It was on the radio', they insisted. In fact, a study had found that among a certain number of high school Ethiopian students, two were infected, yet the Ethiopian presenter on the Amharic radio chat-show had broadcast the information in such a way that most Ethiopians interpreted it erroneously.

Kaplan provides a further example of the dissemination of 'alternative discourse': 'Long after the Israeli Chief Rabbinate had dropped its demand for ritual re-circumcision by Ethiopian immigrants, some Ethiopian activists continued to claim both verbally and in writing that the requirement to 'drop their pants' was still in force'.[7] Similarly, an elaborate discourse about *mikve* (ritual bath) has been elaborated. Many Ethiopians claim that Israelis want them to go to the *mikve* as a form of symbolic conversion.[8] Young educated Ethiopians, who know that this is not true, do not attempt to dispel such rumours.

> Qes Mulugeta told me that, out of all the Israelis, only Ethiopian women were required to go to the *mikve* before marriage. I told him that I had recently been with an Ethiopian bride-to-be to a *mikve* and that there were several other brides-to-be, none of whom were Ethiopian. He looked at me incredulously.

> I ask a young girl on the eve of her wedding to which *mikve* she is going to. She answers in a whisper: 'Shh! Not in front of my mother! She would be furious if she knew that I am going! She thinks it has to do with the conversion issue.'

Preoccupation with perceived racism achieves a number of results. First, it allows young people to ignore their personal difficulties and blame society for any difficulty experienced. Second, their heightened awareness and constant discussion of the racism they feel threatened by allows young people to perceived themselves 'above' it, cleverer than their aggressors. To overcome feelings of powerlessness and regain a sense of control, they propagate alternative knowledge and fight back, if only in words. As one woman said: 'Now that I am fighting about my feelings [of being discriminated against], I feel equal!' Finally, the strong rhetoric of racism creates a discourse which marks Ethiopians off as a group. For young people, the act of self-consciously calling themselves a low-status group provides a sense of unity and shared identity while they struggle to find their place in Israeli society, and fight their perceived 'low-status'.

Modeling themselves on Blacks in the USA, a number of young Ethiopian Israelis develop 'a Black oppositional identity which can serve protective functions. It allows for an anticipation of racism regardless of social, education or economic status and for defenses to be employed when faced with racism. It allows a youngster to find fault in the circumstances rather than in himself'.[9] Similarly, Ballard & Ballard argue that racial discrimination is a factor in preventing the successful 'Anglicisation' of young Sikhs: 'They know that however much they try to conform, they can never really be British because of the colour of their skin'. This feeling becomes the catalyst for the formation of an overt ethnic identity so that practices such as wearing a turban become 'a reaffirmation of ethnic pride in the face of white rejection'.[10]

Voluntary Deafness

The older generation feel that they are 'becoming deaf' in Israel, that they have become ignorant in their new homeland. It seems to me that 'becoming deaf' may be another strategy used to confront the difficulties of immigration. In Chapter Seven, I took the older generation's claims of 'deafness' at face value. But is the Ethiopians' much bemoaned 'deafness' purely an inevitable outcome of their cultural and educational background, or is there also a voluntary aspect to it? Ethiopians complain of their inability to communicate in Hebrew – but how hard are they trying to learn the language?

Based on my observations and Anteby's study of Ethiopian immigrants' Hebrew acquisition, I concluded that older Ethiopians did not put as much effort as they could have into learning Hebrew. This is surprising given the importance they attach to language and their frequent complaints about their 'deafness'. I never heard anyone express unwillingness to learn Hebrew, but a lack of overt statements does not preclude a more subtle form of resistance.

It was Workie, a young married mother of four, who alerted me to the possibility of a mild form of 'passive resistance'. I asked her why her husband's Hebrew was so poor compared to hers. She sighed and answered 'He does not like this country, he is not happy here'. Learning Hebrew is the first step for integration into Israeli society, which is why, given the ideology of the 'mixing of the exiles', the state lays such stress on Hebrew teaching. There is no better symbolic way to express dissatisfaction with Israel than to fail to learn Hebrew. Kaplan[11] came to the same conclusion: "Everyday resistance'[12] would suggest that many adult Ethiopians do not learn Hebrew because their 'failure' to do so insulates them against all the demands that Israeli society normally places on its citizens. Their lack of Hebrew provides them with a powerful symbolic barrier to the hostile penetration by outside forces into their lives.'

This form of resistance is limited because basic Hebrew is essential for Ethiopians who work and/or have children. Elders do not have such pressing daily requirements for Hebrew language and it is therefore no surprise that their Hebrew remains, other than few exceptions, minimal. The older a person is, the harder it is to learn a new language, but efforts were minimal despite this handicap. Anteby suggests that 'for those who hold a position as persons of learning in traditional society, [learning Hebrew] is not regarded as a means of maintaining authority.'[13] She points out that priests, generally the most literate members of the community, do not tend to learn Hebrew.[14] Clearly, if elders, particularly priests, were able to speak Hebrew as well as young people, their authority would be enhanced, or more precisely, their loss of authority would be lessened since they would 'have a mouth' in Israel. But, given their age and reduced contact with Israeli society, they cannot learn the new language in the same depth as young people, and however hard they tried, would remain deficient; they would always continue to speak 'like babies', and not as was their custom in Amharic, as artful masters of the language. Thus, precisely because of the importance given to language, they prefer to have no mouth at all for Hebrew, rather than a mouth which opens them to derision. Elders would rather cut themselves off completely from Hebrew than be deficient in it and become subordinate to their subordinates. Without Hebrew, they can remain masters within their universe, however archaic and reduced it becomes.

Elders, who are rarely able to express more than the most basic greetings in Hebrew, love to show off their words of Italian, which they remember from the time of the Italian occupation over fifty years ago. Speaking Italian is reminiscent of their time as proud soldiers; speaking in Hebrew reminds them of their status as 'deaf' babies.

Passive resistance is also practiced in other domains. The term '*dinkoro*' (deaf) denotes not only a lack of Hebrew, but also a general sense of ignorance in Israel. Just as many Ethiopians have resisted learning Hebrew, this general ignorance is also to an extent cultivated.

Ethiopian parents do not get involved in that part of their children's wedding preparations which take place in an Israeli hall. They say 'I am deaf, what do I know about weddings in this country?' Judging from their ease at learning new practices when they want to, I am convinced that they are well able to engage in wedding hall preparations if they choose to. Their avowed 'deafness' is a means of subliminally resisting the culture of Israeli weddings by total non-involvement. Instead, they occupy their thoughts and minds in setting up a local celebration for the wedding, which involves considerable planning and engagement with Israelis (e.g. hiring video equipment and a DJ, purchasing a cow and transporting the meat) for which they are not deaf.

This wedding example illustrates well the voluntary aspect of 'becoming deaf'. Adults choose what they want to become deaf about. The resultant 'deafness' (ignorance) is then a perfect excuse to withdraw from what they dislike. For example, they can be 'ignorant' about dates and times when it comes to appointments with unpleasant Israelis at the unemployment offices or the hospital, but they understand the Israeli calendar when they have a wedding celebration to attend. Likewise, they say that their deafness, and lack of Hebrew, prevents them from attending Israeli synagogues. Yet they are accustomed to prayers in a liturgical language (Ge'ez) which is not meant to be understood. The older generation also make little effort to adopt even basic Israeli Jewish custom, such as dipping apples in honey at Rosh-Hashanah, which requires no Hebrew whatsoever, or starting the observance of Sabbath restrictions before sundown on Friday. In my view, ignoring *farenj* religious practice is a reaction to the disrespect they experience in Israeli society.

Cultural change: balancing integration and ethnic identity

These last chapters have shown the tenacity with which Ethiopian Israelis hold onto their traditions, at least in discourse. Whilst a number of traditions have remained more or less identical to former practice (e.g. eating *injera* and mourning rituals), most have undergone considerable modification (e.g. female purity laws), and a minority have been totally abandoned (e.g. female circumcision) and new ones taken on (e.g. Bar Mitzvah). What factors influence how specific practices are modified[15]?

The Beta Israel are faced with a dilemma. On the one hand, they want to integrate into the country and merge with their fellow Jews. In this mind-set, they would seek to abandon Beta Israel customs, and drop their customary communal boundaries, and adopt host society ones as much as possible. On the other hand, integration comes at a price: to join the bottom of the socio-economic hierarchy and become 'deaf' (*dinkoro* lit.: ignorant, stupid). For abandoning traditional customs would in effect be admitting to an inferior form of Judaism, and vindicate the Rabbinate's questioning of their Jewish authenticity. Ethiopian Jews aspire towards integration on the one hand while resisting it on the other and these contradictory pulls are reflected in the way they are modifying their customs.

At one end of the spectrum, certain customs have barely been modified in Israel: preparing Ethiopian food, the coffee ritual, meat slaughtering, and mourning rituals (excluding the actual burial of the body which is no longer in Beta Israel hands). The older generation only eats meat from animals which they themselves have slaughtered according to Beta Israel custom. They refuse to eat meat from supermarkets, leave untouched Israeli wedding food dishes which contain meat and refuse to even try a falafel (a popular chick-pea-based fried patty) in case it contains meat 'in disguise'. Given that sharing meat is a central expression of commensality and that meat-eating for the Beta Israel is a prime ethnic marker (recall that Beta Israel did not eat Amhara meat), there is no better way to express ethnic separateness.

Resistance to integration is further apparent in the lack of interest in Israeli religious customs.[16] For example, the Beta Israel could have chosen to adopt Orthodox Jewish female purity practice to replace the loss of their own. According to Orthodox practice, when a married woman is menstruating she must not have any physical contact with her husband, and sleep apart from him for a minimum of seven days for her period plus five 'clean days'. Then she must go and immerse herself in a *mikve* (ritual bath) to become pure (*tahor*) once more. Other than young religious Ethiopian Israelis who were educated in religious boarding schools, Ethiopian Jews do not adopt this purity practice. Freeman[17] seeks to explain this with reference to the 'incongruent symbolism' between Beta Israel and Israeli purity practices. Beta Israel differentiate between the inside and outside of the house, and menstruant women were *outside* the house in Ethiopia. But the Orthodox practice allows women to be *inside* the house, which defeats the purpose of separation in the first place. Moreover, Beta Israel purification rituals took place in a flowing river while a *mikve* is a pool of still water which the Beta Israel consider unsuitable for purification.

While incongruent symbolism may account in part for the lack of adoption of Orthodox Jewish purity rituals, the reasons are more complex. Indeed, Ethiopian Israeli women do in fact observe seclusion within the home – after giving birth – which suggests that when they want to, they can modify the symbolism of their purity practices. The Beta Israel, it seems to me, reject the *mikve* for political reasons. The *mikve* is associated with the Rabbinical demands for Beta Israel to 'convert' to Judaism, and thus represents a direct assault on their religious and ethnic pride. As Kaplan & Rosen aptly put it: the Beta Israel have gone 'from purity to politics.'[18]

Most Ethiopian Jews make few compromises to adopt other normative Jewish religious practices. When I asked a priest whether he had learned Israeli religious practices, he said 'Why? What for?' According to him, his religious knowledge was in no way deficient, so what is there to learn? Holidays which were unknown to most Ethiopian Jews prior to migration are barely taken into account, and are celebrated only in so far as community workers or teenage children organise rituals and parties. When religious traditions conflict, most Ethiopian adults are reluctant to make concessions to the Israeli way.

> According to Beta Israel practice, the Sabbath is the holiest of holidays and grave illness or acute danger are the only legitimate excuses to desecrate it. When the day for the circumcision of a boy (the eighth day) falls on a Saturday, it is postponed until the day after.[19] For other Jews, however, circumcision on the eighth day is imperative, even if it falls on a Saturday. Rows erupt between young Ethiopian parents who wish to comply with the Israeli way, their parents, and Israeli circumcisers. The elders are usually forced to back down when the circumciser refuses to carry out the operation on the ninth day.

Younger Ethiopian Jews (sixteen to thirty age group) are more orientated towards integration. They do wish to maintain an Ethiopian identity in Israel but purity rituals are not their chosen ethnic markers. There are two reasons for this. First, *practicability* is key. Adherence to Beta Israel purity laws is not consistent with a modern urban Israeli lifestyle and full-time studies or employment. The younger generation eat Israeli meat at school and at the army and they feed it to their children, and Beta Israel female purity laws are impracticable for working women and students. Second, whilst young Ethiopian Jewish immigrants want to maintain Ethiopian ethnic identity, they also wish to integrate into Israeli society as much as possible. Beta Israel purity practices are unhelpful in this respect since they overemphasise the difference between Ethiopians and other Israelis, marking out the Beta Israel as essentially different. They choose instead ethnic traditions relating to food, music, sociability, and social etiquette which allow for the maintenance of ethnic distinctiveness and pride, while retaining an ideology of 'sameness to other Israelis'.[20]

Thus, while older immigrants still use the practice and rhetoric of purity as an identity marker, the younger generation is shifting its focus. For them, celebrations of life-events (e.g. circumcision, *cristenna*, *bar mitzvah*, and weddings) are becoming the prime ethnic marker. Celebrations have several advantages: they are practicable in the context of a modern Israeli lifestyle; they are isolated from everyday life; they display 'ethnic' colour to other Israelis; and they enable the strengthening of Ethiopian communal ties, allowing Ethiopian Jews to enact the central idiom of 'being together.' The energy and resources put into such events is phenomenal and as the Ethiopian standard of living increases, so do the size and 'glamour' of celebrations.

In sum, Ethiopian Jews are selecting a number of their former practices with which to cultivate ethnic pride and they choose for this purpose the practices that are compatible with Israeli lifestyle. Clearly, the specific practices chosen, and the extent to which they are modified, vary according to individuals, age-sets, and circumstances. But in all cases, the choice of ethnic custom depends on the balance sought between integration and cultural preservation, the requirements of daily life, and the symbolic significance of the practice in question.

Conclusion

My discussion of the changing customs has stressed the voluntary and deliberate nature of Beta Israel cultural change. It is the

Ethiopian Jewish immigrants themselves, as individuals and as a group, who decide what changes and how. The literature abounds with comparable cases of immigrants clearly *choosing* the nature and degree of change in the traditions that they imported from their homeland. Many political migrants, such as Chilean refugees in the USA, do not want to assimilate or identify with their host country because they see this as a betrayal of their political commitment to those left behind.[21] The Maltese in London present an opposite case. After the group was stigmatised for the criminal activities of a few people, the Maltese sought to deny their cultural heritage and to opt for cultural assimilation.[22]

Anwar paraphrases Muslim Pakistanis in Britain in the mid-1970s: 'They were in Britain to work and not change their culture.'[23] Pakistanis explicitly saw cultural change as a matter of choice, and they *chose* to maintain their native culture as much as possible within the constraints of their new environment. The Pakistanis had to adapt their behaviour – e.g. by accepting manual work and mixed-sex education – but they have not done so willingly and would revert to behaviour which they value more highly if and when they could.[24] Indeed, twenty years later, the social scientists' predictions were borne out: Pakistani corner shops, where the ideals of family business could be put into practice, had flourished, and several Muslim single-sex schools opened.

Similarly, it seems to me that Ethiopian Israelis will continue to evolve their customs and culture in a dynamic fashion. Depending on the relations with the host society, and the degree of integration sought, they will reinforce some elements of their 'tough' traditions, and put others aside. Culture is not lost or preserved in a passive way, but different aspects change in different ways, and the actors themselves play a large part in determining the nature of this change.[25] Peter Gow, concludes his study on a group of Amazonian Indians: 'The native people of the Bajo Urubamba do not see their ancestral cultures as heritable property, but as weapons for the defense of kinship. At particular times such weapons may be useless, and are dropped, to be picked up later when circumstances change ... Native people fear the loss of their children, not their culture.'[26] Cultural traditions are important only insofar as they are perceived to maintain the continuity of the group. For the Ethiopian Jews, such continuity may lie in full integration into the land of Jews – and if maintaining cultural traditions *threatens* such a future, then they are unhesitantly dropped: to the extent that continuity lies in upholding strong ethnic identity, their traditions are upheld and amplified. Their visions of cultural continuity are the subject of the next chapter.

13

The Homeland Postponed

Although the Beta Israel appreciate many aspect of their new country, the much dreamed-of homeland has been ultimately disappointing. The former homeland, on the other hand, is recreated with rich and positive imagery and it begins to rival the present one. But a return is not an option. Instead, the Beta Israel imagine a better place still: the homeland postponed.[1]

Beta Israel aspirations for the future comprise three principal visions: purity, integration, and maintenance of Ethiopian identity. Clearly, these visions are *not* distinct and individuals combine and recombine images from all three.

> Eli presented the perfect image of a young trendy Ethiopian: dreadlocks, a red-yellow-green striped cap and wrist-band, an earring, and a Bob Marley T-shirt. He explained the earring: 'In this country, the *farenj* boys wear one. I wear one to be like them so as to have better communication with them.' [Image of integration] 'And you know, they do not do it so much now, but in Ethiopia, some of the knowledgeable old men, the *awaki* (herbal doctors, men of knowledge) wore an earring – my grand-father who was a great man (*tillick saw*) wore one!' [respect for Beta Israel traditions, and implicitly, purity]. He paused and added: 'The wrist-band, the colours of the Ethiopian flag, is a memory of Ethiopia to remember where I am from' [maintenance of Ethiopian identity]. Eli's clothes and dreadlocks identify him with Rastafarianism, which, for him, connotes a proud Black identity.

Purity restored

A Beta Israel blessing on the occasion of a Bar Mitzvah: '... May He return us to the old days like those of our forefathers ... May

He bring us a time when everybody can live according to his beliefs and according to his forefathers.'

Traditionally-minded elders imagine a golden future in which 'tough traditions' and strict religion will return. Given that the Beta Israel practice of Judaism is more authentic, and 'purer', than that of other Israelis, when 'the time of religion', as one of my informants called it, returns, it will have an Ethiopian religious nature. Beta Israel purity laws and marriage rules will be respected, not just by the Beta Israel themselves, but by all Israelis.

The wife of a priest explained that, at present, while the country was being built, and there was war, and all Jews had not yet in-gathered, the country could not be clean (i.e. ritually clean). The time will arrive however when all Jews will in-gather and the Messiah will come. The country will then become clean and pure and everyone will once more use the menstrual hut [for the seclusion of menstrual women].

Trevisan Semi, who studied Ethiopian Jews who came in the first waves of immigration, also found that an image of future purity brought about by the advent of the Messiah helped to cope with present impurity. She notes that a number of her informants 'resolved the conflict [between their purity norms and Israeli ones] by deferring all problems until the advent of the Messiah. His authority would be supreme, superseding all earlier authorities, and he would institute fresh modes of purification.'[2] The belief amongst other groups of Israeli Jews that the Messiah will come after the in-gathering of the Jews, and that the temple will then be rebuilt and strict religious practices (such as sacrifice) re-instated,[3] lends legitimacy to Beta Israel images of a future 'pure' homeland.

While awaiting the complete restoration of purity practices, many Ethiopian Israelis try to uphold as much Beta Israel religion and purity as possible. A number of priests renew their calls for greater observance of purity laws in the present. The priest who settled in my neighbourhood with his pregnant wife wanted to petition the social services for a council house to be granted for the common use of the local Ethiopian population for impure women. More widespread, is the call for the construction of Ethiopian synagogues for prayer in Ge'ez (the Ethiopian liturgical language) according to Ethiopian custom. As of 1997, there were, to my knowledge, three designated Ethiopian synagogues, although many neighbourhoods used community centres, as make-shift synagogues.

However, even the strongest proponents of the restoration of Beta Israel religion and purity are uncertain about their advocacy; they are aware of the need, in the short term at least, for their children to adopt *farenj* Jewish practice.

> The following words from a priest illustrate the indecision, confusions and contradictions with respect to the desire for a religious future: 'We have many prayers in our language, called '*zamari*' (sung prayers). Our traditions are different – the *farenj* do it by the book (i.e. read). So we want to perform according to our customs. We have one synagogue in Beer Sheva, and one under construction in Kiryat Gat, and we want this in all places where Ethiopians live. There are synagogues for the others in each place – Moroccan, Yemeni. We are Black but we are 'Israel' [i.e. Beta Israel], we preserve the law ... the young people think 'let's forget the Ethiopian ways and pass over to *farenj* ways.' We old people, we don't know Hebrew, so we cannot pray in Hebrew and we continue to perform prayers as we used to. Old people stick to old ways. The young people go to boarding school and learn to speak with the *farenj*, and to pray with them. After a while, after this generation, all will go to Hebrew. [I ask at this point whether he thinks that this is a positive turn of events] Yes, it is good. The meaning is the same – in Amharic or in Hebrew, all prayers are for *Eloe* (the God of Israel) ... It is ending. We tell our children: 'We have a lot, the Torah, Dawit – learn these. This is our language.' We want it to stay – just like you speak to people in English, and you keep the language and the Russians speak and pray in Russian.'

The priest reassures me, and himself, that it is acceptable for his prayers to be forgotten in the next generation since Hebrew prayers are 'the same' as Amharic ones. In the same breath, he says that he wants to encourage children to learn prayers in Amharic so that they are *not* forgotten. From my personal knowledge of this man, the order of what he says is significant. He starts by stating the facts: Ethiopian synagogues are being built but at the same time the young people are learning prayers in Hebrew and will switch to these. When I ask him his opinion on this development, he starts by giving a positive answer as any polite Ethiopian would, and then he switches to his own view: he would like his prayers, and language, to survive.

The following argument between Abba Mucha and his wife also demonstrates the conflicts inherent in maintaining Ethiopian purity given Ethiopian Israeli aspirations for their children to integrate.

After Abba Mucha had explained why he considered Israeli meat impure, I asked if he minded his children eating it. He answered: 'We completely disapprove! They go off the whole time, to the army, to the boarding school. They have strong hunger and thirst and they eat what they are given. But, in Ethiopia, if you went out and stayed with the Amharas, even for a whole year, you did not eat any meat that you were given, you waited for your return home. The religion is tough! But here the kids, they eat meat wherever they find it. I feel very bad about this!' His wife interrupted: 'They [the children] must integrate with others, so we cannot tell them to follow this difficult religion of ours. Time has taken it away and until time brings it back, we cannot force our kids. When God wants to bring religion back, like it was before, he will do so.'

Even though the return to 'tough traditions' – to strict religion and purity – is projected into a mystical future, Ethiopian Jewish immigrants hold more concrete aspirations for the near future, and even the greatest of all complainers, Alequa Ayelign, expressed hope:

When I went to bid farewell to him, at the end of field-work, he told me: 'Now, without our rights [by which he means religious rights] and our own synagogues, we have so many problems. Come back to see us when we are more settled.'

Becoming *Farenj*

Introduction

A Beta Israel priest at a public inquiry about the blood scandal: 'This is our country and we want to defend the country together [with the other Israelis] and in times of peace we can live side by side. This is the justice that we want for our people.'

Abba Negusse imagines the future: 'Education, the army – that civilises the children. They are beginning to work in 'stundry' [Abba Negusse's way of pronouncing 'industry']. The children are being spread in every direction. They apply to the offices to work there. Now Ethiopians and Whites are getting married together ... Ethiopians will acquire knowledge from the Whites. They will travel around together. There will be [Ethiopian] sergeants, officers, generals ... The Ethiopians are learning! There was one Ethiopia and one Israel, but in the future we will all be together!'

Many visions of the future, such as those above, do not focus on the 'Ethiopianisation' of Israel, rather they stress integration of Ethiopian children and young people into Israeli society. Ethiopians will intermarry and have beautiful light-skinned babies. Ethiopians will get good jobs, own cars, and enjoy the same material wealth as their White neighbours. Young people will become good citizens of the country, and acquire the same status as the Whites.[4]

In such visions, the focus is placed on the young. First generation adult immigrants do not imagine themselves integrating into Israeli society. Many adults explicitly say that for them, life was better in Ethiopia, but they are happy to have come because the children can become educated, with all that education entails. For them, the future belongs to the children.

Aster, a young mother of two: 'When you see the children, you think "There is no limit for them."'

Mama Turuwork told me that the *farenj* suggested that she should learn (i.e. go to classes), but she feels that she cannot for she is too old. She wants her kids to learn: 'I tell them to work hard because I cannot learn. I would eat soil for my children to learn!'

Worku, a young man who is bitter that his parents did not send him to school as a child, plays affectionately with his two-year-old son. He looks over to me and, with a huge smile, says: 'He will go to University!'

I learned of these images and aspirations of the future as much from criticisms of the present as from overt aspirations: by complaining about what was not happening now, my informants were implicitly revealing what they would like to happen in the future. The following account, for example, a tirade against Israeli 'racism' reveals the nature a young woman's aspirations: to be accepted as a Jew, and learn her new country's traditions.

Efrat is a young mother who immigrated with cousins in 1984 at the age of sixteen. She was educated and trained in Israel and is now a 'modern' young woman: she works in a semi-skilled job, wears jeans, uses her Hebrew name and is generally outspoken. She was speaking to me shortly after the blood incident: 'There is a lot that we need to learn. For example, *farenj* religion because there are many religious holidays that we did not know in Ethiopia, or how to cook *farenj* food – these are the country's traditions. How can we learn these things? When they integrate us. But when we approach them, they refuse to accept us. So we feel very bad. This widens the gap for the future. If they do not accept us in good spirit, in the future we will be apart from each other. If it continues like this, it will deteriorate and the young people's love will decrease and those who are committed to sacrificing their life for the county will just go abroad. If I am not accepted as a Jew here, why should I stay?'

Visions of an Israeli future

Ethiopians want to become full citizens of Israel and they enjoy imagining the future which their Israeli children might enjoy.

Work

Abba Negusse often admired me because I was a person of knowledge and would therefore obtain a good job in an office or with the government. His children did not have good jobs, making jewellery (he mimicked a fiddling gesture with his hands), and building roads ('outside, under the sun'). Ayelign, his grandson, however, was studying hard and would get a good job.

The most potent and widespread image of the future is that of young well-educated Ethiopians working in 'good' jobs, which for Ethiopians means white collar occupations, such as clerical, management, teaching, and business. Ethiopians have resisted Israeli attempts to settle them in rural areas in agricultural communities (Hebrew: *moshav, kibbutz*) for the image of Ethiopian Jews working the land of Israel is not attractive to them. Working the land, which in their hierarchy of jobs is lowly, would keep them at the bottom of society.

The idiom of integration motivates educated young Ethiopian Israelis to work with other Ethiopians in Israel – as interpreters, social workers, housing advisors, and community workers. They say that they want Ethiopians to 'integrate' and they consider themselves in the best position to enhance the process.[5]

The vision of the well-integrated Ethiopian is manifest in the growing rise in national political aspirations. Already, the Israeli Parliament boasts an Ethiopian MP, who took office in 1995, just twelve years after immigrating.

> Fantaun, who works in a national bank, is an extremely bright and confident young man. He studied teacher training in Gondar and was a teacher in village schools before emigrating to Israel. He started working here with new immigrants before taking a degree in Social Work. After two years working as a social worker, he entered his present job. He finished his narrative with 'Maybe I will stand as an MP for the Likud party.'

Fantaun recounted his life story and finished with his political aspiration, as if this was a direct continuation, a realisable goal. On the one hand, there is no stronger image of integration: Fantaun sees a future for himself in parliament, at the heart of the Israeli system. On the other hand, Fantaun knows that were he to succeed in his ambition, he would do so *as an Ethiopian*, that is precisely by campaigning on his ethnic background. These two perspectives are not as contradictory as they seem, for two reasons. First, just as young Ethiopians want to work 'with Ethiopians' to help them integrate, so too do aspiring Ethiopian politicians know that they have to first battle on ethnic grounds in order to achieve their longer-term aspirations of integration. Second, Israel is a multi-ethnic country, where a large majority of the population classify themselves along ethnic lines;[6] thus forming an ethnic identity does not preclude forging a strong national identity as Israelis.

Lifestyle

Ethiopian Israelis love to imagine living in a materialist utopia. Ethiopians often complain about their current relative poverty, but in more positive moods, they often describe an idyllic future in which the house is filled with mod-cons, a good car is parked outside, and the house itself is well-built and large.

> Zemene, member of an elite family, was asking me to assess his two elder brothers' apartment in a relatively smart urban residential areas. 'Me though,' he exclaimed, 'I want a villa!'

Whenever I walked around town with Worku, he always stopped to admire various cars, and claimed that he too would own such a car one day.

Owning a spacious solid house is a potent aspiration. The house will be beautifully decorated, with large framed pictures, fake tapestries, and large framed photos of family members, including photos of deceased kin taken in Ethiopia which are touched up so that the traditional *gabi* is replaced with a suit and tie. A large display cabinet will exhibit a range of dishes, ornaments, and religious items, including a bible. Furniture will be plentiful and include a dining table, a sofa set, a bedroom set for adults, bunk beds for children, and a well equipped kitchen with a large fridge. All items will be frequently replaced so that they are always new. The house will be situated in a clean leafy quiet neighbourhood where the wind does not blow too hard and there is plenty of shade from the sun. There will be plenty of Ethiopian neighbours, but not exclusively Ethiopian so that 'integration' takes place.

Residents in the densely Ethiopian populated neighbourhood in which I lived sometimes complained: 'How can we integrate when so many Ethiopians live together?'

In the ideal future, Ethiopians will dress Israeli-style.

My neighbour Fantanesh began to prepare the celebration for her son's *bar mitzvah* months in advance. But a few days before the event she had still not decided what to wear. At first, she said she would wear her new Ethiopian dress. However, on the day, she had a last minute change of heart and rushed off to town to buy an outfit, which was several sizes too big and cost her over £100.

On her big day, Fantanesh wanted to wear the 'right' thing, which she decided was not an Ethiopian dress, however beautiful it may be, but an elaborate flowery oversized *farenj* outfit. When display is particularly important, such as for a son's *bar mitzvah*, Ethiopians choose Israeli dress; the vision in which Ethiopians are integrated into a modern Israeli lifestyle is yet again reaffirmed.

In the imagined Ethiopian-Israeli lifestyle, couples and families go on '*shirshir*' (trips) around the country and abroad.

One young friend of mine told me of her plans to take her son to see the country when he is older so that he can learn, and she added that going on a '*tiyul*' (trip, Hebrew) is what Israelis do with their children.

Religion

Young religious modernising Ethiopians envisage a religious future, Israeli style. These young Ethiopians have generally spent a few years in Israeli religious boarding schools and learned there religious practices such as the use of *tiphillin*, the wearing of a *kippa*, the appropriate prayers and blessings for everyday, Sabbath, and holidays, and how to maintain a *kosher* household. When they have children of their own, they want them to follow these practices. They teach them the Israeli version of religious practice rather than the Ethiopian one, even though they themselves may still continue elements of the latter, such as the semi-seclusion of post-partum women. Older Ethiopians who arrived in the early to mid-eighties also adopt a number of Israeli religious practices (such as lighting candles, and Hebrew blessings), and attend Israeli synagogue occasionally.[7]

Intermarriage with *farenj*

Intermarriage is at present uncommon, but widespread enough not to be an anomaly. I estimate from hearsay that in the mid-1990s, there were at least several dozen mixed couples. In-coming partners, both women and men, are drawn from all sections of Israeli society – Moroccan, Yemeni, English, American, and in one case I knew a Swedish (Christian) tourist.

Intermarriage has a positive image.

> My adoptive father often said that he would like his two unmarried children to marry *farenj*. And more than one person joked that he took me into his house with a view to his unmarried son ... One of his sons had a *farenj* girlfriend for a while and Abba Negusse was very sorry when their relationship broke up. When his last daughter eventually married an Ethiopian he lamented more than once 'I would have liked her to marry a *farenj*'.

Intermarriage is an ideal and the resulting light-skinned 'beautiful' children highly desirable. Intermarriage also accords with Zionist ideology, which Ethiopians share, of the mixing of Jews from all regions of the world so that the Jews truly become one people once again.

Fighting to integrate

Just after the blood crisis, a political leader made an impassioned speech to a gathering of Ethiopian Israelis: 'Many of our youth are disgusted. They want to leave this country. But I tell them: "No, you must stay! This is our homeland! Our ancestors dreamed of returning here for generations! This is our country, and we shall fight till we obtain the same status and rights as other Israelis!"'

The image of a homeland in which Ethiopians are integrated into society is not merely dreamed of, it is fought for. Young Ethiopians, especially the educated, choose to dedicate much of their energies to this 'fight'. Without 'fighting for their rights', Ethiopians, they maintain, will remain part of the 'poor, primitive' sector of Israeli society.

Solomon, who has aspirations to leave the country, said of the blood episode: 'It did not affect me. It just confirmed everything that I have always felt. In one way, it was good: it has made people, young people, who felt that they were part of things here, taking things for granted, realise where they stand in this country. It has made them realise that they must fight for whatever they want.'

Zemene, a young man who works in a government department to improve the standards of education for Ethiopians in boarding schools while completing his MA told me: 'We want to integrate but it is difficult. When an Ethiopian buys an apartment in a building, the Israeli neighbours leave. We have the ability to become part of Israeli society, but the gate is narrow. We need to fight, to demonstrate, to shout. I do not like that – we are a quiet people. But even if life in Ethiopia were better, I would not leave, I cannot, this is my homeland. We have many fights ahead for our rights in terms of religion. I am part of Israeli society and we must foster more social relations between them and us. They must learn our language and we theirs. We must build a bridge to cross.' And Zemene is a prime bridge builder. I met him for the first time while we were both canvassing for the first Ethiopian to be elected on the Labour list of MPs. He explained that he was a Likud supporter himself, but having an Ethiopian elected was so important to him that he took the day off work and overlooked party affiliations.

Maintaining Ethiopian identity

While the ideal of integration is nearly universal amongst Ethiopian Israelis, so too is the upholding of 'traditions' in order to remain proud Ethiopians in Israel. Although Zemene (see above) stresses integration, he sees it as a two way process: 'We must learn their language and they must learn ours,' he says, using the word language in the widest sense, as a symbol for 'way of life'. In other words, if Ethiopian Jews must accept Israeli ways, so too must Israelis accept theirs. He thus implies that he fully intends to hold onto 'our language'. His words were also meant literally: he hopes to write an Amharic language textbook in Hebrew for both young Ethiopian and non-Ethiopian Israelis.

To whatever extent Beta Israel fear the loss of their cultural traditions, most of them imagine a proud future in which essential features are upheld. Jan Abbink lists cultural elements which the first Ethiopian Jewish immigrants told him they would like to maintain in Israel: respect and honour for parents and elders, the style of personal behaviour, good and intensive family relations, the wedding and other family religious celebrations, Ethiopian dance, song and music, food, and language.[8]

> Efrat, a young modern woman, speaks of her future in Israel: 'I want to keep our traditions: holidays, *mesquerem* (national Ethiopian holiday), weddings, music, *injera* ...'

> Babu is a teenager. If he won the lotto, he would build a lot of bungalows together, and a swimming pool, near Tiberias, like a kibbutz, for his relatives to live together.

Babu's vision is modern yet it also upholds the primary Ethiopian idiom of 'being together' as kin.

Even when full integration is sought for, Ethiopians are keen that future generations should at least know Ethiopian customs, even if they hardly practice them.

My study was always received warmly when I portrayed it as an attempt to put on paper the richness of current Ethiopian traditions for the sake of future generations.

Young political activists speak of 'preserving our culture' and raise funds to establish cultural centres so that the young people 'will not forget'. After Stevie Wonder (the Black American pop star) came to visit Israel, an Ethiopian Jewish organisation wrote him a fund-raising letter: 'Although we are working hard to enable a successful integration into Israeli society, we are also extremely concerned that our African traditions should be kept alive in Israel ... [support is required for:]
- the creation of a cultural centre for the Ethiopian community
- the documentation of our cultural traditions by means of video and tape-recording
- the creation of a traditional folklore group to keep our Ethiopian musical traditions alive.'

A teenager came to spend his school vacation with his uncle, a Beta Israel priest, to learn, as he put it, 'the prayers in Ge'ez' so that Beta Israel religion will not be completely forgotten once the current generation of priests pass away.

Building tomb-stones

Ethiopian Israelis are increasingly pooling resources to send a couple of family members to Ethiopia to build tombstones (*ault*) on their ancestors' graves and a low wall around their former village's Jewish cemetery.

My neighbour Abba Mahari called me in to his house: 'My brother has returned from Ethiopia where he was making a tombstone for our parents. Come and watch the video he made!' The video began with the unmarked graveyard, and Abba Mahari pointed to the tree under which his father was buried. The following scenes showed the local villagers, which Abba Mahari's brother had hired, building a low stone wall around the cemetery. The next scenes depicted the construction of the cement gravestones. Images of a local *zamari* (a singer with the traditional stringed-instrument, *masenko*), onlookers and interviews of the travellers were interspersed throughout. Close-ups of the two completed tomb-stones were shown: large rectangular cement structures with dedications in both Hebrew and Amharic. The video ended with Abba Mahari's brother riding a White horse in the green hills.

Tombstone building, which requires a large input of time, energy and money, has become a central preoccupation for Ethiopian Jews. The practice embodies reverence for the past together with a long-term vision of the future: future generations will continue to live in Israel but will want to maintain their link to Ethiopia and in particular to their ancestors.

Witness Abba Mahari's comments: 'In Ethiopia, graves were marked with just a tree. How would the little ones,' he said pointing to his three year grandson, 'be able to visit the graves? Now, when he grows up and visits Ethiopia, he will be able to see his ancestor's grave.'

Israelis in Ethiopia

The growing orientation towards Ethiopia as Ethiopian Israelis is apparent in the increase in the trips to Ethiopia and in the form of these visits.

Worku is obsessed with buying a car. However, were he given the choice to buy a car or visit Ethiopia, he would chose the latter. He wants to go with a group of cousins, and rent a jeep to travel back to the village.

Every week, dozens of Beta Israel visit Ethiopia, especially during the temperate months of September and October.[9] The stated purposes are many-fold: for health reasons, to purchase goods, for a holiday, to help a relative who still awaits immigration, or to build tomb-stones. They rarely go to the villages, and those who do, make day trips by car. They complain that the distances are too long, the roads too muddy and that, coming from abroad, the locals will rob them. When they want to see former neighbours and give them cash donations, they summon them to the town hotel where they reside.

At the Ethiopia Hotel in Gondar, I met a group of four middle-aged Ethiopian Israeli men on a three-week trip to Ethiopia. They spent their days meandering around town, and enjoyed the bars in the evening. A couple went by car to a nearby village to meet some former neighbours. Others received former neighbours in their hotel rooms.

A woman recently returned from Ethiopia and I asked if she visited her former village. 'No', she said, 'it was raining and a car could not go.' I asked about walking. She changed tack: 'Who do I have there? All my relatives are here. I just have someone [a fictive kin] in Infraz [a local small town].'

This comment and many other similar ones suggest that Ethiopians do not choose to return to their village, to see the land or village for its own sake. Ethiopian Jews return to Ethiopia as modern Israelis: travelling to former distant villages by foot is too reminiscent of the life they have left behind and compromises their image of modernity.

Young people 'dream' of going to Ethiopia, and after the army, many of them set off. They say that they want to see their birthplace and make a video of it, although I hardly met any youths who actually did return to the natal village, unless the latter was easily accessible. One young woman, who arrived in Israel as an infant, was considering a special package deal, a two-week holiday to Ethiopia, costing $850, which takes you to see the 'interesting' areas, that is the tourist attractions. Mostly, they travel in groups of two to four relatives. They start in Addis, enjoying the night life and their new-found wealth. Then they fly to Gondar.[10] They hire cars to reach the accessible villages and visit distant relatives (from intermarriage with Christians) and Godparents, and give them cash-gifts. Visiting prostitutes is another priority for a number of Ethiopian Israelis on trips to Ethiopia.

Mesganow recently returned and although adamant that he himself had not visited a prostitute, explained the process: 'They pay very little money and get a beautiful virgin'. I asked about condoms, and he and his companions laughed further: 'The young people know about condoms, but the old people do not use them. They say: "The pleasure is for me, not for the rubber!"'

Young men frequently return from Ethiopia with bags full of cloth, spices, incense and jewelry, which they then sell to relatives and neighbours. The profits made cover the cost of the trip and sometimes yield a little extra.

These visits symbolise the attitudes of Ethiopian Israelis towards their 'Ethiopianness'. They uphold their Ethiopian heritage but at the same time they distance themselves from it, and return to Ethiopia not as poor villagers but as wealthy foreigners, who travel only by car, visit prostitutes, and stay in hotels. The tombstones and videos 'to show the children' demonstrate that they desire their children to maintain their Ethiopian identity, at least to the extent of knowing and being proud of their origin. Although the Ethiopian Israeli visitors do not want to *stay* in the villages, they want to visit and video them to show not the poverty there but the beauty of the landscape and the traditional way of life. They want to maintain a link with the past, but they want to sanitise this link, so that the future is built on a rich colourful past, and not a low status impoverished one. Moreover, it is on their return to Ethiopia, when they see quite how much their life has changed, that they feel the most Israeli.[11]

Business in Ethiopia

The desire to maintain a link with Ethiopia in the future was expressed by a few individuals who claim that they wish to work in Ethiopia. Some spoke of setting up Israeli businesses for imports and exports to Ethiopia. Relatively large-scale operations in the import of *teff* flour have begun. Idealist youths would like to do development work 'using the skills acquired in Israel to teach people in Ethiopia' while a few have ambitions to farm land using hired labourers and tractors.

> Worku claims to be a *'balarist'* (lit.: an owner of land rights) thanks to his Amhara father. He would like to claim these rights one day and maybe start a cow heard. He would continue to be based in Israel, albeit with extended trips to Ethiopia, and in his absence, the land and cows could be looked after by his Christian relatives. Before putting this plan in action, he must make some money in Israel. His brother has similar ambitions and he made me write a letter (in English) to the Israeli Ambassador in Ethiopia asking him to investigate some land in which Beta Israel have rights.

> Avi, a young twenty-two-year-old, wants to open a coffee shop in Addis Abeba. He would then divide his time between Ethiopia and Israel.

Solomon, one of the most successful young Ethiopians – a former officer in the army, top government jobs – whose disdain for Israel I quoted above, told me that he had already secured a World Bank loan and had rented seven million square meters of land in Tigre with his brother. He intended to move out there to cultivate cotton for export. I asked if his wife and new-born baby would accompany him. 'No', he said, 'it might not be healthy for the baby'. I teased him: 'Where were *you* born, Solomon?!' We laughed at our simultaneous realisation that you can never go back in life: Solomon, however much he hates Israel, was now Israeli and would not have a child of his grow up in Ethiopia.

Conclusion

In their current daily life, Ethiopians experience continual conflict between their desire to uphold Beta Israel custom and their desire to integrate. For example, young people wish to marry for love – Israeli-style – but they also want to obey traditional Beta Israel marriage rules; a priest experiences inner conflict between his wishes for young people to learn Israeli religious practice and for them to preserve Beta Israel Ge'ez prayers. In their ideal image of the future, such conflicts will dissolve and they will be able to lead full Israeli lifestyles whilst maintaining a degree of cultural heritage.[12] Israel is increasingly adopting a pluralist identity and all around them, Ethiopians witness other ethnic groups upholding customs from their countries of origin.[13] The ideal of being Israeli *and* Ethiopian is therefore a realistic goal. But for this, they have to win their battles for religious and cultural recognition. To cope with an uncertain present, Ethiopian Jewish immigrants create an ideal image of their past and imagine an ideal future in which all Israeli citizens will be colour-blind and the Beta Israel's cultural and religious heritage will feature prominently in the rich mosaic of Jewish ethnic traditions.

Conclusion

The prayers of generations of Beta Israel finally came true: they reached their long dreamed-of homeland, the land of Israel; they were soon to be disappointed.

Ethiopian Jews admire and appreciate their new country, both as the land of the Jews, to which they held a prior sense of belonging, and as a developed country, where their children can be educated and never go to bed hungry. They soon set up strong networks of kin and neighbours, tightly interwoven with continuous coffee drinking, visiting, telephone calls, mourning rituals, prayers, and celebrations. Unpleasant aspects of daily life – 'dirty' work in the factory, 'rude' Israelis, uncontrollable children – are cast aside or 'socialised' in the next round of coffee. The majority of Ethiopian young people have an overall positive attitude towards work, studies, and the army, and they strive for success in these fields.

However, in a manner reminiscent of their experience in Ethiopia, the Beta Israel have acquired low status in their new country. In Ethiopia, they were excluded from land ownership rights and were regarded by the dominant Amhara society as low status craftsmen and blacksmiths associated with evil, supernatural forces. In that milieu, they cultivated their ideology of difference and superiority by inverting Amhara ideology and casting the Amhara as the 'dirty' and 'polluting' group. Moreover, while the Amhara claimed Israelite descent, the Beta Israel described themselves as the 'true Israelites' and upheld a vision of a return to Jerusalem where they would live as equals amongst fellow Jews. Yet, after arriving in Jerusalem, they felt that once again they were despised; in their view, the authenticity of their Judaism was doubted, their skin was dark, and they came from a 'primitive' country. In addition, they soon found that their standard of living was lower than most of their non-Ethiopian fellow citizens, and their jobs less prestigious.

Therefore, while integration was a definite option, it came at a price: to join the bottom of the social and religious hierarchy.

The older generation assert that they have 'become deaf' in Israel: they are unable to become artful masters of the Hebrew language and feelings of ignorance overcome them when they face Israeli institutions. Whilst they can minimise such difficulties by restricting their use of the Hebrew language and their contact with other Israelis, the repercussions within Beta Israel society are harder to bear. Their 'deafness' reduces their status and authority in the eyes of their children and as the younger generation adopt new norms and gain greater relative control, old forms of hierarchy are jeopardised. Ethiopians feel that their ability to socialise their children according to either their own norms or those of the new society is being lost. This loss of control is epitomised by their inability to cure illness: while children wander off into an 'immoral haze', powerful medicine men are impotent to cure the troubles and tribulations within Beta Israel's tummies, heads and hearts.

However, Ethiopian Jewish immigrants do not let themselves be defeated by such feelings. They resist. They took to the streets in 1985 to protest against the Rabbinate's demands for conversions, and again, in 1996, against the policy of discarding their blood donations.

Ethiopian Jewish immigrants also resist in more indirect ways, which are no less powerful. When it suits them, older Beta Israel feign ignorance about the workings of Israeli society and make little effort to learn the Hebrew language, the prime symbol of integration into Israeli society. They also refuse to adopt normative religious practices and instead uphold Beta Israel religious rituals as far as possible. For the older generation, better to remain proud Beta Israel than struggle to become second-class Ethiopian Israelis devalued in the eyes of society at large, especially in those of their own children.

Ethiopian Israelis develop powerful counter-rhetoric to challenge dominant society's negative ascriptions as they understand them. They cast themselves as the 'true Jews', who unlike all other Jews, respect the laws of Moses as set out in the Bible, unadulterated by later words 'written by men'. Whilst purity laws – including marriage rules – are much modified in practice, older Ethiopians often speak of them as if they were unchanging. As in Ethiopia, their discourse on purity allows Beta Israel to imagine themselves as superior to the mainstream. Indeed, they go so far as to refuse meat slaughtered by other Israelis, even when it is labelled 'kosher'.

Young people are less concerned with purity and develop instead a rhetoric of race. While they might have tried to ignore or downplay manifestations of Israeli 'racism', they chose instead to exaggerate and fight against it. This is a means of taking control of the situation, making themselves feel 'cleverer' than Israelis who are unable to dupe them. A minority of young people go further by adopting counter-cultures modelled either on Evangelical Christianity or on American Black culture. In this way, they challenge the prevalent assumptions of what it is to be an Israeli.

Given the Israeli ideology of the 'fusion of the exiles', which assumes assimilation of incoming groups, another strategy for the Beta Israel to overcome their marginality is to consciously develop tight communal bonds and strong ethnic pride. In a continuous round of celebrations, Ethiopian Jews of all ages enact the prime idiom of 'being together'. In this comforting and warm milieu, Beta Israel's low status is irrelevant as they celebrate – or mourn – as proud Ethiopian Jews. Such occasions are communally financed by donations which bind the group together in a never-ending cycle of debt repayment. Weddings are apt manifestations of the dual orientation of Ethiopian Israelis, for the wedding starts Israeli style, in an Israeli Hall, and with the serving of Israeli food, including meat. But here, Ethiopians are not lavatory cleaners, they are masters of the occasion, paying non-Ethiopian staff to serve them, and they spend lavish sums of money. At the same time, these occasions are eminently 'Ethiopian' in form and content, with Ethiopian music, dance, social etiquette and a week-end-long feast at home afterwards, for which a cow is slaughtered according to Beta Israel custom.

Finally, Ethiopian Jewish immigrants seek to overcome the difficulties of the present by creating a perfect past and an ideal future. In what I have called the 'homeland postponed', all Jews will be united in a colour-blind world of material plenty and purity; this is the vision which sustains Beta Israel strength in the face of adversity and enables them to assert 'We are well in Israel'.

Notes

1 Introduction

1. French orientalist Joseph Halevy describing in 1869 an event which took place between 1862 and 1864 (quoted in Rosen 1986: 75).
2. Joseph Halevy travelled to Abyssinia in 1867 on behalf of the Alliance Israelite Universelle of Paris to report on the situation of the 'Black Jews'. Jewish attention to the Beta Israel was ironically fomented by Protestant missionaries, namely the London Society for Promoting Christianity Among the Jews, which established a mission amongst the Beta Israel in 1860 (Seeman 1997, Kaplan 1992). James Bruce was the first Western scholar and explorer to write about the Beta Israel (Bruce 1790).
3. I am grateful for the encouragement and advice given to me at that time by Steven Kaplan, Shalva Weil, Alex Weingrod, Malka Shabtay, Michael Ashkenazi, Chaim Rosen, and Gadi Ben Ezer.
4. Dani Budowski was particularly friendly and helpful, and introduced me to a number of English-speaking Ethiopians.
5. Addissu Messele and Addis Aklum were most helpful and welcoming to me.
6. Appleyard (1995)
7. Benita et al (1994)
8. I subsequently employed English-speaking Ethiopian Israelis to help me transcribe difficult sections of the tapes into English.
9. Ben-Rafael & Sharot (1991: 27–8)
10. Ben-Rafael & Sharot (1991: 232)
11. Several social scientists have pointed out that the term 'Orientals' has little explanatory value given that so-called Orientals do not think of themselves as such (Loeb 1985: 213, Lewis A. 1985: 151, Gilad 1989: 240–1).
12. Ben-Rafael & Sharot (1991: 24–35)
13. Cohen (1972: 95)
14. Ben-Rafael & Sharot (1991: 31), Gonen (1985)
15. Many societies have experienced such a rise in ethnicity. Obvious examples include the former Yugoslavia (Banks 1996), religious fundamentalism in the Middle East (Jewish and Muslim), and

immigrant groups in Israel, USA and in New Zealand, where Leckie (1995: 159) notes an 'increased institutionalisation and overt expressions of ethnic and religious identity among South Asians'.
16. Ben-Rafael & Sharot (1991: 32)
17. Kaplan & Rosen (1993: 35)
18. See Halper (1987) for a powerful critique of recent government policies on the integration of new immigrants.
19. For an excellent review of the academic study of immigrants in Israel, see Alex Weingrod's account in Weingrod (1985).
20. Frankenstein (1953: 33)
21. Frankenstein (1953: 33)
22. As Weingrod (1985) points out, the titles of these studies reveal their theoretical macro-social and comparative orientation: *Israel: Group Relations in a New Society* (Weingrod 1965), *Social Mobility in Israeli Society* (Lissak 1969), and *Israel: Pluralism and Conflict* (Smooha 1978).
23. Patai (1953: 334), see Weingrod (1985)
24. E.g. Weingrod (1966), Goldberg (1972)
25. Deshen & Shokeid (1974)
26. Eisenstadt (1974: 15–6)
27. Deschen & Shokeid (1974)
28. For example Goldberg (1984); Lewis (1985, 1989).
29. Avruch (1981)
30. Avruch (1981: 172)
31. Lewis (1985, 1989)
32. Gilad (1989)
33. Gilad (1989)
34. Kaplan (1995: 20)
35. For a comprehensive discussion on the group's collective designation, see Kaplan (1992: 53–78), Quirin (1992: 11–27), Weil (1995).
36. Ge'ez is the Ethiopian liturgical language
37. Quirin (1992: 11–27)
38. Seeman (1997: 3)
39. Weil (1995)
40. Seeman (1997) hyphenates the term: Ethiopian-Israelis
41. See Salamon & Kaplan (1998) for a comprehensive bibliography.
42. Leslau (1951, 1957)
43. Krempel (1972), Schoenberger (1975), Kahana (1977)
44. Abbink (1984: 402)
45. Schoenberger (1975)
46. Shelemay (1989)
47. Salamon (1994)
48. Levine (1965)
49. Hoben (1973)
50. Messing (1956)
51. Gamst (1969)
52. Pankhurst H. (1992)
53. Pankhurst A. (1992)
54. I borrow this term from Parfitt (1995).

55 I have been unable to access the literature in Hebrew on the Beta Israel – please see Salamon & Kaplan (1998) for a comprehensive up-to-date bibliography of the Hebrew material.
56 *Pe'ammim* 22, 33, 58 (Hebrew); *Les Temps Modernes*, n. 474, 1986; *Israel Social Science Research* 1985 (later to become published in a collection, Weingrod and Ashkenazi 1987), and *Israel Social Science Research* vol. 10, n.2, 1995.
57 Conference papers have been published: Kaplan et al. (1995); Parfitt (1999)
58 Kaplan & Ben Dor (1988); Salamon & Kaplan (1998); see also Weil (1989)
59 Weistheimer & Kaplan (1992), Wagaw (1993), Friedmann & Santamaria (1994), Waldman (1985)
60 From an ethnographic point of view, I have appreciated the most the works of Lisa Anteby, Don Seeman, Chaim Rosen and Hagar Salamon.
61 For an excellent discussion of these contradictions in the case of Yemeni immigrant women in Israel, see Gilad (1989).
62 Kaplan (1995: 19–20)
63 Kaplan notes that by 1992, there were already four books devoted to the subject of Ethiopian Judaism, but that all of them say more about the authors' religious Zionism than they do about Ethiopian Jews (Kaplan 1995).
64 Waldman (1985: 25)
65 Asians in Britain, for example, maintain strong links and orientation to their home country, even if they are firmly anchored in Britain. They thus have a comparison and reference point in India as they develop their Asian British identity (Shaw 1988). Like the Ethiopian Jews, Jews from Yemen, Iraq and Libya, were transplanted in their quasi-entirety to Israel (Gilad 1989: 215). They are therefore left with no reference group back home and have to recreate themselves anew in the host country. While the Beta Israel do still have compatriots awaiting emigration in Addis Abeba (I thank Lisa Anteby for drawing my attention to this point), Jewish life as they knew it, has all but disappeared in Ethiopia.
66 Anwar (1979: ix), also Margolis (1994), Jeffery (1976)
67 American Jewish migrants to Israel present an extreme case of the ideological basis for migrating for they were not suffering political oppression and migration to Israel usually entailed a decrease in their standard of living (Avruch 1981). Clearly, many Jews come to Israel with economic and political motivations as well as ideological ones. Yemenis in the 1950s were ideologically drawn to their homeland, but they were also fleeing the Yemen during the Israel-Arab war after the declaration of statehood (Gilad 1989). Similarly, while Zionism motivated many of the first North African Jewish immigrants to the new state of Israel, more assimilated Jews were later forced to emigrate by the increasing nationalism of North African Moslems (Deshen & Shokeid 1974: 34). But when Jews come to Israel for economic and political reasons, there is no chance to return, their future is imagined in their new country.
68 Salamon & Kaplan (1998: 22)

69 Gilad (1989: 105)
70 Fernea (1985: 301) quoted in Gilad (1989: 105)
71 Abu-Lughod (1986)
72 In this vein a recent publication on Ethiopian Jews is entitled 'The Trauma of Transition: The Psycho-Social Cost of Ethiopian Immigration to Israel' (Schindler, Ruben & Ribner, David, 1997).
73 Quoted in Lewis (1989: 232)
74 Buijs (1993: 10)
75 Bhachu (1993: 106–8)
76 Goldberg (1985: 188)
77 Bilu (1987: 288–9)
78 Bilu (1987: 291), see also Ben-Ari & Bilu (1997b), Deshen (1974: 151–209)
79 Ben-Ari and Bilu (1997) indeed suggest that these practices are signs of the 'Israelization' of the Jewish Diaspora, for the erection of Saints' tombs and synagogues is part of the Zionist ethos of appropriating the land. For a detailed discussion of the centrality of the landscape to Israeli ideas of nationhood, see Selwyn (1995, 1996).
80 Abbink (1984)
81 See Kaplan (1992).
82 For a discussion of the motivations of international migrants see Watson (1977: 6–7), Gold (1992), Camino & Krulfeld (1994)
83 Anwar (1979: ix)
84 Staub (1989: 71)
85 Margolis (1994: 192–4)
86 Anwar (1979: ix), also Margolis (1994), Jeffery (1976)
87 This is not to say that there are not many Israelis who emigrate, but such emigration is not generally towards the country of origin or their parents' country of origin but rather towards the United States or Western Europe.
88 Jeffery (1976)
89 See also Anwar (1981: 216)
90 Anwar (1981: 166)
91 Tambs-Lyche (1980)
92 Jeffery points out that this self-identification to Christianity rather than to their country of origin is difficult because British people do not accept this claim to common allegiance, and for them, Christian Pakistanis remain 'Pakistani', Christian or not (Jeffery 1976: 154).
93 Jeffery (1976: 150–1)
94 Weingrod (1985), Ben-Rafael & Sharot (1991)
95 Gamst (1969)
96 Quirin (1992)
97 Salamon (1993, 1994)
98 Following Amhara origin myths – particularly the legend that the first king of Ethiopian, Menelik, was the illegitimate son of King Solomon and the Queen of Sheba – the Amhara are descendants of ancient Israelites (see Ullendorf 1956).
99 Roland (1996: 172)
100 Mortland (1994: 17)

101 Mortland (1994: 20–1)
102 Gilad (1989: 230)

2 From Ethiopia to Israel

1 See Salamon (1993)
2 Kaplan (1992: 13)
3 Quirin (1992), Abbink (1990)
4 See for example Halevy (1869), Kessler (1982).
5 The Agaw are the indigenous population of Ethiopia, a group present before the creation of the Axumite kingdom in the first century AD. They are considered to be the source of the various Cushitic peoples who form the ethnic base of the population of the Horn of Africa (Levine 1974: 37). Until the twentieth century, the Beta Israel still spoke an Agaw language amongst themselves (Appleyard 1995b).
6 Quirin (1992: 9). In both these views, the history of Judaism and Christianity in Ethiopia is portrayed as a parallel development to the history of the faiths in the rest of the world, a 'microcosm of World Jewish history': a small early Jewish population is said to have been superseded by a later Christian community with only a tiny remnant of Jews surviving (Kaplan 1993: 646). Kaplan characterises the image as follows. 'Having left the Land of Israel, the Jews of Israel wandered in 'exile' until they settled in Ethiopia. There they rose to prominent positions but only to be supplanted by Christians and Christianity. After centuries of persecution and suffering, during which they clung tenaciously to their ancestral faith, they were finally able to return to the Promised Land; spared from a holocaust by the initiative and daring of the Jewish state' (Kaplan 1993: 651). Further parallels were created by viewing the Beta Israel as sufferers of Anti-Semitic persecutions. Then, the final airlifts (or as usually called 'rescue operations') came to be appear as a vindication of the entire Zionist enterprise. Kaplan quotes an official after the airlift of over 14,000 Ethiopians in less than 36 hours: 'if the State of Israel had existed in the 30s and 40s, we could have brought all six million [who perished in the Holocaust] in six months!' (Kaplan 1993: 651).
7 Kaplan (1992), Quirin (1992), Shelemay (1989). James Quirin conducted extensive oral history amongst the Beta Israel. Kay Shelemay studied Beta Israel liturgy and showed that many texts were derived from Ethiopian Christian sources – with the specifically 'Christian' elements removed.
8 Many Christian Ethiopians that I told about my studies to in Ethiopia, England and Israel said proudly 'We are all Israel!' Ethiopians have a long tradition of claiming Israelite descent and national myths and epics draw on this claim – the ancient ark of covenant is thought to be in Axum and the Ethiopian monarchs were direct descents of King Solomon (see Abbink 1990).
9 Ethiopian Christians' observance of the Saturday Sabbath has eroded in recent decades.

10 Kaplan (1993: 647), see also Kaplan (1992), Ullendorff (1956), Pankhurst (1995)
11 Pankhurst (1995). The Beta Israel are not unique as an African group claiming Judaic ancestry and exhibiting a number of Hebraic practices, note also the Lemba of Zimbabwe for example (Parfitt 1995). In Ethiopia, Pankhurst (1995) writes about the Beta Abraham or Bala-Ejj, a group of craftsmen 'almost a separate caste' that have retained customs reminiscent of early Ethiopian Judaic Christianity.
12 Shelemay (1991: 150–1)
13 Kaplan (1992: 65)
14 For a thorough discussion of land ownership in Gondar and Tigre region, see Hoben (1973).
15 Kaplan (1993: 155–6)
16 Kaplan (1992: 69–77), Abbink (1987: 144–5), Shelemay (1989), Quirin (1992)
17 ibid.
18 I borrow the title from Abbink's (1987) article.
19 Beta Israel lived principally in the most densely populated temperate *wayna daga* zone which lies at an altitude of 1,500 m to 2,500 metres, where a mixed farming system of animal husbandry and grain cultivation is practised. The other two altitude zones in North-West Ethiopia are the *daga*, which is above 2,500 metres, and the *qolla*, below 1,500 m. These different altitude zones have different climates and therefore vegetation, but also somewhat distinct economic and cultural life-styles (Quirin 1992: 2).
20 Quirin (1992: 3)
21 Abbink (1987). The Beta Israel were not the only subjected group in the region – Others include the Qemant (see Gamst 1969), Wayto and Berta (Abbink 1987: 145), and the Balla-Ijj (Pankhurst 1995).
22 See Schoenberger (1975: 238–48) and Salamon (1993).
23 On my visit in 1995 to the villages in which the Beta Israel lived, the local Christians bemoaned their departure: 'It is difficult to find a good blacksmith now, or a person to replace a broken pot'.
24 Abbink (1987: 143–5)
25 Abbink (1987: 147), Leslau (1951), Schoenberger (1975: 86–97)
26 ibid
27 Kaplan (1992: 130–2)
28 Leslau (1951: xli), Kaplan (1992: 135)
29 Kaplan (1992: 136).
30 1874 issue of Jewish Intelligence quoted in Kaplan (1992: 137)
31 Kaplan (1992: 116–35)
32 Kaplan (1992: 143–54), Summerfield (1997: 44–94)
33 A few years earlier, direct contact with World Jewry was initiated by the Beta Israel themselves. In 1855, and Ethiopian Jew arrived in Jerusalem with his thirteen-year-old son for the latter to study the Torah with the Rabbis in the Holy City (Kaplan 1992: 139).
34 Kaplan (1992 116–42)
35 Summerfield (1997: 94–232)

36 To this end, Faitlovitch organised the education of a number of young Ethiopian Jews. I met one of his alumni, who had studied in Alsace from the age of sixteen, in an absorption centre in Netanya. A frail old man in a suit and tie, he spoke to me in immaculate old-style French: 'Qu'est-ce que vous prendrez, Mademoiselle? ... Je vais vous éclaircir ... Je ne suis pas un homme de faculté, mais j'aime les gens de faculté.'
37 Kaplan & Rosen (1994: 60–1)
38 See Summerfield (1997: 159–88). In 1908, Faitlovitch was granted an audience with Emperor Menilick II. He pleaded with the Emperor to intervene on behalf of the Falashas, who were sometimes led in chains to work as masons in towns and were accused on supernatural grounds (*buda*). The Emperor issued an order to stop the maltreatment of the Falashas. Faitlovitch also met several times with Ras Tafari in the 1920s, who also issued decrees against false supernatural accusations and forced labour (Summerfield 1997: 182–6).
39 Summerfield (1997: 202)
40 Summerfield (1997: 228–22)
41 Kaplan (1992: 151–2)
42 Faitlovitch in various reports to the Pro-Falasha committee (Shelemay 1989)
43 Summerfield (1997: 255–66)
44 Faitlovitch (1905: 26–7) quoted in Kaplan (1993: 649): 'When I was in Africa among the Falasha, surrounded by tribes of semi-savages, I felt an inexpressible joy in observing the energy, intelligence, and moral qualities that distinguish them. We can be proud to count among our own these noble children of Ethiopia, who, with a no less legitimate pride, trace their origins back to our own, worship our God, and practise our cult. The fervour with which they seek to progress, to exit this African barbarism which envelops and suffocates them, proves that they have maintained the distinctive characteristic of our people ... how different to the other Abyssinians, uninterested in study and in the progress and civilisation of Europeans, to whom they naively imagine themselves superior!' (my translation based on an abbreviated translation in Kaplan & Westheimer 1992: 18).
45 Kaplan (1993: 649)
46 Rabbi Waldman (1990) quoted in Kaplan & Rosen (1993: 37)
47 Quoted in Kaplan & Rosen (1993: 37)
48 Quoted in Summerfield (1997: 330)
49 Summerfield (1997: 302–36), Schoenberger (1975: 210–14)
50 Kaplan (1992: 162)
51 Quoted in Kaplan (1993: 161)
52 Schoenberger (1975), Summerfield (1997: 334)
53 Kessler (1982: 11), Schoenberger (1975: 179f)
54 Abbink (1984: 113), Parfitt (1985)
55 Quoted in Winn (1981: 4)
56 Kaplan & Rosen (1994)
57 Schoenberger (1975)
58 Personal communication with Ethiopian Israelis who migrated in the 1970s, see also Abbink (1984: 105–6).

59 Abbink (1984: 112)
60 Abbink (1984: 115-6), Yilma (1996)
61 Parfitt (1985), Abbink (1984: 118-20)
62 Parfitt (1985)
63 This money was raised from Jewish sources internationally by the Israeli government and pro-Falasha groups in Israel and North America (Parfitt 1985).
64 For a full account of Operation Moses, see Parfitt (1985). For a critical account of Israel's motives, see Karadawi (1991).
65 The Sudanese government had agreed to turn a blind eye to the Operation as long as it was kept secret, so that it was not openly seen to be negotiating with the Israelis, who were 'the enemies' in the eyes of most Arab countries. However, media leaks were unavoidable, especially since the Jewish Agency used the operation to stage a large scale international fund-raising operation to pay for it (Parfitt 1985: 103).
66 Parfitt (1985)
67 These migrants included Beta Israel as well as Falas Mura, former Beta Israel who converted to Christianity in earlier generations.
68 Westheimer & Kaplan (1992), Wagaw (1993: 241-3), Jewish Agency (1994)
69 I thank Lisa Anteby for drawing my attention to this point.
70 Salamon & Kaplan (1998: 6). For an in-depth discussion of the Falas Mura question and Falash Mura integration into Israel, see Seeman (1997).
71 Source: Central Bureau of Statistics, Jerusalem.
72 Ministry of Immigrant Absorption (1996)
73 Salamon & Kaplan (1998: 6) The Ethiopian birth-rate is about thirty per thousand, about 50 per cent higher than among the general Israeli population.
74 See Hertzog (1995)
75 Kaplan & Salamon (1998: 8)
76 The development of 'ethnic' neighbourhoods is common in Israel (see for example Lewis 1995 on a Yemeni ethnic neighbourhood). As in the case of the Ethiopians, ethnic residential proximity are the result of government policies, housing shortages, and the immigrants' own choices (see Holt 1995, Gonen 1985, Ben-Rafael & Sharot 1991).
77 Kaplan & Salamon (1998: 8)

3 An Ethiopian Village in Urban Israel

1 Benita et al. (1994)
2 At the time of field-work, several thousand Ethiopians had still not acquired permanent housing, and lived in absorption centres and mobile home sites. For a description of accommodation and daily life there, see Anteby (1996).
3 See also Anteby (1996: 379)
4 An article in *The Jerusalem Post* (Upper Afula, 15/7/1992) reported that dozens of angry residents of the new neighbourhood in Afula demonstrated against the influx of immigrants from Ethiopia.

5 See Anteby (1996)
6 Here are a few examples of donations received (£1 = NIS 5, approximately). A wedding in a hall drew in a total of NIS 51,360. from 473 donations:

Bride's parents	NIS 6,000
Groom's father	NIS 1,200
Groom's mother	NIS 1,000
Bride's grandmother, bride's uncle	NIS 500 each
10 guests	NIS 250–300
19	NIS 200
36	NIS 150
232	NIS 70–100
169	NIS 50
2	NIS 20

The profit, once all costs were taken into account, was marginal in this instance. A larger wedding yielded intakes of NIS 25,000 at home, resulting in a profit of NIS 10,000, and an intake of NIS 75,000 at the hall, and a NIS 25,000 profit (approximate figures, unverified by me). A small celebration at home to mark a son's wedding yielded NIS 9,470 of which NIS 1,000 were profit, at the same home, an engagement party made a NIS 2,000 profit. A larger neighbourhood celebration for a *cristenna* (the birth of a child) received NIS 17,395. The cost was about NIS 9,000 (one cow NIS 3,400, video man NIS 2000, beer NIS 3,100, flour NIS 140, rented freezer 200), yielding a profit of about NIS 8,000.

Funeral donations are much lower and profits minimal. In one relatively small funeral gathering, 600 people donated NIS 7,450. Mostly 10 shekel notes, a good number of 20 shekel notes, and the odd 50 shekel and 100 shekel note from close relatives.

7 Janet Carsten, in her study of rotating saving societies, *kut*, in Malaysia, stresses their purpose as a means of socialisation of money: although ethnographers and participants alike tend to stress their value as 'saving' societies, in fact, they are more about *consumption*. By pooling resources, kin, affines, and neighbours, more than *saving* together, *consume* together (1989).
8 See Schoenberger (1975: 44)
9 See also Anteby (1996)
10 Occasionally, the counting starts from the common ancestor. Alternatively, the counting is reversed, starting instead with ego and going backwards. Ego is 'one' and the final number of generations is found when the original joint sibling pair is reached.
11 Visiting kin who live far away was an integral part of daily life in Ethiopia. When my informants described the seasons, they said that after the sowing of seeds came the 'time of visiting' – a whole season whose chief purpose was to visit kin who lived in distant villages (see also Schoenberger 1975, Salamon 1993).
12 Gow details the way in which for the Piro of the Bajo Urubamba in Peru, the problem of wanting to be with kin while still getting married with non-kin and therefore having to live away from the kin group constitutes the drama of everyday life: 'choosing to live with one set of

close kin necessarily means abandoning another set' Gow (1991: 225).
13 In this respect there are winners and losers in Israel. In Ethiopia, the traditional pattern was for women to marry out of the village, and male siblings build their houses around the parental home. Thus women generally did not live with close kin. However, I know of many instances when women returned to the home village after divorce, or when she succeeded in making her husband move to her natal village. In Israel, there are men who live within walking distance of several siblings, while they lived far away in Ethiopia, and similarly women who live close to kin, while her husband's kin are far off.
14 Shokeid (1974: 210-34)

4 Israel the Homeland

1 Italics added. Yilma (1996: 60)
2 Abbink (1990) provides a comprehensive survey of Beta Israel origin myths, contrasting them to the dominant Amhara-Tigray origin myths.
3 The dynasty of the seven King Gideons was said to have began when the Israelites migrated from Egypt towards Quwara after the destruction of the Second Temple (see Schoenberger 1975: 11-14. Abbink 1990).
4 Personal communication from Steven Kaplan in November 1994
5 Immigrants who have spent several years in absorption centres and mobile homes begin buying new household goods there.
6 See Wagaw (1993: 104-8)
7 My impression was that the worst racism towards Ethiopian Jews from veteran Israelis actually comes from Sephardi populations rather than from the Ashkenazi (other than the Orthodox who are openly hostile on religious grounds). Israelis of European extraction tended to speak positively of Ethiopians, even if somewhat condescendingly 'oh aren't they lovely!' 'so beautiful!' 'so polite' 'to think of where they came from ...'. Many Sephardi Israelis that I spoke to used overtly hostile words such as 'dirty', 'primitive', 'lazy', and 'smelly' to describe Ethiopians. The worst and most open hostilities however came from Russian new immigrants.
8 Rosen (1987)
9 I noted that in public, Ethiopians referred to Israeli Arabs they share a hospital waiting room with or a drink in the café on the square as 'Qemant'. The Qemant were a Judaic-pagan group, neighbours to the Beta Israel with whom they used to share a common language. The Qemant have all converted to Christianity (Gamst 1969). Ethiopians told me they used this term in public because it would not be nice for the Arabs to know that they were being talked about.
10 In a Joint-Brookdale Institute and Ministry of Immigrant Absorption study of 5,300 Ethiopian home-owners, 15-27 per cent of respondents said that they do not talk with their neighbour and 77-90 per cent said that they were interested in closer contact (Ministry of Immigrant Absorption, April 1996).

11 Whilst 11 per cent of pre-1989 immigrants in Afula say that their children only play with other Ethiopian children, up to 59 per cent of new immigrants assert this (Benita & Noam 1995: 91).
12 Beta Israel practised excision and infibulation (Trevisan Semi 1985: 105, Schoenberger 1975: 88).
13 Weistheimer & Kaplan (1992)
14 Budowsky, personal communication, 12/95.
15 Anteby (1996: 524)
16 Herman (1994: 160). A survey of the literature shows that other immigrants, from a variety of urban and rural areas of developing countries, adapt equally well to Western urban life. See, for example, Foner (1977) on Jamaicans in England and New York, Gold (1992) on refugees from Cambodia, Shaw on Pakistanis in Britain, and Goldberg (1972) on Lybian Jews in an Israeli rural environment.

5 Young Ethiopian Israelis

1 Horwitz (1999)
2 Most youths do not have a detailed understanding of Rastafarianism, but they associate it with Black American power and Black pride. They like the fact that its three main identifying colours are green, red and yellow, the colours of the Ethiopian flag. They are proud of the reverence shown to Ethiopia, thanks to Rastafarian idolisation of former Emperor Haile Selassie. In fact, the term 'Rastafari' is the original title and name of the emperor, Ras Tafari (for a discussion of Rastafarianism, see Jones (1988).
3 Kaplan & Rosen (1994: 86–91)
4 For a discussion of Ethiopian Jewish immigrants' education see Wagaw (1993: 130–190) and for a critical discussion of education policies see Holt (1995).
5 *Ha'aretz* 10/2/97.
6 See Wagaw (1993: 191–214) for detailed discussion of the adult vocational schemes. In a survey carried out by the JDC in 1992 among 2,800 young Ethiopian adults (age 22–35) who came between 1984 and 1985 as part of Operation Moses, 85 per cent males and 39 per cent females participated in vocational training courses (Lifshitz & Noam 1993).
7 Kaplan & Rosen (1994: 93)
8 In 1995/6, there were 891 Ethiopian students in higher education, of which 411 were in special one year preparatory courses, and 480 were regular students (Ministry of Immigrant Absorption, April 1996). I knew several University students well, and spent several days in Haifa University and the Technion dormitories with Ethiopian undergraduates. The students were happy, boisterous, hard-working, and appeared to be enjoying their student life to the full, chatting and listening to Bob Marley till two a.m. The dormitory rooms were chiefly for Ethiopians, and social life was almost exclusively with Ethiopians.

9 In 1996, there were 1,500 young Ethiopians serving in the army, of which 62 were officers (34 in regular service and 28 in the reserve forces) (Ministry of Immigrant Absorption, April 1996).
10 Shabtay (1995 and 1999)
11 Shabtay (1995, 1999)
12 Kaplan & Salamon (1998: 11)
13 In the JDC 1992 survey of 2800 young adults, 83 per cent males were absorbed in jobs, army or further courses. 68 per cent men and 41 per cent women were working (most of the women were in the younger age group, since they tend to stop work after marriage). Three quarters of men and just under half the women who work, do so in a variety of skilled jobs: primarily as skilled labourers in industry and construction or as high-level service workers, women primarily as assistant nurses, dental technicians and assistant nursery school teachers (Lifshitz & Noam 1993).
14 Rosen (1995)
15 See also Rosen (1995)
16 Ethiopians who arrived as infants or who were born in Israel present a different scenario. Few of them had reached their late teens at the time of fieldwork given that few Ethiopians had arrived in Israel more than eleven years earlier. Judging from my observations and from conversations with Ethiopians and Israelis who work with Ethiopian youngsters, those Ethiopian Israelis who arrived before the age of about eight to ten have a more difficult time at establishing their identity and many are apparently under-performing at school.
17 Shaptay (1999: 177)
18 For example, religious youngsters wear *kippa* (skull cap) outside of school, recite appropriate blessings and prayers, attend the synagogue, and celebrate annual holidays in keeping with standard Sephardi practice.
19 Only a small percentage of the 2,800 adults in the JDC 1992 survey were found to meet with non-Ethiopians with any frequency (Lifshitz & Noam 1993).
20 Ethiopian youths are not alone and other immigrants also combine, and switch between, elements of two different cultures. Psychological studies of immigrant youth use the term 'biculturalism' to depict this process (Garcia Coll & Magnuson 1997: 108–9). Asian youths in Britain provide good examples of 'bicultural' identities, blending different norms with remarkable grace (Anwar 1979, Shaw 1988). Outsiders often assume that British Sikhs will inevitably experience major problems of 'culture conflict' between 'traditional' parents and freedom-seeking 'anglicised' youngsters. Ballard & Ballard who conducted fieldwork in the 1970s conclude that Sikh youths went through a period of rebellion against their parents' values (as, they point out, do any other adolescents in Britain), juggling different expectations such as socialising with schoolmates versus attending the temple, or abiding by family orientation at home versus the individualist ethos of school. However, most eventually returned to follow a 'modified version of Punjabi cultural norms in their late teens and early twenties' (Ballard & Ballard 1977: 44–5).

21 Bloch (1989), Leach (1970 [1954])
22 Gilad (1989: 230)
23 See also Gilad (1989)

6 Rejected

1 See also Nudelman (1995: 207)
2 Yilma (1996: 63)
3 Kessler (1982)
4 Elon (1987), see also Kaplan (1988)
5 Herman (1994: 154)
6 Kaplan (1988). The Bene Israel (Indian Jewish immigrants) also conducted a successful struggle for wholesale recognition as an equal Jewish community in the 1960s (Weil 1977: 80).
7 Jews of all ethnic origin marrying in Israel need to provide proof of their claim to Judaism.
8 See Kaplan & Rosen (1993) for a discussion of this linkage between ritual immersion and baptism
9 See Ojanuga (1993)
10 Kaplan & Salamon (1998: 11)
11 Kaplan & Salamon (1998) quote the following figures from the Navon Commission's Report (Jerusalem, July 1996): HIV was not found among Ethiopian immigrants prior to 1990; 226 of approximately 10,000 immigrants tests in 1991 were found to be carriers; of the 1,386 identified HIV-positive cases in 1996, 550 were Ethiopian immigrants; in 1996, overall figures of identified cases of HIV are 2.8 per cent Ethiopian males, 1.6 per cent Ethiopian females as compared to a rate of .0004 per cent among the general population; and the rate of HIV infection rose from 3 per cent for Ethiopian immigrants who arrived in 1992 to 8 per cent for Ethiopian immigrants arriving in the first three months of 1996.
12 For a full discussion on the symbolism of blood for the Beta Israel, see Salamon (1993) and Seeman (1997: 210–14).
13 Anteby (1996: 527–30)
14 See also Schwarz (1998)

7 On Becoming Deaf

1 Levine (1965)
2 Molvaer notes that 'seats' are located in the body for various mental faculties amongst the Amhara. Thoughts and feelings originate in the heart. Strong feelings such as love are 'seated' in the stomach or intestines e.g. 'Anjet bellagn' 'my intestines eat me/I feel sorry/regretful' (Molvaer 1995: 55).
3 Levine does not mention the Beta Israel directly, but since the Beta Israel are culturally similar to Amharas – at least as far as language is concerned – Levine's study applies equally well to them (1965).

4. Levine (1985)
5. Levine (1965: 5–10)
6. Levine (1965: 6)
7. Levine (1985: 27–28)
8. Levine (1985: 25)
9. Rosen (1987: 59)
10. Another type of funeral verses, called *fukera*, is reserved for great men, heroes who have killed people or lions. People do not wail while it is sung, instead an even more elaborate dance, involving all the mourners, is performed. Extract from a *fukera* that I recorded:

    '... So many dead bodies, the mother of the killer, why does she not get darker and skinnier, when she held fire in her belly for nine months? ...
    The killer, the organiser of the army with horses, wherever he goes along the valleys, he builds huts of dead bodies ...
    Oh Dessie, the head of a tiger, who could go around your village?. With a long *alvin* [the name of a gun] he kills ...'

11. During the first decades of the state of Israel, the ulpan was given only to educated immigrants who wanted to integrate into Israeli professional life. Others became manual workers with no formal language training. Thus many Israelis who arrived from the Middle East and North Africa in the 1950s and 1960s are illiterate, especially women who did not go out to work. Today, all immigrants are placed in an ulpan few weeks after arrival. This is the fruit of a political choice aimed at 'absorbing' as fast as possible new immigrants in Israeli social fabric (Anteby 1996: 126).
12. Anteby (1996: 127)
13. A JDC survey of all Afula Ethiopian residents analysed their ability to carry out a simple conversation. They concluded that 63 per cent all men, 48 per cent of all women, 79 per cent of the adults under 45, 24 per cent of those over 45, and 29 per cent of new immigrants, could carry out a simple conversation (Benita & Noam 1995: 86). In a survey carried out by the JDC in 1992 among 2,800 young Ethiopian adults (age 22–35) who came between 1984 and 1985 as part of Operation Moses, the majority of men do not have difficulty carrying on a simple conversation and reading or writing a simple letter in Hebrew. The women have more difficulty – one third have difficulty in carrying out a simple conversation, and 70 per cent difficulty to write a simple letter (Lifshitz & Noam 1993).
14. Anteby (1996: 138), my translation. Relative to other immigrants in Israel, Ethiopian performance is poor. A Central Bureau of Statistics study, found that after five years in Israel, 71 per cent of immigrants from the European republics of the Former Soviet Union and 52 per cent of those from non-European ones spoke basic Hebrew. 53.2 per cent from European republics and 32.35 from non-European republics read a Hebrew newspaper (Horowitz 1986: 26).
15. See Doleve-Gandelman (1989), Smadar (1985), Spector (1994)
16. Anteby (1996: 131–145)

17 Anteby (1996: 422)
18 Levine (1965)
19 Anteby (1996: 422–4)
20 There are no accurate figures for literacy levels and schooling for Beta Israel. Anteby (1996: 127) estimates a rate of 90 per cent illiteracy for the adult population which concords with Wagaw's (1993) estimation of a rate of 90 per cent for adults aged over 37 year old. A survey conducted among adult Ethiopian immigrants aged 22 or over in 1994 in Afula, illiteracy in Amharic stood at 75 per cent for men and 89 per cent for women (Benita & Noam 1995: 84).
21 Levine (1965)
22 Levine (1965: 87), see also Anteby (1996: 144), H. Pankhurst (1992: 39)
23 Anteby (1996: 401)
24 Anteby (1996: 101). "A new temporal order governs the life of the group. This temporality – expressed by a fixed schedule, a precise timetable, a rigorous dating system and unknown climate and seasonal variations – imposes on the immigrants foreign accounts, segmentations, regularities, and methods of measuring. Lost, distraught, disorientated in this geometric spatial universe and in this fragmented temporal world, they have at first neither landmarks nor reference points" (My own translation).
25 See also Anteby (1996: 523)
26 However, by 1996, 5,000 families had taken up the house purchase scheme (Jerusalem Report, 30 May 1996).

8 Losing Control

1 Doleve-Gandelman (1990)
2 A JDC survey found that less than half the Ethiopians in Afula of working age (22–64) were employed. The employment rate amongst men was high, standing at 77 per cent (Benita & Noam 1995: 89). This figure seems somewhat high to me – it is possible that Ethiopians doing temporary work said that they were in employment, thereby artificially raising the percentage. Kaplan & Salamon (1998: 12) also dispute these figures, pointing out that the survey was conducted amongst house owners, who are not representative of the Ethiopian immigrant population as a whole.
3 Kaplan & Rosen (1994)
4 In fact, Arabs tend to work in construction while economic migrants from Thailand and Romania are employed in agriculture.
5 See also Abbink (1984: 208)
6 In a survey conducted in 1993 by the JDC, out of 294 working adults, 44 per cent of veterans (pre-1985 immigrants) and 20 per cent new immigrants were employed in skilled jobs (Benita & Noam 1995).
7 Clearly this is an idealised picture. When there was no agricultural work, the Beta Israel occupied themselves with their craft work (Schoenberger 1975).

8 Similarly, Stewart notes that after fifteen months of fieldwork he inadvertently ignored the world of the factory where his Gypsy informants worked. He notes: "My own attitude, it seems to me now, reflected the concerns of the Rom. They might have complained as they walked past my front door in the morning that they were going off to "suffer" again in the factory, but little other reference was made to this crucial part of their lives." (Stewart 1997: 141).

9 I stress that my discussion is focused on women who did not receive education in Israel, that is who arrived after the age of about eighteen/twenty. Younger women have rapidly adopted new norms and expectations.

10 I learned about child-rearing in Ethiopia through conversations and by watching small children during my two month stay in villages in Gondar. Molvaer (1993) corroborates these findings. He discusses the treatment of children at different ages and even attempts a psychological critique of Amhara methods of upbringing, suggesting that this withdrawal of affection has negative psychological consequences.

11 Anteby (1996)

12 Doleve-Gandelman (1990)

13 Kaplan & Salamon (1998: 7)

14 Kaplan (1988)

15 See Schoenberger (1975: 192) for a description of the council of elders in Beta Israel villages.

16 There are no figures, but I rarely met middle-aged persons who were not at least on their second marriage. Alula Pankhurst who conducted research in a neighbouring population which was culturally similar to the Beta Israel notes the very high incidence of divorce (1992: 114). Out of a sample of 95 households, 3 had 12 marriages, and the average number of divorces was 3.3 per adult. 49 per cent of marriages lasted less than 5 years.

17 In a sample of 58 new immigrants, Reiff (1999) found that 50 per cent claimed to suffer from poor health in Israel (compared to a 10 per cent estimation by their doctors). See also Nudelman (1995).

18 Hodes & Kloos (1988), Nuldelman (1995), Reiff (1999)

19 See also Arieli & Ayche (1993). Reiff (1999) notes that 26 per cent (N=14) of her sample of new immigrants reported that their physical symptoms were caused by a specific aspect of living in Israel (such as a housing problem).

20 Young (1975)

21 See Reiff (1999), Youngmann et al. (1998)

22 Nudelman (1995), Reiff (1999)

23 Ethiopian immigrants are not alone in this: many studies of immigrants in Israel have shown that traditional medicine is still used in addition to Western medicine because the latter does not always fulfil immigrants needs (Nudelman 1995 see also Bilu 1979).

24 Nudelman (1995)

25 Nudelman (1995)

26 For a detailed discussion of divination as a source of prevention of illness amongst Ethiopian Israelis, see Nudelman (1999).

27 For a detailed description of contemporary amulet practices and beliefs, see Anteby (1996: 351–6, 1999: 204–5).
28 Nudelman (1995), Kahana (1985)
29 Nudelman (1995)
30 Similarly, Summerfield, who worked for three years as an Immigrant Advisor to Bangladeshi and Somali communities in Tower Hamlets, East London, concluded that 'control over one's own life is a major element in mental health' (1993: 98).
31 Kaplan & Rosen (1994: 105–6), Arieli & Ayche (1993)
32 Kaplan & Rosen (1994: 105–6)
33 Kaplan & Rosen (1994: 106)

9 Being Together as Ethiopians

a Kaplan & Rosen (1993: 43)
1 Weil (1995: 237)
2 Given that Amharic was the national language in Ethiopia, many Beta Israel from Tigre also spoke Amharic as their second language.
3 These ethnic hostilities are apparent today, both in Ethiopia and abroad. In London, at the student bar of the School of Oriental and African Studies, for example, Ethiopians from Tigre keep their distance from Amharas, sitting apart from one another on separate tables (personal conversations with Ethiopian Asylum seekers and students in London, 1994).
4 Kaplan (1988)
5 For a discussion of differences, and perceived differences, between the personal characteristics of the Amhara and Tigray, see Rosen (mns) and Soroff (1995: 145, 212–3).
6 See also Herman (1994)
7 For a detailed analysis of Beta Israel perceptions of *barya*, see Salamon (1994).
8 In accord with Beta Israel kinship theory, a person is *barya* if he has *barya* ancestors within seven generations. After seven generations, with intermarriage with non-slaves, the *baryanett* (slavery) is shed.
9 Salamon (1994)
10 See for example Gans (1962), Fallers (1967), Rogg (1971), Kim (1981), Markowitz 1993, Goldberg (1972).
11 For a similar account of a wedding celebration in 1981, see Abbink (1984: 225–6).
12 See also Anteby (1996: 436–61).
13 In Israel, there is little tradition of overt resistance and demonstrations, and the Ethiopian 1996 demonstration was one of the largest ever staged by Jews in Israel. For a discussion of Moroccan youth ("the Black Panthers") protest against the dominant society from which they felt socio-economically excluded, see Shama & Iris (1977: 141–162).
14 See Kaplan (1988)
15 Abbink (1984: 252)

16. In the case of Pakistanis in the UK, for instance, Anwar argues that together with residential segregation, the formation of an ethnic community and ethnic institutions is instrumental in enabling immigrants to cope with the effects of migration (1979: 11; see also Gold 1992 on Vietnamese in USA).
17. Markowitz (1993: 246).
18. Cohen (1985: 98)

10 Proud Ethiopians

1. By using the term 'traditions', I am not suggesting that the Beta Israel have had an unchanging past characterised by unchanging traditions (See Kaplan & Rosen 1993). As Hobsbawn (1983) points out, traditions which appear very old to the actors, can in fact be recent in origin.
2. Anteby (1999)
3. Ethiopian Israelis are well aware of their relative poverty compared to other Israelis. These former mud-hut dwellers, for whom a tin roof was the height of social ambition, protest of the flimsiness of the walls of their new houses, and the four rooms appear inadequate: after a life barefoot, they complain that their income is insufficient to buy the particular shoes that they want. A twenty-year old: 'This country is hard if you have no money. You cannot call what we have 'a house'. If you see a *farenj* house, there is a TV in each room, and each child has his own room. Look how thin the walls are in our house! The sink is no good, and the cupboards are no good, and we need a new fridge.' The relative poverty of most Ethiopian Jews in Israel is accepted by non-Ethiopian Israelis. The latest report on the situation of Ethiopian Jewish immigrants states: 'the community's economic situation is nothing less than dire' (Kaplan & Salamon 1998: 24).
4. Kaplan (1992), Quirin (1992), Abbink (1987)
5. When referring to Ethiopia, I refer to the Christian Amhara neighbours, without mentioning Muslim neighbours. I am following the Beta Israel in this who hardly even mention the Muslims – their significant 'other' was the Christians (see Salamon 1993).
6. I thank Taddesse Wolde, fellow doctoral student, for alerting me to this other meaning of '*tbeb*' and for telling me the saying.
7. See Salamon (1993) for an in-depth discussion of the relations between Beta Israel and their neighbours in Ethiopia.
8. See Anteby (1999) for a description of the Ethiopian Jewish naming system.
9. Molvaer (1995: 152)
10. Molvaer (1995: 63)
11. Levine (1965: 251–2)
12. Quoted by Kaplan (1999: 119).
13. Ashkenazi (1995)
14. Anteby (1996: 229–33)
15. See Anteby (1996: 179–205) for a discussion of the gender basis and symbolism in Beta Israel cooking.

11 The Purest of Jews

1 The Orit comprises the five books of the Old Testament, called *Torah* in Hebrew. For a good discussion of Beta Israel liturgy, see Shelemay (1989).
2 Soroff (1995: 178); Trevisan Semi (1985: 104).
3 Soroff (1995: 224)
4 For accounts of Beta Israel religious practices in Ethiopia see Leslau (1951, 1957), Schoenberger (1975), Ben-Dor (1986, 1987), Shelemay (1989).
5 See Shelemay (1989)
6 For complete descriptions of religious belief and practice in Ethiopia, see Leslau (1951, 1957) and Shelemay (1989). A detailed account of religious practice in Israel has yet to be published.
7 *Moadonim* are small concrete buildings which have been built in every residential area of Israel for citizens to take refuge in an emergency. They are open for use by the public, and are home to community groups such as elders' clubs and youth groups.
8 Shelemay describes services in Beta Israel synagogues in Ethiopia (1989, 1991: 39–41).
9 In some households, where teenagers are religious and have attended religious boarding school, some Hebrew prayers are added and grape juice is drank prior to eating the *dabbo*.
10 Religiously observant Israeli households use a hot plate to keep food and water hot throughout the Sabbath without contravening the Sabbath injunction not to light a fire.
11 Soroff (1995: 202–6)
12 Shelemay (1991: 45)
13 Schoenberger (1975: 222)
14 Leslau (1951: xxix–xxxvi)
15 Shelemay (1991: 39–41)
16 Messing (1956), Leslau (1951: xiv), Schoenberger (1975: 86–97).
17 Leslau (1951: xix), Trevisan Semi (1985: 105–6).
18 Trevisan Semi (1985: 106–7).
19 See Kaplan & Rosen (1993)
20 Educated Beta Israel and priests do not like this term because of its Christian connotations – Ethiopian Christians hold a christening, called *cristenna*, on the fortieth day for a boy and eightieth for a girl (Pankhurst H.1992: 137–8). They prefer to use the word *qeddesat*, which is derived from the word 'sanctify'. Abbink (1984: 216) also refers to the ritual by the term *arde'et*.
21 Leslau (1957: 55)
22 Muslims and Christians in Ethiopia also only consume meat from animals slaughtered by their co-religionists.
23 Since Beta Israel marriages were identical to their Christian neighbours, they were not mentioned in their rhetoric of purity with respect to Amhara. However, given that other Israelis, especially Arab Israelis 'marry their cousins', Beta Israel include marriage rules in their discourse on communal purity in Israel (see Anteby 1996: 500–17).

24 Schoenberger (1975: 70–4); Anteby (1996: 333–37).
25 See Hoben (1973) for a functional explanation of Amhara marriage rules, similar to the Beta Israel ones, and Anteby (1996) for a symbolic analysis.
26 The importance of the sibling bond is affirmed in numerous daily situations. For example: 'My brother' and 'my sister' (*wandimye, ihitye*) are affectionate terms of address which connote closeness; I was told about my relationship with Aveva, my adoptive sister 'You eat and drink together; you are just like sisters'; and the recounting of kinship genealogies often start from a sibling bond, e.g. 'Tauvesh and Melash were sister and brother, etc.)'.

12 Subverting Negative Ascriptions

1 Similarly Margolis describes how Brazilian immigrants in New York 'use humour to deal with their plummeting employment status'. Young women, employers of domestic servants in their home country, recount with amusement their experiences as domestics for New Yorkers, using humour to create a distance between their *real* status, as judged by their previous position in life, and their current one (1994: 130).
2 See also Anteby (1996: 495–6)
3 Anteby (1996: 490)
4 This argument has been influenced by Michael Stewart's analysis of Hungarian Gypsies. The Rom define themselves as 'clean' compared to 'dirty' Hungarians. They use this ideology to subvert dominant society's negative representations of them and proclaim their 'distinctiveness and moral/cultural superiority over others' (Stewart 1997: 234).
5 I was told of a simple ritual, called *memfeq*, which was performed for boys around the age of ten. This was little more than a blessing by a priest and it allowed the meat of animals that the boy killed henceforth to be eaten.
6 Kaplan (1999)
7 Kaplan (1999: 121–2)
8 Kaplan & Rosen (1993)
9 Cross (1995: 187)
10 Ballard & Ballard (1977: 47)
11 Kaplan (1999: 117)
12 Scott (1985: 29)
13 Anteby (1996: 146), my translation
14 Younger priests, who arrived in Israel in their early twenties have learned Hebrew, and several of them enrolled in Rabbinical training programmes.
15 In discussing cultural change amongst immigrants, it is important to maintain a long term perspective and not automatically attribute changes to the immigration experience *per se* for many changes were already inherent in the pre-immigration culture and society. Shaw makes this point in relation to changing Pakistani marriage practices in Britain. She concludes, after studying marriage practices in the

Pakistani village that her British informants come from, that 'the incidents [of changing marriage practices] are symptomatic not of a wholesale desire to adopt a western lifestyle and its values but of stresses inherent in the culture itself, for such disputes occur within a wholly traditional framework (1988: 179).'
16 Abbink (1984: 256) suggests that the emphasis Beta Israel place on the lack of a place for the seclusion of impure women expresses not only a reluctance to give up an 'emotionally deeply engrained' practice, but also can be seen a kind of '*protest*' and affirmation of their 'authenticity' in religious matters. Anteby (1996: 525) states that a group of practices can be considered 'resistances' to integration – mourning ritual, food, and traditional medicine. Kaplan (1999) explores the concept of 'everyday forms of resistance' in Ethiopian Israeli life.
17 Freeman (1994)
18 Kaplan & Rosen (1993)
19 See also (Leslau 1951: xvi)
20 Freeman (1994). Similarly, young Bene Israel, the Jews from India, wanted to integrate fully into Israeli society and gain equality and acceptance. They too chose which ethnic traditions to uphold. They shed Indian cultural patterns which have kept their parents apart, while at the same time they cultivated elements of Indian folklore and behaviour which does not interfere with an Israeli lifestyle and reinforces their ethnic identity (Roland 1996: 185–6).
21 See Eastmond (1993: 50), see also Gold (1992: 18), Kim (1987)
22 See Dench (1975)
23 Anwar (1979: 165)
24 Jeffery (1976: 106–7)
25 See Goldberg (1972: 76) for a similar point in relation to Lybian Jews in Israel.
26 Gow (1991: 286)

13 The Homeland Postponed

1 The term 'homeland postponed' is my own, and although Beta Israel never used an equivalent term, I hope that the following discussion will show its resonance.
2 Trevisan Semi (1985: 110)
3 See Johnson (1993: 266–74).
4 While Ethiopian Israelis do recognise differences in status among other Israelis, they tend to view all Israelis as undifferentiated – in much the same way as most Israelis, unless specifically asked to differentiate, will tend to think of Ethiopians as one uniform group.
5 Young educated Ethiopians have more pragmatic motivations too in taking such jobs – they are the best paid white collar work that they can obtain (see also Rosen 1995).
6 Ben-Rafael (1982); Ben-Rafael & Sharot (1991).
7 Soroff (1995: 145–74).
8 Abbink (1984: 236)

9 I obtained this information from the 'requests for visa' file at the Ethiopian Embassy in Tel Aviv.
10 Ethiopian Israelis from Tigre continue their journey North to reach their native region.
11 Levy accompanied a group of Moroccan-born Israelis on part-pilgrimage and part-tourist excursion to Morocco. He concludes that the journey was not a return to the past in a straightforward sense. A clear sense of being Israeli grew during the trip and present-day Morocco was alien to the travellers. 'We could argue that the travellers left to search for their Maghrebi roots, and thus manifested a trend towards segregation. But we could equally, and perhaps more forcefully, argue that in Morocco they found the roots of their Israeli identity.' (Levy 1997: 42).
12 A small, but growing, minority of Ethiopian Israelis turn towards an altogether different image of a future homeland: the coming of Christ on earth. Espousing Evangelical Christianity, they have opted for a minority which gives them better status than the one their skin-colour condemns them to. They become a child of God, equal to every other human being and loved by Christ. They take control over their lives by gaining a vital mission in life – to convert others to the faith – and they can withstand current difficulties thanks to their dream of redemption. See Seeman (1997, 1999) for a full discussion of Evangelical Ethiopian Israelis.
13 Since the mid-eighties, the melting-pot ideology has increasingly given way to pluralism and commentators note the effervescence of cultural identity in Israel (Weingrod 1985, Ben-Rafael & Sharot 1991).

Bibliography

Abbink, Jan. 1983. '*Seged* celebration in Ethiopia and Israel: Continuity and Change of a Falasha Religious Holiday', *Anthropos* no. 78, pp. 789–810.

Abbink, Jan. 1984. *The Falashas in Ethiopia and Israel: the Problem of Ethnic Assimilation*, PhD thesis, Nijmegen University.

Abbink, Jan.1987. 'A socio-structural analysis of the Beta Israel as an 'infamous group' in traditional Ethiopia,' *Sociologus* XXXVII, 2, pp. 140–154.

Abbink, Jan. 1990. 'The enigma of the Beta Israel ethnogenesis: an anthrohistorical study' in *Cahiers d'Etudes Africaines*,120, XXX–4, pp. 397–449.

Abu-Lughod, Lila. 1986. *Veiled Sentiments: Honour and Poetry in a Bedouin Society*. Berkeley: University of California Press.

Anteby, Lisa. 1994. 'Print, magic and videotapes: new patterns of orality and literacy among the Ethiopian Jews in Israel', in H. Marcus (ed.) *New Trends in Ethiopian Studies*. New Jersey: Red Sea Press.

Anteby, Lisa. 1995. 'Rituals of Birth and Death: the construction of identity for Ethiopian Jews', in *Israeli Social Science Research*, vol. 10 (2), pp. 41–54.

Anteby, Lisa. 1996. *Voies de l'Integration, Voix de la Tradition: Itinéraires socioculturels et pratiques de communication parmi les Juifs Ethiopiens en Israel*. Unplished PhD, Université Rene Descartes, Paris.

Anteby, Lisa. 1999. 'Of Names, Amulets and Movies: Some Patterns of Oral and Written Tradtitions – Analysis of a Service for the New Moon' in T. Parfitt (ed.) *The Beta Israel in Ethiopia and Israel*. London: Curzon.

Anteby, Lisa. (in press). "There's Blood in the House: negociating female rituals of purity among the Ethiopian Jews in Israel", in R. Wasserfall (ed.) *Female Rituals of Purity in Judaism*.

Anwar, Mohammed. 1979. *The Myth of Return*. London: Heinemann.

Appleyard, David. 1995. *Colloquial Amharic – A Complete Language Course*. London: Routledge.

Appleyard, David. 1995 b. 'The Beta Israel names for God in Agaw prayer texts,' in S. Kaplan, T. Parfitt, E. Trevisan Semi (eds.) *Between Africa and Zion: Proceedings of the First International Congres of the Society for the study of Ethiopian Jewry*. Jerusalem: The Joint Distribution Committee.

Arieli, Ariel & Seffefe, Ayche. 1993. "Psychopathological Aspects of the Ethiopian Immigration", *Israel Journal of Medical Science*, vol. 29 no. 6–7, pp. 411–418.

Ashkenazi, Michael. 1988. 'Political organisation and resources among Ethiopian immigrants' in *Social Science Information*, 27(3), pp. 371–89.

Ashkenazi, Michael. 1995. 'Ethiopian immigrants, 'malevolent coincidence' and the idea of the limited good' in S. Kaplan, T. Parfitt, E. Trevisan Semi (eds.) *Between Africa and Zion: Proceedings of the First International Congres of the Society for the study of Ethiopian Jewry*. Jerusalem: The Joint Distribution Committee.

Avruch, Kevin. 1981. *American Immigrants in Israel: Social Identities and Change*. Chicago: University of Chicago Press.

Ballard, Roger & Ballard, Catherine. 1977. 'The Sikhs: the development of South Asian settlements in Britain' in J. Watson (ed.) *Between two Cultures: Migrants and Minorities in Britain*. London: Basil Blackwell.

Banks, Marcus. 1996. *Ethnicity: Anthropological Constructions*. London and New York: Routledge.

Ben Ezer, Gadi mns 'Ethiopian Jews Encounter Israel: narratives of migration and the problem of identity'.

Ben-Ari, Eli and Bilu, Yoram. 1997. 'Introduction'. in E. Ben-Ari & Y. Bilu (eds.) *Grasping Land: Space and Place in Contemporary Israeli Discourse and Experience*. Albany: State University of New York Press.

Ben-Ari, Eli & Bilu, Yoram. 1997b. 'Saints' sanctuaries in Israeli development towns' in E. Ben-Ari & Y. Bilu (eds.) *Grasping Land: Space and Place in Contemporary Israeli Discourse and Experience*. Albany: State University of New York Press.

Ben-Dor, Shoshana. 1986. 'Le Probleme de l'identité religieuse des Beta Israel' in *Les Temps Modernes*, no. 474, pp. 101–116.

Ben-Dor, Shoshana. 1987. 'The Sigd of Beta Israel: testimony to a community in transition' in M. Ashkenazi & A. Weingrod (eds.) *Ethiopian Jews and Israel*. New Brunswick and London: Transaction Books.

Benita, Esther & Gila, Noam. 1995. 'The Absorption of Ethiopian immigrants' in *Israel Social Science Research*, vol. 10(2), pp. 81–96.

Benita, Esther, Noam, Gila. & Levy Ruth. 1994. 'The Absorption of Ethiopian Immigrants: Findings from a survey in Afula'. Jerusalem: JDC-Brookdale Institute.

Ben-Rafael, Eliezer & Sharot, Stephen. 1991. *Ethnicity, Religion and Class in Israeli Society*. Cambridge: Cambridge University Press.

Ben-Rafael, Eliezer. 1982. *The Emergence of Ethnicity: Cultural Groups and Social Conflict in Israel*. London: Greenwood Press.

Bhachu, Parminder 1993 'Identities constructed and reconstructed: Representations of Asian women in Britain' in G. Buijs (ed.) *Migrant Women: Crossing Boundaries and Changing Identities*. Berg. Oxford.

Bhachu, Parminder. 1985. *Twice Migrants: East African Sikh Settlers in Britain*. London: Tavistock.

Bilu, Yoram. 1987. 'Dreams and wishes of the Saints' in H. Goldberg (ed.) *Judaism viewed from within and without*. Albany: State University Press.

Bilu, Yoram. 1979. 'Demonic explanations of illness among Moroccan Jews in Israel' in *Culture, Medicine and Psychiatry* 3, pp. 363–380.

Bloch, Maurice. 1989 [1976]. 'The past and the present in the present', in M. Bloch (ed.) *Ritual, History, and Power: Selected Papers in Anthropology*. London: Athlone Press.

Bruce, James. 1790. *Travels to discover the sources of the Nile*, vol. 111. London: G.G.J. and J. Robinson.

Buijs, Gina. 1993. 'Introduction' in G. Buijs (ed.) *Migrant Women: Crossing Boundaries and Changing Identities*. Oxford: Berg.

Camino Linda. & Krulfeld R. (eds.). 1994. *Reconstructing Lives, Recapturing Meaning: Refugee Identity, Gender, and Culture Change*. Basel: Gordon and Breach.

Carsten, Janet. 1989. 'Cooking money: gender and the symbolic transformation of means of exchange in a Malay fishing community' in M. Bloch & J. Parry (eds.) *Money and the Morality of Exchange*. Cambridge: Cambridge University Press.

Cohen, Eric. 1972. 'The Black Panthers of Israeli Society' in *Jewish Journal of Sociology*, 14(1), pp. 93 – 104.

Cross, William. 1995. 'Oppositional identity and African American youth: Issues and prospects' in W. Hawley & A. Jackson (eds.) *Toward a common destiny: Improving racd and ethnic relations in America*. San Fransisco: Jossey-Bass.

Dench, Geoffrey. 1975. *Maltese in London: a Community Study in the Erosion of Ethnic Consciousness*. London: Routledge.

Deshen, Shlomo. 1974. 'The situational analysis of symbolic action and change' and 'the varieties of abandonment of religious symbols' in S. Deshen & M. Shokeid (eds.) *The Predicament of Homecoming*. Ithaca and London: Cornell University Press.

Deshen, Shlomo & Shokeid, Moshe. 1974. 'Introduction' in S. Deshen & M. Shokeid (eds.) *The Predicament of Homecoming*. Ithaca and London: Cornell University Press.

Doleve-Gandelman, Tamar. 1989. "Ulpan is not *Berlitz*: adult education and the Ethiopian Jews in Israel", *Social Science Information* no. 28 (1), pp. 121–144.

Doleve-Gandelman, Tamar. 1990. 'Ethiopia as a lost imagainary space: the role of Ethiopian Jewish women in producing the ethnic identity of their immigrant group in Israel' in J. Flower MacCannell (ed.) *The Other Perspective in Gender and Culture*. New York: Columbia University Press, New York.

Eastmond, Marita. 1993. 'Reconstructing life: Chilean refugee women and the dilemmas of exile' in G. Buijs (ed) *Migrant Women: Crossing Boundaries and Changing Identities*. Oxford: Berg.

Einsenstadt, Shmuel. 1954 *The Absorption of Immigrants*. London: Routledge and Kegan Paul.

Einsenstadt, Shmuel. 1974. Preface to S. Deshen & M. Shokeid (eds.) *The Predicament of Homecoming*. Ithaca and London: Cornell University Press.

Elon, Menachem. 1987. 'The Ethiopian Jews: a case study in the functioning of the Jewish legal system' in *Journal of International Law and Politics*. vol. 19, pp. 535–563.

Faitlovitch, Jacques. 1905. *Notes d'un voyage chez les Falachas (Juifs d'Abyssinie)*. Paris.

Fallers, L (ed.). 1967. *Immigrants and Associations*. The Hague: Mouton.

Fernea, Ruth. 1985. *Women and the Family in the Middle East: New Voices of Change*. Austin: University of Texas Press

Flad J. M. 1869 [1862] *The Falashas (Jews) of Abyssinia*. London.

Foner, Nancy. 1977. 'The Jamaicans: cultural and social change among migrants in Britain, in J. Watson (ed.) *Between two Cultures: Migrants and Minorities in Britain*. London: Basil Blackwell.

Frankenstein, C. 1953. *Between Past and Future*. Jerusalem: Szold Foundation.

Freeman, Dena. 1994. *A contextual perspective on Beta Israel ritual and ethnicity*. BA thesis, Cambridge University.

Friedmann, Daniel & Santamaria, Ulysses. 1990. 'Identity and Change: the example of the Falashas, between assimilation in Ethiopia and integration in Israel' in *Dialectical Anthropology*, no. 15, pp. 56–71.

Friedmann, Daniel & Santamaria, Ulysses. 1994. *Les Enfants de la reine de Saba: les Juifs d'Ethiopie – histoire, exode et integration*. Paris: A. Métailié.

Gamst, Frederick. 1969. *The Qemant: a Pagan-Hebraic Peasantry of Ethiopia*. New York: Hold, Rinehart and Winston.

Gans, Herbert. 1962. *The Urban Villagers*. New York, Free Press.

Garcia Coll, Cynthia & Magnuson, Katherine. 1997. 'The Psychological Experience of Immigration: A developmental Perspective' in A. Booth, A. Crouter A. & N. Landale (eds.) *Immigration and the Family: Research and Policy on U.S. Immigrants* Mahwah, New Jersey: Lawrence Erlbaum Associates.

Gilad, Lisa. 1989. *Ginger and Salt: Yemeni Jewish Women in an Israeli Town*. Boulder, Colorado: Westview Press.

Gold, Steven. 1992. *Refugee Communities: A Comparative Field Study*. Newbury Park: Sage Publications.

Goldberg, Harvey. 1972. *Cave Dwellers and Citrus Growers: A Jewish Community in Libya and Israel*. Cambridge: Cambridge University Press.

Goldberg, Harvey. 1985. 'Historical and cultural dimensions of ethnic phenomena in Israel', in A. Weingrod (ed.) *Studies in Israeli Ethnicity: After the Ingathering*. New York: Gordon and Breach Science Publishers.

Gonen, Amiram. 1985. 'The changing ethnic geography of Israeli cities' in Weingrod, A. (ed.) *Studies in Israeli Ethnicity: After the Ingathering*. New York: Gordon and Breach.

Goulden, David. 1998. "*Out of Africa? An Appraisal of the Israeli government's special mortgage scheme for Ethiopian immigrants*", BA Thesis, The Victoria University of Manchester.

Gow, Peter. 1991. *Of Mixed Blood: Kinship and History in Peruvian Amazonia*. Oxford: Clarendon Press

Halevy, Joseph. 1869 'Exursion chez les Falachas en Abyssinie.' *Bulletin de la Société de Géographie*, March-April, Paris.

Halper, Jeff. 1987. 'The absorption of Ethiopian immigrants: a return to the fifties' in M. Ashkenazi & A. Weingrod (eds.) *Ethiopian Jews and Israel*. New Brunswick and London: Transaction Books.

Herman, Marilyn. 1994. *Concepts of honour among the Beta Israel*. PhD thesis, University of Oxford.

Herzog, Esther. 1995. 'The bureaucratic absorption of Ethiopian immigrants in Israel: integration or segregation?' in in S. Kaplan, T. Parfitt, E. Trevisan Semi (eds.) *Between Africa and Zion: Proceedings of the First International Congres of the Society for the study of Ethiopian Jewry*. Jerusalem: The Joint Distribution Committee.

Hoben, Alan. 1973. *Land tenure among the Amhara of Ethiopia: the dynamics of cognatic descent*. Chicago: University of Chicago Press.

Hobsbawm, Eric. 1983. 'Introduction: Inventing Traditions' in E. Hobsbawn and T. Ranger (eds.) *The Invention of Tradition*. Cambridge: Cambridge University Press.

Hodes, Richard and Kloos H. 1988. 'Health and medical care in Ethiopia' in *The New England Journal of Medicine 319*, pp. 918–923.

Holt, David. 1995. 'The culture cluster: a comparative perspective on Ethiopian Jewish problems in Israel' in *Israel Social Science Research* vol. 10 (2) pp. 97–116.

Horowitz, Tamar. 1986. 'General Perspective' in T. Horowitz (ed.) *Between Two Worlds: Children from the Soviet Union in Israel*. Lanham: University Press of America.

Horwitz, Dawn Lille. 1999. 'Dance at the Ethiopian Disco: Tradition or Change' in T. Parfitt (ed). *The Beta Israel in Ethiopia and Israel*. London: Curzon.

Jeffery, Patricia. 1976. *Migrants and Refugees: Muslim and Christian Pakistani families in Bristol*. Cambridge: Cambridge University Press.

Johnson, Paul. 1993. *A History of the Jews*. London: Phoenix.

Jones, S. 1988. *Black Culture, White Youth: The Reggae Tradition from JA to UK*. London: Macmillan Education.

Kahana, Yael. 1977. *Black Brothers: Life among the Falashas*. Tel Aviv: Am Oved (Hebrew).

Kahana, Yael. 1985. 'The Zar Spirits: a category of magic in the system of mental health care in Ethiopia'. *Journal of Social Psychiatry* no. 31 (2), pp. 125–143.

Kaplan, Steven. 1988. 'Leadership and communal organization among the Beta Israel (Falasha): an historical study', in *Encyclopedia Judaica Yearbook 1986–1987*. Jerusalem: Keter, pp. 154–163.

Kaplan, Steven. 1988b. 'The Beta Israel and the Rabbinate: law, ritual and politics' in *Social Science Information*, vol. 27 (3), pp. 357–370.

Kaplan, Steven. 1990. *Les Falashas*. Paris: Editions Brepols.

Kaplan, Steven. 1992: *The Beta Israel (Falasha) in Ethiopia: from Earliest Times to the Twentieth Century*. New York: New York University Press.

Kaplan, Steven. 1993. 'The Invention of Ethiopian Jews: Three models', in *Cahiers d'Etudes Africaines*, 132, XXXIII-4, pp. 45–658.

Kaplan, Steven. 1995. 'Beta Israel studies towards the year 2000' in S. Kaplan, T. Parfitt, E. Trevisan Semi (eds.) *Between Africa and Zion: Proceedings of the First International Congres of the Society for the study of Ethiopian Jewry*. Jerusalem: The Joint Distribution Committee.

Kaplan, Steven. 1999. 'Everyday Resistance and the Study of Ethiopian Jews' in T. Parfitt (ed) *The Beta Israel in Ethiopia and Israel*. London: Curzon.

Kaplan, Steven & Ben-Dor, Shoshana. 1988. *Ethiopian Jews: an Anotated Bibliography*. Jerusalem: Ben Zvi Institute.

Kaplan, Steven and Parfitt, Tudor and Trevisan, Semi Emanuela (eds.). 1995. *Between Africa and Zion: Proceedings of the First International Congres of the Society for the study of Ethiopian Jewry*. Jerusalem: The Joint Distribution Committee.

Kaplan, Steven & Rosen, Chaim. 1993. 'Ethiopian immigrants in Israel: between preservation of culture and invention of traditon' in *The Jewish Journal of Sociology*, vol. 35, no. 1, pp. 35–48.

Kaplan, Steven & Rosen, Chaim. 1994. 'Ethiopian Jews in Israel' in *American Jewish Year Book 1994*, vol. 94 D. Singer & R. Seldin (eds). New York: The American Jewish Committee.

Kaplan, Steven & Salamon, Hagar. 1998. *Ethiopian Immigrants in Israel: Experience and Prospects*. London: Institute for Jewish Policy research.

Karadawi, Ahmed. 1991. 'The smuggling of the Ethiopian Falasha to Israel through Sudan' in *African Affairs*, 90, pp. 23–49.

Kessler, David. 1982. *The Falashas: the Forgotten Jews of Ethiopia*. New York: Africana.

Kim, I. 1981. *New Urban Immigrants: The Korean Community in New York*. Princeton: Princeton University Press.

Krempel, Valerie. 1972. *Die Soziale und Wirtschaftliche Stellung der Falascha in der Christlich-Amharischen Gesellschaft Nordwest Athiopiens*. Berlin: Frei Universitat (Dissertation).

Leach, Edmund. 1970 [1954]. *Political Systems of Highland Burma: a Study of Kachin Social Structure*. London: Athlone Press.

Leckie, Jacqueline. 1995. 'South Asians: old and new migrations' in Greif S. (Ed.) *Immigration and National Identity in New Zealand: One People, Two People, Many People?* Palmerston North, NZ: the Dunmore Press.

Leitman, Eva. 1995. 'Migration and Transition: Three Generations of Ethiopian women', in S. Kaplan, T. Parfitt, E. Trevisan Semi (eds.) *Between Africa and Zion: Proceedings of the First International Congres of the Society for the study of Ethiopian Jewry*. Jerusalem: The Joint Distribution Committee.

Leitman, Eva and Weinbaum, Elisabeth. 1999. 'Israeli Women of Ethiopian Descent: The Strengths, Conflicts and Successes' in T. Parfitt (ed) *The Beta Israel in Ethiopia and Israel*. London: Curzon.

Leslau, Wolf. 1947. 'A Falasha religious dispute' in *Proceedings of the American Academy for Jewish Research* 16: 71–95

Leslau, Wolf. 1957. *Coutumes et Croyances des Falashas*. Paris: Institut de'ethnologie.

Leslau, Wolf. 1969 [1951] 'Introduction' in *Falasha Anthology*. New York: Schocken Books.

Levine, Donald. 1965. *Wax and Gold: Tradition and Innovation in Ethiopian Culture*. Chicago: University of Chicago Press.

Levine, Donald. 1974. *Greater Ethiopia: The Evolution of a Multiethnic Society*. Chicago: University of Chicago Press.

Levine, Donald. 1985. *The Flight from Ambiguity: Essays in Social and Cultural Theory*. Chicago: University of Chicago Press.

Levy, Andre. 1997. 'To Morocco and back: tourism and pilgrimage among Moroccan-born Israelis' in E. Ben-Ari & Y. Bilu (eds.) *Grasping Land: Space and Place in Contemporary Israeli Discourse and Experience*. Albany: State University of New York Press.

Lewis, Herbert. 1985. 'Ethnicity, culture and adaptation among Yemenites in a heterogeneous community' in A. Weingrod (ed.) *Studies in Iraeli Ethnicity: After the Ingathering*. New York: Gordon and Breach Science Publishers.

Lewis, Herbet. 1989. *After the Eagles Landed: The Yemenites of Israel.* Boulder, Colorado: Westview Press.

Lifshitz, Chen and Noam, Gila. 1993. 'A survey of young Ethiopian immigrants', JDC paper. Jerusalem: Joint Distribution Committee.

Lissak, Moshe. 1969. *Social mobility in Israeli Society.* Jerusalem: Israel Universities Press.

Loeb, Laurence. 1985. 'Folk models of Habbani ethnic identity' in Weingrod, A. ed. *Studies in Israeli Ethnicity: After the Ingathering.* New York: Gordon and Breach.

Margolis, Maxine. 1994. *Little Brazil: An Ethnography of Brazilian Immigrants in New York.* Princeton: Princeton University Press.

Markowitz, Fran. 1993. *A Community in Spite of Itself: Soviet Jewish Émigrés in New York.* Washington and London: Smithsonian Institution Press.

Messing, Simon. 1956. 'Journey to the Falashas', *Commentary,* XXII, p. 28–40.

Ministry of Immigrant Absorption. 1996. *Immigrant Absorption: Situation, Challenges and Goals.* Jerusalem: Ministry of Immigrant Absorption.

Molvaer, Reidulf. 1995. *Socialization and Social Control in Ethiopia.* Wiesbaden: Harrassowitz Verlag.

Mortland, Carol. 1994. 'Cambodian refugees and identity in the United States' in L. Camino & R. Krulfeld (eds.) *Reconstructing Lives, Recapturing Meaning: Refugee Identity, Gender, and Culture Change.* Basel: Gordon and Breach.

Nudelman, Anita. 1995. 'Health Behaviour and traditional healing among Ethiopian immigrants in Israel' in S. Kaplan, T. Parfitt, E. Trevisan Semi (eds.) *Between Africa and Zion: Proceedings of the First International Congres of the Society for the study of Ethiopian Jewry.* Jerusalem: The Joint Distribution Committee.

Ojanuga, Durrenda. 1993. 'The Ethiopian Jewish Experience as Blacks in Israel' in *Journal of Black Studies,* vol. 24. No.2. pp. 147–158.

Pankhurst, Alula. 1992. *Resettlement and Famine in Ethiopia: the Villager's Experience.* Manchester: Manchester University Press.

Pankhurst, Helen. 1992. *Gender, Development and Identity: an Ethiopian Study.* London: Zed books.

Pankhurst, Richard. 1992. 'The Falashas, or Judaic Ethiopians, in their Christian Ethiopian setting', in *African Affairs,* no. 91, pp. 567–582.

Pankhurst, Richard. 1995. 'The Beta Israel (Falashas) in their Ethiopian setting' in *Israel Social Science Research,* vol. 10 (2) p. 1–12.

Parfitt, Tudor. 1985. *Operation Moses.* London: Weidenfelt & Nicholson.

Parfitt, Tudor. 1995. 'The Falasha phenomenon?' in S. Kaplan, T. Parfitt, E. Trevisan Semi (eds.) *Between Africa and Zion: Proceedings of the First International Congres of the Society for the study of Ethiopian Jewry.* Jerusalem: The Joint Distribution Committee.

Parfitt, Tudor (ed.). 1999. *The Beta Israel in Ethiopia and Israel.* London: Curzon.

Patai, Raphael. 1953. *Israel between East and West.* Philadelphia: Jewish Publication Society.

Quirin, James. 1992. *The Evolution of Ethiopian Jews. A History of the Beta Israel (Falasha) to 1920.* Philadelphia: University of Pennsylvania Press.

Reiff, Marian. 1999. 'Sickness and Medicine: Perceptions of Ethiopian Immigrants and their Doctors in Israel' in T. Parfitt (ed) *The Beta Israel in Ethiopia and Israel*. London: Curzon.

Rogg, Edward. 1971. 'The influence of a strong refugee community on the economic adjustment of its members', in *International Migration Review* 5(4): 474-481.

Roland, Joan. 1996. 'Indian culture and identity among the Ben Israel in Israel' in F. Lazin & G. Mahler *Israel in the Nineties*. Gainesville: University Press of Florida.

Rosen, Chaim. 1986. Ethiopian Jews in Israel in V. Avner (ed.) *The Jews of Ethiopia: a People in Transition*. Tel Aviv: Beth Hatefutsoth.

Rosen, Chaim. 1987. 'Core Symbols of Ethiopian identity and their role in understanding the Beta Israel today' in M. Ashkenazi & A. Weingrod (eds.) *Ethiopian Jews in Israel*. New Brunswick: Transaction Books.

Rosen, Chaim. 1989. 'Getting to know the Ethiopian Jews in Israel by means of their proverbs' in *Social Science Information*. 28(1) pp. 145-159. London: SAGE.

Rosen, Chaim. 1995. 'Working as a government anthropologist among the Ethiopian Jews in Israel', in *Social Science Research*, vol. 10(2), pp. 55-68.

Rosen Chaim. mns. 'The many ways of the Ethiopian Jews: points of comparison and contrast between the Beta Israel of Gonda and Tegre'.

Salamon, Hagar 1994. 'Slavery among the Beta Israel in Ethiopia: religious dimensions of inter-group perceptions' in *Slavery & Abolition*, vol. 15, no. 1 pp. 72-88

Salamon, Hagar and Kaplan, Steven. 1998. *Ethiopian Jewry: An Annotated Bibliography 1988-1997*. Jerusalem: Ben-Zvi Institute and Hebrew University.

Salamon, Hagar. 1993. *The Beta Israel and their non-Jewish Neighbours*. PhD thesis. Hebrew University, Jerusalem (Hebrew).

Schindler, Ruben & Ribner, David. 1997. *The Trauma of Transition: The Psycho-Social Cost of Ethiopian Immigration to Israel*. Aldershot: Avebury.

Schoenberger, Michelle. 1975. *The Falashas of Ethiopia: An Ethnographic Study*. Cambridge M.Litt thesis.

Schwarz, Tanya. 1998. 'Les plus purs des Juifs – D'Ethiopie en Israel, l'evolution des rituels de purification falashas', in *Terrain* 31, pp. 45-58.

Scott, James. 1985. *Weapons of the Weak: Everyday Forms of Peasant Resistance*. New Haven: Yale University Press.

Seeman, Don. 1997. *"One People, One Blood", Religious Conversion, Public Health, and Immigration as Social Experience for Ethiopian-Israelis"*. Cambridge (Mass.) PhD thesis.

Seeman, Don.1999. 'All in the Family: 'Kinship' as a Paradigm for the Ethnography of Beta Israel' in T. Parfitt (ed.) *The Beta Israel in Ethiopia and Israel*. London: Curzon.

Selwyn, Tom. 1995. 'Landscapes of liberation and imprisonment: towards an anthropology of the Israeli landscape' in E. Hirsch & M. O'hanlon (eds.), *The Anthropology of the Landscape*. Oxford: Oxford University Press.

Selwyn, Tom. 1996. 'Atmospheric notes from the fields: reflections on myth-collecting tours' in T. Selwyn (ed.) *The Tourist Image: Myths and Myth Making in Tourism*. Chichester: John Wiley & Sons.

Shabtay, Malka. 1995. 'The Experience of Ethiopian Jewish Soldiers in the Israeli army' in S. Kaplan, T. Parfitt, E. Trevisan Semi (eds.) *Between Africa and Zion: Proceedings of the First International Congres of the Society for the study of Ethiopian Jewry*. Jerusalem: The Joint Distribution Committee.

Shabtay, Malka. 1999. 'Identity Reformulation Among Ethiopian Immigrnat soldiers: Processes of Interpretation and Struggle' in T. Parfitt (ed.) *The Beta Israel in Ethiopia and Israel*. London: Curzon.

Shama, Avraham & Iris, Mark. 1977. *Immigration without Integration: Third World Jews in Israel*. Cambridge, Massachusetts: Schenkman Publishing Company.

Shaw, Alison. 1988. *A Pakistani Community in Britain*. Oxford: Basil Blackwell.

Shelemay, Kay. 1989 [1986]. *Music, Ritual and Falasha History*. Michigan: Michigan University Press.

Shelemay, Kay. 1991. *A Song of Longing: an Ethiopian Journey*. Urbana and Chicago: University of Illinois Press.

Shokeid, Moshe 1974. 'The evolution of kinship ties among Moroccan immigrants' in Deshen S. & Shokeid M. (eds.) *The Predicament of Homecoming*. Ithaca and London: Cornell University Press.

Simon, Rita & Brettell, Caroline (eds.). 1986 *International Migration: the Female Experience*. Towota, New Jersey: Rowman and Allanheld.

Smooha, Shmuel. 1978. *Israel: Pluralism and Conflict*. Berkeley: University of California Press.

Soroff, Linda. 1995. *The Maintenance and Transmission of Ethnic Identity*. Lanham, MD: University Press of America.

Spector, Geoffrey. 1994. *Creating the Space for the First World*, Hebrew University (unpublished mns).

Staub, Shalom. 1989. *Yemenis in New York*. Philadelphia: Balch Insititute Press.

Stern, Henry. 1968 (1862) *Wanderings among the Falashas in Abyssinia*. London Frank Cass and Co.

Stewart, Michael. 1997. *The Time of the Gypsies*. San Fransisco & London: Westview Press.

Summerfield, Daniel. 1997. *From Falasha to Ethiopian Jews: the external influences for change*. PhD thesis, London University (SOAS).

Summerfield, Hazel. 1993. 'Patterns of adaptation: Somali and Bangladeshi Women in Britain' in G. Buijs (ed.) *Migrant Women: Crossing Boundaries and Changing Identities*. Berg, Oxford.

Tambs-Lyche, Harald. 1980. *The London Patidars: A Case Study in Urban Ethnicity*. London: Routledge.

Trevisan Semi, Emanuela. 1985. 'The Beta Israel (Falashas): from purity to impurity'. in *Jewish Journal of Sociology*, vol. XXVII, no. 2.

Tsili, Doleve-Gandelman. 1989. 'Ulpan is not Berlitz: adult education and the Ethiopian Jews in Israel' in *Social Science Information* 28, no. 1 pp. 4–24.

Ullendorff, Edward. 1956. 'Hebraic-Jewish elements in Abyssinian Christianity' in *Journal of Semitic Studies*, 1, pp. 216–256.

Wagaw, Teshome. 1993. *For Our Souls: Ethiopian Jews in Israel*. Detroit: Wayne State University Press.

Waldman, Menachem. 1985. *The Jews of Ethiopia: the Beta Israel Community*. Jerusalem: Ami-Shav.

Watson, James. 1977. 'Introduction: immigration, ethnicity and class in Britain' in J. Watson (ed.) *Between Two Cultures*. Oxford: Basic Blackwell.

Weil, Shalva. 1977. *Bene Israel Indian Jews in Lod, Israel: a study in the Persistence of Ethnicity and Ethnic Identity*. Brighton, Sussex University (unpublished PhD thesis).

Weil, Shalva. 1987. 'Anthropology becomes home: home becomes anthropology' in A. Jackson (ed.) *Anthropology at Home* London: Tavistock.

Weil, Shalva. 1989. 'Ethiopian Jews in Israel: a Survey of Research and Documentation' in *Jewish Folklore and Ethnology Review*, vol. II (1–2), pp. 28–32.

Weil, Shalva. 1995. 'Collective Designations and collective identity among Ethiopian Jews' in *Israel Social Science Research*, vol. 10 (2), pp. 25–40.

Weil, Shalva. 1995b. 'Representations of Leadership among Ethiopian Jews in Israel' in S. Kaplan, T. Parfitt, E. Trevisan Semi (eds.) *Between Africa and Zion: Proceedings of the First International Congres of the Society for the study of Ethiopian Jewry*. Jerusalem: The Joint Distribution Committee.

Weingrod, Alex and Ashkenazi, Michael (eds.). 1987. *Ethiopian Jews and Israel* New Brunswick and London: Transaction Books.

Weingrod, Alex. 1985. 'Introduction' in A. Weingrod (ed.) *Studies in Israeli Ethnicity: After the Ingathering*. New York: Gordon and Breach.

Westheimer, Ruth & Kaplan, Steven. 1992. *Surviving Salvation: The Ethiopian Jewish Family in Transition*. New York: New York University Press.

Winn, Michael. 1981. 'Falashas: doomed to extinction?' in *The National Jewish Monthly*.

Yilma, Shmuel. 1996. *From Falasha to Freedom – An Ethiopian Jew's Journey to Jerusalem*. Jerusalem: Gefen Publishing House.

Young, Allan. 1975. 'Why Amhara get *kureynya*: sickness and possession in an Ethiopian *zar* cult' in *American Ethnologist*, vol. 2, n.3 p. 567–584.

Youngmann, Rafael et al. 1999. 'Idioms of mental health problems among Ethiopian Jewish patients in Israel' in T. Parfitt (ed.) *The Beta Israel in Ethiopia and Israel*. London: Curzon.

Index

Amharic
  identity marker 243-4
  prayers in 236
  richness of expression 131-5
  speaking with children 110, 153
appellation of Ethiopian Jews 11
Arabs
  Ethiopian Jews, relations with 89-91
  population in Israel 8
army 14, 64, 100-5, 221, 224

banks see financial dealings
Bar Mitzvah see celebrations
blessings see religion
blood crisis 117-22, 187, 237,
  references to 87, 163, 224-5, 243
body metaphors, the stomach 122, 124, 138
bureaucracy see social security services
business, in Ethiopia 248-9

celebrations 52-56, 184-5, 241, 261 (fn. 6)
  as identity marker see ethnicity
  bar mitzvah 55-6, 63-4, 216-8
  neighbourhood 51, 63-4
children
  loss of control over 155, 157-62
  rearing 93, 110, 155-7
Christian Evangelicals 14, 252
Christians (Amhara), see Ethiopia, relations with Christians

coffee 47, 96, 190
  conversations over 171, 194, 220, 221
  grinding 4
conflict resolution 59, 68
  loss of control over 164-5
consumerism 80-3
  aspirations for the future 240-2
  buying goods 81-2
consumption, see also credit societies
credit societies 56-8, 83, 155, 166, 191
cultural change, see also integration
  comparative literature 17-23, 232, 264 (fn. 20), 272-3 (fn. 15)
  dual identities 109-13, 230-1, 247-8
  self-conscious 92-7, 189-90, 222-4, 228-33, 236-7
cultural traditions 195-99, 220-1, 228-33, 243-5 see also cultural change and rituals

divorce 165

education 14, 78, see also students
environment, loss of control over 147-50
  as a cause of illness and behaviour change 160, 168
Ethiopia see also purity practices
  daily life 127, 135, see also coffee grinding

ethnographies 12
relations with Christians 21, 26, 28, 194–5, 220
reminiscences 191–4
Ethiopian village 50
visiting 110, 245–9
ethnicity, together as Ethiopians 177–188, 229, 240, 252 *see also* resistance
celebrations as identity markers 184–5, 228, 231, 252
internal divisions 177–83, *see also* slaves
comparative literature 184, 188, 226, 253 (fn.15)
exchange
gifts 52–3
labour 53, 67
money 52–3, 67, *see also* credit societies

Falas Mura 37
female circumcision 94
fieldwork 2–7, 41, 57, 131, 190–1
financial dealings 83–4
food 198–9, 229, 231 *see also* purity practices, meat
at celebrations and rituals 63, 96, 203–4, 223
availability 79–80
children's food 158–9
Israeli 111, 229
preparation 53–4
receiving 45–6
symbolism 56, 95, 105–6, 190, 198–9
funerals 14, 52–3, 96, 109, 184–6, 261 (fn.6) *see also* rituals
funeral verses 134, 266 (fn. 10)

gossip 59, 112, 198
greetings 45, 60, 134
guests *see* social relations

health care, Israeli 14, 77, *see also* illness *and* medical practices
Hebrew *see also* language
learning, motivation 137, 153, 226–8

illiteracy 138–9
proficiency 135–37, 165, 251, 266 (fn. 13)
history 26–34 , *see also* Italian occupation *and* World Jewry
origins 26–7
15th–17th centuries 27–8
18th–19th centuries 28–29
19th–20th centuries 29–30
modernisation and Ethiopian revolution 33–4
homeland *see also* Israel, the homeland
comparative literature 19–20
homeland postponed 234–49
housing 14, 38, 41
difficulties with mortgage 142
ideal 240–1
interior décor and furniture 44, 81–2
humour 94, 135, 220–1

identity *see* cultural traditions *and* young Ethiopian Israelis *and* integration
illness 160–5 *see also* medical practices
causes of illness 161–3
failure to cure 163
immigration
Ethiopian Jews to Israel 34–8
motivations, Ethiopian Jews 75–7, 179, 235
motivations, other migrants 19, 255 (fn. 65, fn. 66)
policies 38, 81
integration *see also* cultural change *and* resistance *and* homeland, postponed
aspirations for 87–94, 237–44
cultural adaptation 94–7, 228–33
participation in civil life 88–9, 240
rhetoric of integration 87–8
young people 105, 106–13, 230–1, *see also* cultural change, dual identity

Israel
  Beta Israel perceptions 77–80
  country of immigration
    ethnicity 8–11
    history of immigration 7–8
    social studies of Israeli
      immigrants 9–11
  the homeland 72–7, see also
    myths of origin
Israelis (non-Ethiopian) see also
    Arabs
  American Jews 11, 255 (fn. 67)
  Ethiopian Jewish perceptions
    90–2, 114–5, 147, 187,
    196, see also neighbours
  Indian Jews 22
  Moroccan Jews 18
  pride in relation to 220–1
  Yemeni Jews 11, 17, 255 (fn. 67)
Italian occupation 32–33, 46

kin, social relations 63–71, see also
    social relations
  mutual help 67–8, 166
  quarrels and reconciliation 68
  telephone 66–7
  visiting kin 65–6
kinship 60–71
  breaking the kin group 216–9
  defining kin 60–2
  feel of kin 63–4, 71, 195
  slaves in the kin group 182–3

language see also Hebrew and
    Amharic
  pride and resistance 220–2,
    214–8, 236
lifestyle see consumerism
literature on Ethiopian Jews 11–5
  Beta Israel in Ethiopia 12–3
  Beta Israel in Israel 13–5
livelihood, loss of control over
    147–50

marriage see purity practices
  with non-Ethiopians 108, 242–3
material goods see consumerism
meat see also food
  slaughtering 89

medical practices 14, 169–72, see
    also illness
missionaries
  Jewish 30–3
  Protestant 12, 29–30
mourning see funerals
myths of origin 72–4

neighbours, social relations 42–60
  difficulties 59–60, 68–70
  formal structure of relations
    46–8
  inside the house 43, 45–6
  mutual help 53–4, 70–1 see also
    credit societies
  non-Ethiopian 43, 50–1, 89
  visiting 52

politics
  internal Ethiopian politics 14,
    178
  Israeli political system 78–9,
    240, 243–4
  participation in Israel's General
    Elections 75, 88–9
prostitution 247–8
purity practices 200, 209–19,
    229–31, see also religion
  birth 205–7
  difficulties of maintaining 59,
    69–70, 95–6, 112, 172–3,
    182, 190, 210–3
  in Ethiopia 21, 28–9, 31,
    209–11
  meat 164, 191, 214–5, 221,
    237
  marriage 209–13 see also
    marriage
  menstruation 210–11
  pride in 221–2, 234–7, 251

racism, perceptions of, see also
    rejection
  blood crisis 117–22, see also
    blood crisis
  discourse on racism 118–20,
    224–6, 252
  effect on integration 107–8
  within Ethiopian Jews 183

Rastafarianism 99, 255 (fn. 2)
rejection *see also* racism
  perceptions of 114–26, 143, 174, 239, 243
  perceptions of religious 116–7, 124–6, 143, 221–2, 239, 249
religion 14–15, 200–9 *see also* Israel, the homeland *and* purity practices *and* rejection, religious
  belief 201–2
  blessings and prayers 41, 85, 204–5, 234–5
  Ethiopian practices
    annual holidays 207–9
    Day of Atonement (*astasreyo*) 95–6, 196, 207, 208–9
    prayer house 202–4
    Sabbath 205–7
  in Ethiopia 31–3
  ideals for the future 234–7
  loss of control over 162–4, 174
  relation to Israeli practice 91, 200–1, 222–3, 225, 229–31, 242
resistance 186–7, 220–233, 243–4, *see also* blood crisis *and* ethnicity
  ideological 224–8, 251
rituals, *see also* Bar Mitzvah *and* coffee *and* purity practices
  birth 14, 51, 211–14
  death *see* funerals
  innovation 18 *see also* cultural change

slaves (*barya*) 181–3
  myth of origin 75
social relations 72–3, 215, *see* celebrations *and* neighbours *and* kinship *and* young Ethiopians
  difficulties 68–70, 251
  hierarchy between individuals 45, 145, 152–65, 195–6
  guests 45–6
  social status 82–3
social security services
  difficulties with 134–7, 139–42, 147–8, 160, 172–3
  getting the better of 59, 84–5, 153–4
spirits (*kole*) 167, 168–72
students 99–100
suicide 165, 172–3

television 89, 92–3
tomb-stones 245–6
transport 80, 138–8

unemployment 146–7

women 14
  ease at running household 80
  men and 96, 108, 152–4, 165
work 14, *see also* unemployment
  aspiration for 239–40
  difficulties 125, 150–2
  young people 105–6
World Jewry 30–3

young Ethiopian Israelis 98–113, **129**, *see also* students *and* army *and* work,
  drop-outs 98
  identity 106–13, 124–6, 225–6, 230–3, 234
  immigration 179–80
  perceptions of racism *see* racism, perceptions of
  social life 99, 108–9, 111–2